THE WHOLE
SCHOOL LIBRARY
HANDBOOK

EDITED BY **BLANCHE WOOLLS & DAVID V. LOERTSCHER**

ala
editions

an imprint of The American Library Association
Chicago 2013

Cover design by Casey Bayer.
Composition by Priority Publishing.
Selected artwork from ClipArt.com.

The paper used in this publication meets the minimum requirements of American National Standard for Information Sciences— Permanence of Paper for Printed Library Materials, ANSI Z39.48-1992.

Library of Congress Cataloging-in-Publication Data
The whole school library handbook 2 / edited by Blanche Woolls and David V. Loertscher.
     p.   cm.
    Includes bibliographical references and index.
    ISBN 978-0-8389-1127-3
    1. School libraries—United States—Handbooks, manuals, etc.
I. Woolls, Blanche. II. Loertscher, David V., 1940–
Z675.S3W662 2013
027.8—dc23   2012028265

Printed in the United States of America.

17   16   15   14   13   5   4   3   2   1

CONTENTS

Dedication

The previous edition of this book was dedicated to Elizabeth T. Mahoney, Librarian's Librarian to the faculty and staff in the School of Information Sciences at the University of Pittsburgh. That dedication gave thanks to Elizabeth for introducing Blanche to George Eberhart's first edition of *The Whole Library Handbook* and it remembered Margaret I. Rufsvold, who, during our doctoral program at Indiana University encouraged us to become educators of school librarians, a challenge we continue to enjoy.

This edition is dedicated to the two people who are most important in our lives: Sandra Loertscher and Don Fadden. To them, this is very small payment for all the things they have contributed to us over the many years.

A special dedication to the contributors

A special dedication to the contributors from the previous edition is adapted here to thank those whose names are over new articles and to the new names that have been added. This book is a collection of articles from books and library journals. It would not exist without the generosity of the authors, the editors, and the publishers involved. These professionals have shared their work for the greater good. This is but a small token of appreciation for their contributions.

These authors, editors, and publishers provide essential information for school librarians on a regular basis. Journals provide articles to help justify programs and to keep school librarians aware of the changes that affect them, such as changes in copyright laws. Journals provide information to help librarians understand federal legislation and to keep up with the newest technologies, the newest educational movements, and the newest research reports.

The publishers, journal and book, and their contact information have been placed at the back of this volume for your convenience in ordering subscriptions and in requesting catalogs.

Preface

The preface to the first edition of *The Whole School Library Handbook* acknowledged the borrowing of the idea from George Eberhart's own "very creative compilation and distillation of information, facts, hints, and suggestions from the professional world. . . ."

This new edition contains all new articles and chapters. Many of the lists you found in the previous edition have been moved to these pages on the ALA website: "Pioneers and Leaders in Library Services to Young People," "ALA Youth Division Presidents," and "State Department Websites." While we continue to want you to have access to this information, we believe it is better in electronic format than on the printed page. This will allow for annual updates in a way that is not possible in a print publication.

We do have an apology. In our previous edition's listing of school library winners of the coveted National School Library Media Program of the Year we missed one. Patricia W. Pickard reminded us that her school system, DeKalb County, Georgia, won the NSLMPY large school district award in 1991. We are delighted to be able to clarify that with this edition.

Our last reminder is that you should follow George Eberhart's advice one more time: "Please keep in mind that many of the selections are only [edited] extracts of longer books or articles. The originals in their full glory are almost always worth seeking out."

Again, we hope our choices please you.

Flip this library: School libraries need a revolution, not evolution

by David V. Loertscher

One of the biggest business battles of our times is between Microsoft and Google. The two have very different business models. Microsoft believes that if they build it, we will come and buy their product. Google's approach is different: If they build it, we will integrate it into our lives. We use Microsoft products on their terms, but we use Google products from iGoogle to Google Docs on our terms, to construct whatever we want.

What does this have to do with school libraries? A lot. School libraries are like Microsoft (without the revenue, of course). We've created and invested in school libraries and, in recent years, their websites, with the expectation that our students will come to these places.

Sorry folks, but the old paradigm is broken. It's time to become part of the Google generation. If we polled our students, we'd probably discover that they're busy searching online, and maybe IMing or texting each other. Our school libraries and websites are the last things on most kids' minds. At some point, we have to admit that our creations have become irrelevant to today's students.

Last year, when I thought of revising my book *Taxonomies of the School Library Media Program* (Hi Willow, 2000), I realized that I had pushed the traditional model of school libraries about as far as it could go. We don't need a revision. We need a reinvention. Experts say that the rank and file of any profession can't recreate itself because it's too enmeshed in the status quo. We're more hopeful.

What has to happen for school libraries to become relevant? If we want to connect with the latest generation of learners and teachers, we have to totally redesign the library from the vantage point of our users. Our thinking has to do a 180-degree flip. In short, it's time for school libraries to become a lot less like Microsoft and a lot more like Google. With this notion in mind, I collaborated with two of my colleagues,  Carol Koechlin and Sandi Zwaan, Canadian educational consultants, to develop an idea we're calling the school library learning commons.

This learning commons is both a physical and a virtual space that's staffed not just by school librarians but also by other school specialists who, like us, are having trouble getting into the classroom and getting kids' attention. Support staff operates the open commons so that the specialists such as literacy coaches, teacher technologists, school librarians, art teachers, music teachers, and physical education teachers can spend time creating learning experiences and co-teaching. The main objective of the open commons is to showcase the school's best teaching and learning practices. For example, a principal who is impressed with the collaborative teaching going on among the school librarian, the teacher technologist, and a social studies teacher may invite the three to demonstrate their next unit in the learning commons. Since their work exemplifies the yearlong school improvement initiative, invitations are sent not just to the faculty but also to the school board. On another day, parents may be invited to the learning commons to observe a jointly designed medieval art fair created by a classroom teacher, the art teacher, and the school librarian.

The learning commons includes an experimental learning center, which occupies a physical and virtual space. The experimental learning center aims to improve teaching and learning by offering professional development sessions and resources that are tailor-made to each school's greatest needs.

What does this new learning commons look like? In the physical space, we enter a room that's totally flexible, where furnishings can be moved about to accommodate different functions and groupings. The open commons, like the traditional library or computer lab, functions as a warehouse for books and other shared materials and is staffed by paraprofessionals and computer technicians. Its flexible space allows individuals, small groups, and classes to visit at their own convenience; but the distinctive feature of the open commons is that it's a place where teachers can demonstrate the very best teaching and learning practices in the school and others can observe excellence in action.

The experimental learning center is the hub for all school improvement initiatives. It's the center for professional development sessions and action research projects, where innovative ideas are presented and new technologies are tried out before being fanned out into the rest of the school.

In the virtual world, the learning commons is both a giant, ongoing conversation and a warehouse of digital materials from ebooks to databases to student-generated content, all available 24/7 year-round. Thanks to social-networking software, information can flow not just from teachers to learners but in multiple directions: among students, from students to classroom teachers, from school librarians to classroom teachers and students. As expected, the virtual learning commons supports the work of both the physical open commons and the experimental learning center. Teachers may go online to meet. Professional development or action-research sessions can also take place online.

Do that 180-degree flip

Thinking differently and creatively is never easy. Here are some exercises to help you make a 180-degree switch.

Resolve to think like a patron rather than a provider, a customer rather than a store owner. For example, right now your library is probably open throughout the school day. Imagine what it would mean to students and teachers if it were open 24/7, 365 days a year.

Let's say each student is currently allowed to check out two books. What if each child could check out an unlimited number of books or download digital or audio books to their Kindle or any such device anytime they wished?

In some schools, students only get credit for reading books in the Accelerated Reader program. How about giving them credit for reading everything and anything?

Many of today's students read textbooks and take notes in class. Imagine a learning environment in which the multimedia world of information fed individual students' needs, and where on-demand digital textbooks/multimedia/databases are available 24/7 and under the control of the user.

Here's another 180-degree flip: A typical classroom assignment and library website are examples of one-way communication. Adults tell learners what to do, how to do it, and where to find information. In the new learning commons, homework assignments and library websites offer two-way communication.

How? It's easy. The teacher posts assignments on a blog that's linked through an RSS feed to individual students in the class, each of whom can access the blog through an iGoogle page or another personal home page. When an assignment is given, everyone—teachers, school librarians, students, and other specialists—can comment, coach, suggest, recommend, and discover together, and push everyone toward excellence. Content flows in and out of students' iGoogle pages via RSS feeds to help them complete their assignments and work together constructively. Involve the tech director in developing this system, and watch the barriers fall.

Flip your problems

Let's take that same 180-degree flip approach and apply it to a simple school library problem, resisting the temptation to say, "It won't work." Instead, think of the reasons it could work and the benefits that would accrue.

Here's a common problem: Professional development sessions take place throughout the school, but seldom in the library and the school librarian is rarely involved. As a result, school-wide improvements in teaching and learning aren't viewed as part of the library program. The 180-degree flip: All professional development programs are held in the experimental learning center, which, of course, is located in the learning commons. Why would that work?

- The learning commons is a politically neutral space.
- Administrators would have one place to go for school improvement programs: the learning commons.
- Even if you weren't "invited," you'd be there anyway.
- The learning commons is where the best resources and technology are located and folks just might stumble over that idea as they work together!

Think over the benefits, and remember, you have to be convinced yourself before you can convince others.

Get spacy

Still not sure? Take a look at your space. How can it function as a learning commons and an experimental learning center? For starters, consider getting rid of the immovable bookshelves cluttering the center of your space and the banks of computers taking up major real estate. Think of alternative solutions: wireless laptops that can connect anywhere. Circulate books to classrooms so you don't have to shelve the entire collection in the learning commons.

Are the "can'ts" and "won't happens" still crowding in? Hold a creative problem-solving session with other colleagues and include some outsiders who might bring fresh perspectives.

Finally, make the learning commons happen today, not tomorrow. Host a professional development session in the library and promise to overcome any problems or barriers. Now that's the spirit! It's going to happen; it will happen; you will make it happen. It will be a success with the resources and technology of the old library now front and center in this new learning commons.

What we're proposing is bold. Gone are the days when we can afford to exist on the periphery. The new learning commons is at the very center of teaching and learning. No longer will the library be something that students and teachers need to remember to come to; instead it will be integrated into their lives. Finally, the library will become the hub of teaching and learning, a place that everyone owns and contributes to, one giant conversation that's both a social and a learning network.

Face it, folks. We're at a crossroads. Doing nothing, trying to shore up the status quo, or attempting to resuscitate a dead model aren't feasible choices. Flip it now!

SOURCE: Adapted from David V. Loertscher, "Flip This Library: School Libraries Need a Revolution, Not Evolution," *School Library Journal* 54 (November 2008): 46–48. Used with permission.

A tribute to a giant: Cora Paul Bomar
by Blanche Woolls

In our first edition, we asked one of our friends, and one of those great school librarians in our lives, Marilyn Miller, to select a number of "Pioneers and Leaders in Library Service to Young People" from her *Dictionary of American Library Biography* and its two supplements and from the *Dictionary of Pioneers and Leaders in Library Services to Youth*, all published by Libraries Unlimited in 1978, 1990, 2003, and 2004, respectively. Miller noted:

> These individuals were selected for inclusion in these volumes for their dynamic leadership and contributions at state, regional, and national levels. Though now deceased, their vision and contributions at state, regional, and national levels live on in the established school library media programs of today.

They remain the giants on whose shoulders we continue to work, fight, lobby, write, do our best to continue the libraries they helped develop where none existed, and improve all of our libraries. The editors also asked school librarians around the United States to name people they considered outstanding school librarians. Our list was to be 100, but some of the nominations came as pairs of names, so that list increased to 103. These two lists appear on this book's website at www.alaeditions.org/webextras/.

One of the nominees has moved to our list of pioneers, those giants on whose shoulders outstanding school librarians build. Her contributions to school librarianship were so powerful that we felt she needed to be remembered and honored here. Cora Paul Bomar (left) was indeed a giant in the field of education and librarianship, providing 50 years of teaching and promoting both school and public libraries. Her teaching career began in 1932 in a one-room rural school in western Tennessee where she was teacher and librarian to students in grades 1–8. She was, at various times, a school librarian at all levels through elementary, high school, and junior college.

Cora Paul Bomar

Her greatest contributions came with her appointment to the staff of the North Carolina Department of Public Instruction. In this role she saw the creation of school libraries not only in North Carolina but also throughout the nation. As the first director of educational media in the department, she built a state educational media program that included school librarians, audiovisual media, and instructional television, and she added a Material Review and Evaluation Center. When she left the department, all secondary schools and 98% of elementary schools had a central library.

In the 1960s, the American Association of School Librarians published its new *Standards*. The association received a grant from the Knapp Foundation to support the education of school librarians and the development of model school libraries across the United States. A motion picture, *And Something More*, presented an exemplary elementary library program, and a report from the U.S. Office of Education showed that fewer than 50% of U.S. elementary schools had libraries.

President Lyndon Baines Johnson signs the ESEA, April 11, 1965, as his childhood teacher looks on. Credit: LBJ Library and Museum.

Working with Mary Helen Mahar and the Office of Education staff, Bomar testified in support of federal legislation before House and Senate committees on six occasions. This resulted in the passage of the dedicated funding for the creation and expansion of school libraries in Title II of the 1965 Elementary and Secondary Education Act.

Improvements in school libraries in Pennsylvania

Should one need any evidence of the importance of this legislation for school libraries, Brenda H. White conducted a doctoral dissertation study of the improvements in school libraries and school library programs as a result of ESEA Title II in Pennsylvania. Based on an analysis of data from various sources—financial records, library records, interviews with superintendents, business managers, and librarians—several important changes occurred.

- Spending for library resources increased during this time period at a faster rate than spending for salaries or teaching supplies.
- The numbers of librarians increased, as did the number of libraries and the size of the collections.
- Circulation policies were liberalized in some cases because of the improved collections.
- Book collections increased from an average of 4.82 books per pupil to an average of 11.02 books per pupil.
- Audiovisual materials became accessible through central cataloging and housing.

These findings led to the conclusion that ESEA Title II had a demonstrable and positive effect on the development of school libraries in the Commonwealth of Pennsylvania. Some facts revealed by the study:

- The average number of centralized school libraries increased by 28.7%.
- The average number of centralized elementary school libraries increased by 38.1%.

- The number of full-time librarians increased from an average of 3.1 in each reporting district to 7.9 per reporting school.
- Financial resources for school libraries, which included local, state, and federal funding, increased by 351.4% over the period.
- Print holdings, counted by volumes, increased by 60.9% over the period.
- Audiovisual holdings showed the most change with school districts consolidating their holdings with their print holdings into central, cataloged collections.
- The numbers of nonprint holdings increased by 314.9% over the period.
- Print material holdings, as a per-pupil measure, increased on average from 4.82 to 10.18.

When Cora Paul left the Department of Public Instruction, she joined the faculty of the Department of Library Science and Technology in the School of Education at the University of North Carolina at Greensboro. She retired from this position in 1979, but in 1986 she was asked to return as interim chair, during which time she had the name changed to Department of Library and Information Studies and saw its program reaccredited by the American Library Association's Committee on Accreditation.

She served as president of the American Association of School Librarians, the Southeastern Library Association, and Beta Phi Mu, the international honor society for librarians. She was a sought-after consultant on developing school libraries, planning school library facilities, the evaluation of school libraries, and library education programs.

Cora Paul Bomar has left us a legacy of actions to follow to improve school libraries in this new century. How to go about empowering school librarians to undertake these actions is unclear. The DeWitt Wallace–Reader's Digest Fund ended in 1998 and school librarians did little to use the results of this project to show how this impacted student learning. The multiple studies conducted by Keith Curry Lance have not been used to their fullest either. The Scholastic publication *School Libraries Work!* is widely distributed, but we still have persons in power who say public libraries are all that is needed for children or that school libraries can be run by volunteers. The path to success might start where Cora Paul Bomar started.

Just discovering exactly how many school libraries exist would be a start. Counting the actual number of elementary school libraries with librarians would compare 1960 with 2011. Do more or fewer than 50% of schools have libraries with professional librarians? At least we would have some concrete evidence to see how steep the climb might be.

Then a national campaign should be designed and launched with as much help as possible from willing sponsors, beginning with those who benefit from selling things to school librarians. Getting parents and communities to understand the value to their children is essential, and having something to show to audiences would be another avenue to pursue.

The greatest challenge would be to get every school librarian ready and willing to carry out the planned program. Too often some school librarians sit back and expect the pioneers and outstanding school librarians to do it all, and "all" is too much for a small group. The numbers needed to carry out such a campaign must come from every school library in the United States. If we can follow the path created by the pioneers in the 1960s, we can move forward.

Conference 101 : Letterman-inspired lists to get you through ALA conferences

by Jeri Kladder

As a seasoned attendee of both ALA's Midwinter Meeting and Annual Conference, I know about the hustle and bustle. In a lighthearted, David Letterman kind of way, I present several Top 10 lists to help conference newcomers get through it all.

Top 10 take-alongs

Several weeks before you leave, designate a laundry basket for collecting what you need. Drop in things as you think of them or notes to yourself if you can't pack it right away. You are less likely to leave behind something crucial.

1. Water. Carry it with you. Filtered water (Brita bottles) work especially well because you can't always find a drinking fountain or a vendor to sell you water at inflated prices.
2. Comfortable shoes. You will do lots of walking.
3. A sturdy, wheeled book bag. The wheels are important because you'll collect lots of stuff, and paper is heavy.
4. Energy assists. Stock up on protein bars or peanuts. The best exhibit viewing is when everybody else is at lunch.
5. Business cards and address labels. Vendors will mail catalogs and you don't want to write your name and address on a mailing list over and over.
6. Highlighter, marking pens, and sticky notes to mark your convention booklet. A mini-schedule on the back of your badge checks what comes next.
7. A nice-sized poster tube and padded mailers with preaddressed labels and mailing tape to mail back literature to your library at the convention center post office.

8. Plastic sleeves and folders to keep important schedules from getting lost. Use one for invitations so you know who invited you and who were the honored authors and illustrators, which makes writing thank-you cards easier.
9. A camera. Document your meeting the Newbery or Caldecott winners or some other legend of children's literature, librarianship, or children's publishing.
10. Your preplanned schedule from the ALA website, ala.org. When choosing what to attend, consider geography and travel time. With four conflicting programs, you and your coworkers should negotiate the schedule and compare notes later.

Top 10 attractions

1. The *Booklist* Forum, held Friday evening during Annual Conference, when *Booklist* invites a panel of authors to discuss writing for youth.
2. The Scholarship Bash, held Saturday evening at Annual Conference, lets you have fun while adding to the scholarship to enable the education of our replacements.
3. All committee meetings during Midwinter Meeting and Annual Conference that are held for all three youth divisions. Members are welcome to attend

and cruise the committee tables to get a good overview of the hard work done by the committees. Find one you are particularly drawn to, grab a seat, and introduce yourself. You may find yourself selected to join a committee.

4. The Newbery/Caldecott/Wilder banquet during Annual Conference. If you can't afford the pricey ticket, come at 9 p.m. and sit on the periphery to hear the winners' acceptance speeches.

5. The youth division President's Programs always feature an intellectually stimulating presentation of some facet of youth library service or advocacy.

6. Polish your book-talk skills at the Association for Library Service to Children's book discussion. You need to have done your homework: Read and be prepared to discuss a selection of five children's books. If you have never participated in professional book discussion, learn here; if you are an old hand at book discussion, you enjoy a rousing oral debate, honing your skills, and helping newcomers.

7. The Coretta Scott King Book Awards Breakfast. Held on the Tuesday morning of Annual Conference, this breakfast is well worth getting up early to honor the author, illustrator, and new-talent award winners.

8. Exhibits. A wonderful opportunity to see advance reading copies of new books, get your name on catalog mailing lists, seek out vendors to provide next year's summer reading club prizes, and talk to sales representatives. Publishers really want to hear how to make their products better or fill a need you have.

9. Attend at least one event or program that is not about youth librarianship. Seeing and hearing issues outside your own service area helps you understand the larger library picture and youth services' place in it.

10. Take the shuttle bus from hotel to the convention center, stand in line (almost anywhere), and talk to people around you. In a city, no matter how large, almost everyone you encounter is connected to libraries in some way. Talk, compare notes, share ideas, bemoan your common problems. You just may come away with a new friend and a new idea to take back to your library.

Top 10 money-saving tips

1. A suite for four to six people may be less expensive than several two-person rooms—and you just might get two bathrooms and more closet space.

2. Bring a water bottle to save money on the pricier bottles available for purchase.

3. Bring protein bars for breakfast and lunch.

4. Some hotels offer complimentary breakfasts, and some have inexpensive room-service breakfast. These hearty choices allow you to run through the normal lunch hour at the exhibits, and your early dinner will be less expensive than a later meal.

5. Register early. The super early-bird registration saves money. If your library can't foot the bill, it won't hurt as much to pay your own way.

6. Accept lunch, dinner, and reception invitations. You meet some wonderful

book people and have some great conversations with authors, illustrators, and editors, and the receptions often include hors d'oeuvres.

7. Take the shuttle bus from the airport instead of a taxi. Shuttles are less expensive and they show you the location of other conference hotels as they drop passengers. Round-trip tickets and the ALA discount save you even more.

8. Use the conference shuttle bus system to get from conference hotels to the convention center. If the program and meeting schedules are posted early, you can save travel time and money by choosing a hotel convenient to your agenda.

9. Share taxis with others going in your direction. After a program or meeting in one hotel, getting to the next event on time might be impossible if you have to take the shuttle bus to the convention center and then a different bus route. If there is a cluster of people from your finished meeting, ask if anybody is going to your next event. You'll make friends, save time, and pay only a portion of the taxi fare yourself.

10. Take advantage of a convenient all-purpose store to stock up on drinks and snacks. It will be less expensive than restaurant food.

Top 10 ways to fit in if you're alone

1. Though we are advised not to wear our badges around town, librarians aren't hard to spot. You are surrounded by helpful folk in the elevators, on the street corners, in hotel lobbies, even in restaurants.

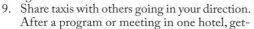

2. Before you go, get a sturdy fold-out map of the city and mark your hotel, the convention center, and other hotels where your meetings are held. Learn the lay of the land before you go.

3. Keep some small bills in your pocket for taxis and small purchases so you aren't opening your wallet or purse all the time. Keep money in two different places. If you lose one, you won't be strapped.

4. A waistpack or neck pouch keeps your money, credit cards, and identification close to your body.

5. Local Arrangements Committee people provide excellent guidance at meeting and program sites. Look for their smiles and signs. They are there to help.

6. Plan your route to meetings and receptions before you go out onto the street. You will feel more in control than if you are pondering a map on a street corner.

7. Plan at least one sightseeing trip to a nearby museum, library, or shopping area so you can feel like you have actually been somewhere.

8. Do your research. Timing is important. Can you make it to the next meeting on the shuttle?

9. Arrange your arrival early enough to pick up your registration materials on Friday afternoon. Plan your conference days leisurely.

10. Strike up conversations with other attendees wherever you are. Share tables at restaurants and exhibit snack areas. The more you connect, the less you will feel alone.

Top 10 follow-throughs

1. Send thank-you notes to the sponsors of invitation-only events.
2. Submit your expenses and reimbursement requests quickly. Don't miss the deadline.
3. Distribute giveaways to coworkers who manned the fort while you were away.
4. Write your report and make it exciting to lure others.
5. Fill out and submit a committee volunteer form for your favorite division.
6. Enthuse about your experience to your coworkers; get them to consider joining you next time.
7. Follow up on activities and ideas you have heard about at conference. Write or email some of the people you met and with whom you exchanged business cards.
8. Make plans to attend again. Request conference time at work. Preregister for the next conference; make hotel reservations.
9. Share and incorporate new ideas and programs you heard about at conference. Consider writing a best-practices article for your division's periodical about how you adapted somebody else's program.
10. Broaden coworkers' perceptions of the larger library world by sharing how other libraries do what they do. Tell your coworkers about practices, events, and programs at your libraries that other attendees want to emulate.

SOURCE: Adapted from Jeri Kladder, "Conference 101: Letterman-Inspired Lists to Get You through ALA Conventions," *Children and Libraries* 3 (Winter 2005): 41–44. Used with permission.

From bossy girls to bug eaters

by Sharon Korbeck Verbeten

Editors' note: Megan McDonald received her MLS from the University of Pittsburgh, where her classes prepared her for a role as a school or public librarian. She has since moved from telling stories in public libraries to writing stories for children. This article showcases someone with an international audience for her books and someone you can point to when you are asked about how to get a children's book published.

Megan McDonald

Megan McDonald ate bugs and lived to tell the tale. In fact, McDonald has told many tales, some about crunchy bugs and some about moody little girls, in her years as a children's book author. With more than 30 titles to her credit, McDonald is perhaps best known as the creator of the Judy Moody fiction series, which has sold more than 3.75 million books.

"Sometimes I think I am Judy Moody," said McDonald. "I'm certainly moody, like she is. Judy has a strong voice and always speaks up for herself."

The Judy Moody series was introduced in 2000, and six years later the then-46-year-old McDonald was busy on her eighth book of the series. In between the series books, she also writes picture books and nonfiction titles. One was *Beetle McGrady Eats Bugs!* (Greenwillow, 2005), a tantalizing tale of tasty insect treats and the girl daring enough to eat them.

And that first bite started with the author herself. "If I'm going to do this right. . . . I made myself eat a toasted mealworm and a roasted cricket," said McDonald, who lives in Sebastopol, California. Bugs have invaded her life, it seems, since she was a little girl, when her mother got her a field guide and a magnifying glass.

"She didn't want [bugs] in the house," McDonald recalled. "I'd hide [dead moths] in my jewelry box. I really had no idea that bugs would become such a part of my life."

"I love to pick up on things I think kids are interested in too," she said. A winsome pair of insect buddies also spotlighted her 2005 title *Ant and Honey Bee: What a Pair!* (Candlewick).

Bugs weren't the only squeamish part of her childhood. The budding scientist in McDonald led her to collect, of all things, scabs. "That was part of the scientist thing when I was little," she said. "If I save it, I can look at it again."

The youngest of five daughters, McDonald had a childhood in Pittsburgh, Pennsylvania, that provided fodder for her future career. "That was really a good training ground," she said. "I kind of get inspired by things that happened with my sisters."

It's possible some of her sisters' personalities and mannerisms may appear in her stories. "My sisters are delighted for me," she said, "but they like to tease."

Schooled in English and library science, McDonald has worked as everything from storyteller to park ranger. But in every career, she felt the same push. "It's all about connecting kids to books," she said.

The Judy Moody series with its bossy, moody big-sister heroine seems to resonate that powerfully. "I'm so lucky to meet fans everywhere I go. The thing that's been amazing to me is how much kids relate to Judy. They treat her like a real person," she noted. "Kids really see themselves reflected in her. Even as adults, we see ourselves in her."

2005 was a banner year for McDonald with as many as six new books, including *When the Library Lights Go Out* (Atheneum), a tale of puppets coming to life after dark. As she sets up shop in her house (yes, she can work in her pajamas), McDonald scribbles down ideas whenever they come, even on napkins. "Ideas can come at any time." And that well is far from dry. "I always get asked, 'How many [Judy Moody books] are you going to write?' I have sort of a bottomless well for Judy," she said. "I try to make every book something special. As long as I have fresh ideas, I'll keep going."

Her legion of fans will be happy to hear that; after all, getting kids to read is a noble goal. "The most gratifying [thing] is I have so many people tell me [my books] have transformed a kid who didn't like to read into a reader.

"That's the highest compliment."

SOURCE: Adapted from Sharon Korbeck Verbeten, "From Bossy Girls to Bug Eaters: Megan McDonald Draws Inspiration from Childhood," *Children and Libraries* 4 (Spring 2006): 39–40. Used with permission.

Did you know?

When Megan McDonald was a child, she collected bugs, scabs, fancy toothpicks, and Barbie doll heads.

Her favorite book as a child was *Harriet the Spy* by Louise Fitzhugh. At age 10, McDonald wrote her first story for her school newspaper; it was about a pencil sharpener. Her middle name is Jo. She wanted to change her name to Megan Jo Amy Beth McDonald so it would contain the names of all four sisters from Louisa May Alcott's *Little Women*. She is the fifth girl in her family; when she was born, the doctor yelled, "It's a boy!" as a joke.

Want to know more? Visit her website at www.meganmcdonald.net.

The inner teacher-leader:
The staff developer

by Pat Franklin and Claire Gatrell Stephens

One important role of a school librarian is that of teacher-leader. This position is a way for the school librarian to be in the forefront of bringing innovations to schools. This role continues to be of great importance as school-reform movements push schools in new directions. The perceptive school librarian recognizes school restructuring as an opportunity to serve in a teacher-leader role and expand it into new spheres of influence.

The increased accountability demands leave little time for the average teacher to invest in identifying and developing best practices for the classroom. This provides a perfect opportunity for the school librarian to demonstrate leadership skills by offering teacher in-service programs to increase professional skills.

If not currently involved in professional development, the school librarian should start reaching out to those in charge. Principals, classroom resource teachers, reading coaches, science and math coaches, team leaders, and department chairs often work together to guide professional learning at the school level. Ask to meet with the team leader individually or to attend a team meeting. Before attending one of these meetings, the school librarian should do some homework. What is there to know about the professional development program of the school, its strengths or weaknesses? Does a particular philosophy guide the program? What skills would the school librarian bring to the table to enhance the program?

When meeting with those making staff development decisions, the school librarian should maintain an open attitude and listen to ideas and concerns discussed. Since good professional learning programs develop from the problems teachers and administrators consider significant, it is helpful to be aware of these concerns. If there is no clear direction for the staff development program, the school librarian can volunteer to organize a needs-assessment survey for the faculty. By identifying areas of strength and weakness in student test scores, the professional development team will gain a clearer vision of instructional needs.

Many teachers need training to assist them in identifying, understanding, and teaching curriculum-based information skills in mastering new information technologies, a place for school librarian leadership. Another asset is the school librarian's network of contacts—knowledge of and links to experts within and outside school. Facilitate in-service activities by bringing in guest speakers or tapping the knowledge of school-based, expert teachers.

Leading effective in-service activities requires a clear plan with goals and objectives for the session. They model best practices for the classroom. Plans should be carefully made for the time allotted. All aspects of the in-service presentation must be relevant to the teachers with content that can be directly applied in the classrooms. Be well-prepared.

If planning and presenting formal in-service sessions is not possible in a particular school setting, consider looking for alternative ways to bring professional development to the school site. Facilitate a book study group for new teachers who read a professional book and meet three to four times over the course of a semester for reading and discussion.

Participating in faculty in-service programs requires a commitment of time and energy on the part of the school librarian and increases influence, allowing teachers to see the school librarian in a different light, as a full educational partner and a leader. In addition, since presentations promote good teaching practices related to use of resources and technology, the use of the school library will improve. In-service opportunities help lessen the isolation many school librarians feel and let them forge relationships with faculty and staff.

Perhaps most importantly, the time and preparation put into developing good staff development enriches the school librarian. By taking time to focus on the qualities of good teaching and sharing that information with peers, school librarians refocus what is done and why. The time and energy spent developing and presenting a staff in-service session ends up being a great experience with incredible value.

Resources

Crowley, John D. *Developing a Vision: Strategic Planning and the Library Media Specialist.* Westport, Conn.: Greenwood Press, 1994.
Hartzell, Gary N. *Building Influence for the School Librarian.* Worthington, Ohio: Linworth, 1994.
Woolls, Blanche. *The School Library Media Manager,* 2nd ed. Englewood, Colo.: Libraries Unlimited, 1999.

How can a professional book study be organized? Here are some titles:

Forsten, Char, Jim Grant, and Betty Hollas. *Differentiating Textbooks: Strategies to Improve Student Comprehension and Motivation.* Peterborough, N.H.: Crystal Springs Books, 2003.
Marzano, Robert J., Debra J. Pickering, and Jane E Pollock. *Classroom Instruction That Works: Research Based Strategies for Increasing Student Achievement.* Alexandria, Va.: Association for Supervision and Curriculum Development, 2001.
Marzano, Robert J., Jennifer S. Norford, Diane E. Paynter, Debra J. Pickering, and Barbara B. Gaddy, eds. *A Handbook for Classroom Instruction That Works.* Alexandria, Va.: Association for Supervision and Curriculum Development, 2001. A good companion book for *Classroom Instruction That Works.*
Rutherford, Paula. *Instruction for All Students,* 2nd ed. Alexandria, Va.: Just Ask, 2008.
Rutherford, Paula. *Why Didn't I Learn This in College? Teaching and Learning in the 21st Century,* 2nd ed. Alexandria, Va.: Just Ask, 2009.

SOURCE: Adapted from Pat Franklin and Claire Gatrell Stephens, "The Inner Teacher-Leader—The Staff Developer," *School Library Media Activities Monthly* 25, no. 7 (March 2009): 44–45. Used with permission.

Have MLS, will travel
by Helen R. Adams

Here are four questions that could change your life: Do you like to travel and have a spirit of adventure? Are you interested in learning firsthand about other cultures? Do you enjoy being a librarian but want a change from your current position? Have you considered becoming a librarian in an international school?

At the 2005 East Asia Regional Council of Overseas Schools Teachers' Conference in Vietnam, I met more than 40 school media specialists who served in 14 countries and interviewed nine of those from the United States and Canada about their experiences.

What brought them to such work? The reasons are as varied as the countries they serve in. Three factors drew Rob Rubis to his current position as high school librarian at the International School Bangkok: He sought escape from cold Canadian winters, wanted to satisfy a wanderlust, and felt a "dissatisfaction with the status of teachers in Canada."

Former public librarian Beth Gourley found her way to the International School of Tianjin, China, more serendipitously: While deleting messages from an email list in 1997, she saw an opening for a school librarian and applied.

A birthday prompted Barbara Kieran to go after her first international position as a school librarian in Saudi Arabia. "I turned 50 and suddenly realized I was closer to the end than the beginning of my life and it was time to get busy in realizing a lifelong dream of living internationally."

Betsy Piper's life as a "trailing spouse" to her journalist husband led her from being an elementary school librarian in Baltimore to schools in Moscow, London, and Japan, and, most recently, the Seoul Foreign School in Korea.

Carol Van Brocklin's impetus came during a stressful time in her job as a government librarian. "A friend reminded me that I had been interested in mission work years before and maybe this was the time to trust God and make the move," she says. That move eventually guided her to library positions in Bolivia, Ecuador, and the Philippines.

International schools are independent schools that operate autonomously in countries around the world, often serving the children of personnel employed in diplomacy, foreign service, multinational corporations, and the military. While the instruction is usually in English, each school and its library situation is unique.

The Seoul Foreign School serves students from 49 countries, and ethnic Koreans comprise 44% of the student population. Carolyn Kitterer, the school's former middle and high school librarian, says the library is large, located on two floors, and houses a collection of about 28,000 items. With flexible scheduling, the library is used by small groups, full classes, and individual students from 7:30 a.m. to 4:30 p.m. As in most international schools, parents are able to use the library for reading and research.

Kirk Palmer, media specialist for the Primary Library at the Singapore American School, reports that 85% of students there hold U.S. passports, and that 40 nationalities are represented. "Although we follow curriculum from the U.S. in all levels, we do introduce Asian cultures and a certain amount of multiculturalism in every level," he points out. The Primary Library, "a huge space soaring in some parts up to three stories high" began renovation in 2005 to add a television studio with editing capabilities, a larger storytelling area, and 25% more floor space, with a goal of expanding the collection to 35,000 items.

Mary Ellen Scribner, the first librarian at the relatively new Saigon South International School in Ho Chi Minh City, Vietnam, has spent much of her time organizing current resources and expanding the collection to include periodicals and electronic databases. Parents of the 250 mainly American, Korean, Taiwanese, and Vietnamese students may also borrow books from the collection since the city has no English-language public library. While elementary students use the library on a fixed schedule, Scribner says she is

Beth Gourley and students at the International School of Tianjin celebrate Book Week dressed as their favorite characters.

"working hard to develop more collaborative opportunities with middle and high school teachers."

The Surabaya International School Library in Indonesia is "the only English-language library in the city of 7 million, so I get a lot of visitors who like to see what a U.S. educational standard library looks like," explains Barbara Kieran. She finds one thing that makes an international school different is "the fact that all aspects of the students' lives really do revolve around the school. The school community is more like a large family."

Ups and downs of the job

"The best thing about working in the overseas schools is the students," reveals Kitterer. "I really enjoy the mix of nationalities and cultures and their interest in learning. The other outstanding feature is the opportunity to meet and know people from all over the world. There are other very positive aspects such as supportive administration and community, the strong sense of community, and the variations of curriculum dependent on where in the world you are located."

Van Brocklin adds that one thing she finds in international schools is "a much higher percentage of parents who are actively involved with their students' education and wanting to help their children. I have an average of one to three parents per day who come into the library to ask for help in finding books for their children to read, and I don't think there are many schools in the States that can say that."

Opportunities for travel and exposure to other cultures are another major advantage of teaching overseas, notes Candace Aiani, upper school librarian at the Taipei American School in Taiwan. "We have traveled to many wonderful places multiple times including China, Thailand, Cambodia, Egypt, Vietnam, the Philippines, and Indonesia," she says. "We plan to travel to India and Myanmar this coming year. Previous to our teaching overseas, we could not have imagined that we would have the opportunity or the money to travel so much."

However, as with every experience in life, there are some negative aspects about serving in an international school. One downside "is the transition issues of students, colleagues, and friends moving out of your life, coupled with the fact that you are often away from your own family and close friends," explains Kitterer. Aiani also cautions that "if someone has aging parents, as we do, it is difficult, if not impossible, to provide much support from a distance."

Finding a position

Many placement agencies are available; however, the two mentioned most frequently by the librarians interviewed in this article were International Schools Services and Search Associates. A less obvious source for international positions is the University of Northern Iowa, which has been holding recruitment fairs since 1976.

Additionally, two print sources can help interested librarians gain a sense of the range of opportunities in international education: *The ISS Directory of Overseas Schools* is a valuable annual guide listing international schools, and *The International Educator* newspaper lists current openings and maintains an interactive website.

Association of Christian Schools International, www.acsi.org.
Council of International Schools, www.cois.org.
International Schools Services, www.iss.edu.
Search Associates, www.search-associates.com.
The International Educator, www.tieonline.com.
University of Northern Iowa, www.uni.edu/placement/overseas/.

In China, Beth Gourley reports, "overall, we have good broadband access, but internet filtering is pervasive. Noise levels, constant construction, and pollution can all be a grind." Another frustration can be "the distance that our materials have to travel to reach us," adds Piper. "We have only one big order a year, with perhaps one supplementary order arriving later." The materials are gathered in a warehouse, she says, "and must wait until enough accumulates to warrant sending an order."

Finally, Scribner cautions, "Educators who work in international schools have little if any legal recourse when the school doesn't fulfill its contractual obligations or arbitrarily decides that the employee hasn't fulfilled hers or his, or in any grievance or dispute for that matter."

Advice for others

What do these international librarians advise others considering such a move? "Make sure to research the schools you are interested in applying to," counsels Gourley. "There are many different types of international schools throughout the world—packages, perks, and workplace atmospheres can vary widely. Be aware of the difference between a not-for-profit and a proprietary school."

Aiani recommends librarians seeking employment abroad "be willing to take a position in a less desirable assignment in order to move to a more desirable location later."

Above all, Kitterer urges, "Be a risk-taker. If you want to work in an international school, you must be flexible and adaptable in ways you might not have considered. The perfect job may be there, but more likely you may find yourself in situations that are unique to the country, the times, or subject to economic or political situations. Be open and willing to try or accept things that are new or different."

Just as the libraries and positions are unique, Aiani points out, "The schools are very different from one another in size, ownership, etc., so don't be afraid to ask all the hard questions about pay and benefits." She notes the great difference in taxes and other benefits from country to country, and says to be sure to consider the whole package such as housing, overseas allowance, and travel home rather than just the base pay. "Americans living overseas do not pay federal income tax on approximately the first $80,000 of their income [the foreign earned income exclusion], so consider that when looking at income," she adds.

Kitterer cautions, "One thing you must consider when looking at a dollar amount is the cost of living in a country, as it may be that a low salary (and whatever additional, if any, benefits) will allow you to live very comfortably and save money as well, while another place may offer what looks to be a lot of money, but you will struggle from month to month."

"Generally, librarians are on the same salary schedule as classroom teachers and receive the same benefits as other employees," explains Palmer. "The main difference in any school would be from locally employed faculty and overseas hires."

Piper, who was a local hire, agrees. "Overseas and local-hire employees do not receive the same benefits," she laments. "If I were hired from abroad, I would also receive housing, access to a shared car, and an annual round-trip ticket to my home country."

Rob Rubis counsels taking the long view with regard to financial planning, since many international

Barbara Kieran at the Surabaya International School.

schools don't have true retirement plans. "Although the salary and benefits packages seem wonderful, if you do not have a retirement plan, you will need to have invested heavily in a personal savings plan or investment portfolio to offset the lack of a fixed retirement income," he urges.

Without a doubt, all nine international school librarians interviewed felt fortunate to be experiencing their profession with a global twist. "I think that my enduring memories have to do with the small cultural experiences that I encounter in everyday life," says Aiani. "The wonder and beauty of other cultures never ceases to impact my thinking and my perspective in life. It is hard to explain what is special about eating beef noodle soup with chopsticks, or riding the local bus #601 past the hospital, or climbing 1,500 stairs to the top of Yangmingshan Mountain to see the talking bird, or stopping for the millionth time to pose for a picture with strangers because the locals are fascinated by our western faces."

SOURCE: Adapted from Helen R. Adams, "Have MLS, Will Travel," *American Libraries* 36, no. 10 (November 2005): 54–56. Used with permission.

Opening the door to leadership: The key
by Sharon Coatney

School librarians have the capacity to become school leaders. But to accomplish this goal, they need to cultivate and develop the dispositions, responsibilities, and skills necessary to become lifelong learners. As the old saying goes, school librarians must "practice what they preach" and expectations for students must also be expectations for themselves. Modeling is the best teacher.

Lifelong learners

The American Association of School Librarians *Standards for the 21st-Century Learner* (ala.org/aasl, 2007) speaks to the lifelong learning needs of all ages. Learners are not just students in grades preK–12. In any school building, there are many adults (staff, administrators, teachers, and parents) who can be encouraged to demonstrate the characteristics of lifelong learners by the presence, modeling, and active leadership of a school librarian. Developing and displaying the dispositions of curiosity, openness to new ideas, and the motivation to seek information to answer personal questions is imperative (*Standards,* Dispositions in Action 4.2.1, 4.2.2, 4.2.3.). Becoming a model for lifelong learning should be a goal of every school librarian.

What do students see as they enter the school library? Are the adults in the room engaged in learning activities? Perhaps the school librarian is personally interested in the workings of the internal combustion engine, narrow-gauge steam locomotives in America, the glaciers of Alaska, the culture of the Middle Ages, the architecture of New England, or the quilt patterns of southern Appalachia. No matter what the topic is, the demonstration of that interest, the sharing of findings with others by constructing creative school library displays, the writing of newsletter articles, and posting to blogs serve to model research accomplished through constant reading, inquiry, and sharing new findings (Skills 1.1.6, 2.1.4, 4.1.7, 3.1.3).

Research pursuits

Though personal passions may not be of particular interest to the other learners in the school, the demonstration of the disposition towards continually learning and pursuing new information (Disposition 1.2.7) about the topic is a model that must be shown. This concept can be expanded by the school librarian who can encourage adults to display their own interests in the school library and show them how to find the information they need, how to construct interesting projects (electronic, print, visual), and how to discuss their research pursuits (Responsibilities 1.3.5, 3.3.5). This modeling by adults is a powerful tool in fostering curiosity in students (Skills 1.1.9). Teaching students, faculty, and staff how to do research using all types of media, how to evaluate and synthesize the information, and how to construct the final products is an opportunity to show the school librarian's skills in information searching, evaluation, organization, synthesis, and creation (Skills 2.1.1, 2.1.2, 2.1.3).

The recitation bench

It is well established that learners learn from repetition. In the one-room school-house, teachers across America long ago capitalized on that fact by using the concept of the recitation bench. Students were called to the front of the room to recite their lesson, read aloud, work math problems on the board, and demonstrate geography skills using maps displayed at the front of the room. Students at their desks worked quietly at other tasks while they waited their turn to recite. By hearing these daily recitations, they were constantly exposed to reviews of previous lessons and previews of upcoming materials, thus cementing the learning in their long-term memory. A placard at the one-room schoolhouse at the Tallgrass Prairie National Preserve near Strong City, Kansas, quotes Lloyd Smith, former country school student: "As for book learning, I think I can truthfully say that I learned more hearing the older pupils recite than from poring over my own lessons."

The school library, through the leadership of the school librarian, can become a living recitation bench, a richly blended tapestry of sounds and sights that reflect all of the learning, both informal and formal, going on in schools (Disposition 3.2.1). By providing the vision to use the library as a place to display student work, begin electronic real-time discussions, host programs that reinforce and pique student learning, and preview interesting new concepts, the school librarian both provides a forum for that repetition of learning and models the disposition to continually find new interest in learning about everything and anything in our world (Dispositions 3.2.2, 3.2.3).

Learn, teach, lead

School librarians need to know what is critical to the curriculum and should continually look for and learn about new information, new materials, and new findings related to curricular areas so they can share the information with students and faculty. It is a big job and never-ending, but interesting and rewarding. The job of school librarian is to consistently and continually learn in all areas covered by the curriculum, providing what David Loertscher describes as "the best educated member of the faculty."

The tagline of ASCD (www.ascd.org) states, "Learn, Teach, Lead." ASCD Executive Director Gene R. Carter emphasizes this concept when he says, "For more than 65 years, ASCD has provided educators with the tools, resources, and leadership they need to respond to our constantly changing world. We help educators learn, teach, and lead beyond boundaries." "Learn, Teach, Lead" also describes the role of school librarians. School librarians need to learn in order to teach and fulfill the job as the curriculum leader in the school.

School librarians are, first and foremost, educators. They have the skills necessary to learn about the curriculum in depth, to keep abreast of what is new, and to help teachers teach it. School librarians have the responsibility to provide the model for lifelong learning by demonstrating the dispositions, responsibilities, and skills called for in the AASL *Standards for the 21st-Century Learner.* School librarians are the learning leaders in schools.

SOURCE: Sharon Coatney, "Opening the Door to Leadership: The Key," *School Library Monthly* 26, no. 4 (December 2009): 43–44.

50 ways to succeed @ your library: Making you a professional
by Blanche Woolls

That old adage: If it looks like a duck and quacks like a duck, it must be a duck. If we are to assume our rightful place in the professional community, we need to make sure that we look like professionals and sound like professionals. At some recent school library conferences, this author has presented a program called "Fifty Ways to Succeed @ Your Library." A list of ways was distributed and participants at the sessions were asked to add to the 50 ways. The original ways are shown below with some expansions of the discussions. Because most of them have no real cost attached, implementing these will help you become the professional you should be. They are divided into four categories: managing, teaching, public relations, and "that extra effort."

Managing

1. Make your library media center appealing to all who enter. Close your eyes and do a virtual walk into your media center. What does the visitor see? How can you make it more attractive?
2. Don't put up with broken, scarred, wrong-size, and mismatched furniture and shelving. This one could cost you some money, so you need to take your principal, a teacher, and a member of your advisory committee to a national or state association meeting where many furniture vendors display their wares and show what the library could look like. Know the amount that needs to be raised and have some thoughts about how you would raise that money.
3. Improve your signage. If you can't figure out how to do this, look around at your local bookstores and see what they do. You could ask the art teacher to help with this.
4. Take some hints from public librarians. Children's librarians often put their bookshelves on wheels to make rearranging spaces quite easy. They also sometimes hang bookracks on the end of shelves and do other things to make spaces more useful.
5. Merchandise your collection. Visit the local bookstore or even a local department store and look at how they entice customers to want to buy their products.

6. Weed your collection. Nothing is as negative as shelves and shelves of old, unattractive, out-of-date things that nobody wants. Shelves crowded with "dogs" will keep your teachers and students away because they won't think you have anything that is modern.
7. Change displays, bulletin boards, and exhibitions frequently. What's on that bulletin board or in that display case will draw students into the media center.
8. Be sure you help students learn about continuing their educations. Guidance counselors cannot reach students as easily as you can because their offices are small and usually require an appointment to enter. You can help every student find something to do when they finish high school. If students knew how to enroll in programs after high school, quitting school might be less of an option. Most of us came from homes where parents let us know what we were supposed to do after high school, so we stayed in high school. You need to do this for students who don't have parents who see any advantage (or possibility) for study after high school.

Teaching

9. Work with teachers and students, making the teaching job easier for teachers and the learning job easier for students. Collaborate with your teachers.
10. Meet with teachers informally and formally and plan. Collaborate with your teachers.
11. Teach, with their teachers, the things students need to learn. Collaborate with your teachers.
12. Teach your teachers all the new bells and whistles technology has to offer. This makes you the hero in the battle to stay current.
13. Take all teachers with a smile. Yes, the football coach does like to send his class to the library before the Friday game. You should be thankful that you aren't responsible for the arms, legs, necks, backs, and heads of 100 young men who may come away from that game with something wrong with any or all of those body parts. Make sure you have a collaborative assignment for the class, and be a good sport.
14. Share with your teachers new articles from your professional collection. They will look to you for leadership in educational innovation.
15. Dream up new ways to approach the same old same old. A teacher may be bored to death with some or all assignments, which means students are going to be equally bored. Help spruce up assignments and learning will increase.
16. Be especially helpful with new teachers or things new to a teacher. In both cases, the teacher may be at borderline panic. This is an easy way to become a hero and leader.
17. Encouraging reading has always been our assignment. Students today are bombarded by so many opportunities to do anything except read. Use all the ideas you can find in your head, on the internet, or in professional books and other publications to increase the reading skills of your students.

Public relations

18. Copy Walmart's greeter scheme. Assign students to stand at the door and welcome students into the library. This might be a good assignment for an escapee from study hall (if your school still has them).

1

19. Watch rules. My principal always told me that a rule meant a punishment for breaking the rule, and keeping up with those who break ineffective rules and their punishment is more difficult than not having the rule in the first place. Two all-encompassing rules are: Do unto others what you would have others do unto you, and Do not do unto others what you would not want others to do to you.

20. Watch and remove rules that limit students. Things like "Two-week checkout only" or "You can't come to the library if you have an overdue book" or "One book only."

21. Make sure the students understand it is *their* library. This means you ask them what they want and then you try to provide it. After all, it is *their* library.

22. Overcome overdues. If you lengthen the checkout time (as you do for teachers) and only require that a student return the book when another student requests it or at the end of the semester, you won't have overdues.

23. Forget fines. Fines cost more in bad public relations and bookkeeping than you could possibly earn.

24. Resist broadcasting any negative messages over the public address system. Make these messages about good new books, new things available, new opportunities.

25. Resist negative reminders in the library. If your library media center has rules, they should begin with something other than "No" or "Do not."

26. Have great programs. Schedule exciting things in the media center. Shopping centers and airports bring automobiles in for people to see. Ever think about a motorcycle in the library?

27. Encourage students to volunteer in the library media center. This helps them understand what goes on in there. If they understand a database well, they can help teach others how to search, effectively easing your teaching load. It also makes the media center *their* media center.

28. Keep the principal informed of exciting things going on in the library media center. Give him things to brag about to other principals.

29. Maintain a great website where you have links to great information. If you can't do this alone, draft a reliable student or two.

30. Keep your principal informed about what is new in the professional literature. When principals are cutting-edge aware of all the newest educational trends, they won't be embarrassed at a district meeting when something is proposed that is new.

31. Have an advisory committee for the library media center. What they can help you do will surprise you. They become your advocates.

32. Hold at least one event in the library each semester to show parents. When you do this, make sure the students are doing the showing.

That extra effort

33. Watch for opportunities for proposal writing. This can be time-consuming at the start, but once you get a list of places and their offerings, you can pick and choose. Also, you need not do this alone. Get your advisory committee members or other teachers to help you; or, if you want to get a bigger grant, get other media specialists in the district to join you.

34. Find out about contests in which your students can participate. You may have to help the teachers collect and submit entries, but a winning student makes the newspaper.

35. Find out about field trips. Sometimes you can tell teachers about special opportunities for students and how to get to the place. Sometimes you can do the training offered by the museum or gallery and become the "teacher" for all the students, thus relieving all other teachers in your building from participating in the training.
36. Don't miss school events. Students really know who attends their special functions, whether it is a football game, the class play or musical, or a field trip. An easy way to become a mentor.
37. Show your worth. You may have to gather some statistics, but when you make a difference, you need a record of that.
38. Keep records of your successful experiences. If something worked well, do it again.
39. Conduct real research. For this you may need to find a local college or university and an assistant professor in need of research for tenure, but what you discover may have more value than action research you did on your own.
40. Make frequent reports. These should be short and sweet and interesting.
41. Visit your legislators. Take students, teachers, and parents to show off your program. That way they will know who and what you are when you need to ask for legislation.
42. Invite the school board and your legislators to your school. This needs to have your principal's approval, but it may not have occurred to your administrators that having the school board or your legislators visit the school and library just to show off the great programs there would bring applause to your school. It is another way to help them understand education and school library media programs.
43. Be a problem solver for little, middle, and big problems. Gain a reputation for getting things corrected, made better, made possible. You may not always be able to do this alone, but you should learn who are the best people to work together to make things happen.
44. Volunteer to provide a session at your state conference. This way you should be able to get funding to attend. If you really want to ensure this, ask your principal and a teacher to present with you.
45. Volunteer to write for a professional periodical. Your teachers, principal, and community will love seeing their school featured.
46. Bring in the media as often as you can. When you can do something in the library, perhaps invite legislators to your building; the media will come mostly because the legislator will want this featured in the media.
47. Make sure students understand Frances Henne's description of the ultimate in information literacy: "For some students, and in certain schools this may be many students, the only library skill that they should have to acquire is an awareness imprinted indelibly and happily upon them that the library is a friendly place where the librarians are eager to help." This is what we are all about.
48. Think before you whine, then don't.
49. Most of all, enjoy your job, all day, every day. The contribution you are making to the teachers and students in your school cannot be measured.
50. Smile.

SOURCE: Adapted from Blanche Woolls, *School Library Media Manager*, 4th ed. (Westport, Conn.: Libraries Unlimited, 2008).

Professional development through Learning Circles
by Peggy Mourer

Learning Circles, as defined by Michelle Collay in her 1998 book *Learning Circles: Creating Conditions for Professional Development,* are: "Small communities of learners among teachers and others who come together intentionally for the purpose of supporting each other in the process of learning." Another way to envision Learning Circles is to compare them to the ever-popular reading circles or book clubs that have sprung up in recent years. Everyone in the group will read a specific assignment prior to the meeting and then get together to share, to reflect, and most importantly to learn.

Learning Circles present a unique opportunity for school librarians to offer professional development activities to their fellow faculty and administrators either after school or during in-service days. Normally they will involve reading two or three short articles or looking at a few chosen websites, and then getting together for discussion. Focus questions will help direct the discussion.

You should allow 8 to 16 participants, but that's entirely up to you. The focus questions are designed to provide approximately one-and-a-half hours of discussion, but again this depends on the number of participants and the degree of discussion. You should set a time frame so that teachers that need to be home at a certain hour will feel comfortable leaving, even if the discussion continues.

Try to keep planning and preparation to a minimum. Basically, you will need to establish your group and give them the assignment one to two weeks in advance of your meeting date. You might want to make two or three photocopies of the readings to circulate among your group or have them on reserve in the library so that participants can read them before or after school or during their planning periods. A major recommendation is to hold your circle in the library. This is a great opportunity for networking.

SOURCE: Peggy Mourer, "Professional Development through Learning Circles," *Learning and Media* 34 (Spring 2006): 11. Used with permission.

Working together internationally
by Terry Freedman

Defining "collaborative project." Let's start by defining what we mean. To a large extent, schools encourage collaboration all the time, especially in countries such as the United States, Britain, and Australia. At least, you will have to look quite hard to find classrooms with rows of children silently hanging onto the teacher's every word.

An increasing number of teachers are seeing the potential value in longer-term projects in which students have to work together. Various reports that have come to my attention over the years, along with anecdotal evidence and my own experience, strongly suggest that knowledge discovered or created together is more likely to be retained.

It's actually quite difficult to define "collaboration," especially when it comes to assessment. Should you define it in terms of quantity or quality? I remember establishing some group work in one of my classes, and one boy's contribution to his group consisted mainly of ignoring them altogether and chatting to his friend in a neighboring group about football. Not much collaboration there? Yet every so often he would turn back to his group and say, "Why not try X?" and the others would invariably take up his suggestion.

Given that the group's completed work was outstanding, largely because of these interventions, one might be tempted to say that he collaborated well. I would disagree. If you think about it, he didn't collaborate at all; he just made some suggestions that the others regarded as good. Collaboration is not about making great suggestions, but playing a full part in a project, discussing issues and working together through disagreements to find a solution that is agreeable to all.

I am particularly interested in online collaborative projects working across international boundaries. In that context, collaboration or lack of it tends to show up very quickly because the tools that are used to facilitate discussion leave a trail, a record that can be scrutinized at leisure.

Photo: Association for Achievement and Improvement through Assessment

Why should treachers set up collaborative projects?
A very quick answer would be: because they have to. Take the new secondary curriculum in England, and the more specialized curriculum for ages 14 through 19, for instance. They both involve teaching students personal learning and thinking skills, so students can be independent enquirers, creative thinkers, reflective learners, team workers, self-managers, and effective participators.

Recent research indicates that employers regard the top generic skills as literacy, teamwork, responding positively to change, organizing, and prioritizing. These were followed by communication, numeracy, customer care, general IT skills, personal presentation, problem-solving, timekeeping, enthusiasm/commitment, business awareness, and enterprise.

This kind of requirement is not confined to students. In the training guidance for teachers about to teach the new Diploma qualification in England, there is this rather telling paragraph:

> To deliver the Diploma and achieve the outcomes for learners, institutions will have to review their existing practice and the training of their workforce. In many cases this means taking a radical look at deployment of staff, collaborative planning and timetabling, mentoring and support, the learning environment and pedagogical practice. Institutions will need to create the climate for these changes.

In the National Educational Technology Standards for Students, collaboration is listed almost at the top of the list. You will also find collaborative skills embedded in the 2007 AASL *Standards for the 21st-Century Learner*. We find, also, the following in the NETS Standards for Teachers: "model collaborative knowledge construction by engaging in learning with students, colleagues, and others in face-to-face and virtual environments."

If we were to base our decisions about activities on whether or not we had to run them, the curriculum arid school life would be very arid indeed. Fortunately, collaborative projects are intrinsically beneficial. In a survey I carried out in 2008, a female student from Canada gave the following response to the question "Did you regard the project as a success overall? Why/why not?": "Yes, because it was fun to compare our lives and see the similarities and differences between our lifestyles."

Neil Winton, a principal teacher in Scotland said, "Yes, it engaged the pupils and has been an overwhelming success for motivating them to become more independent in their learning." Kim Cofino, a teacher who is a 21st-century literacy specialist in Thailand, reflects: "Success, for me, is determined by the process, not the product. Have students learned how to connect, collaborate, and create across time and distance? Do they understand the ever-changing nature of our society, that one tool is not the learning, but rather learning how to learn independently. If so, the project has been a success."

Finally, Anne-Maree Moore, a teacher and technology coordinator in Australia, maintains that her students "were very motivated by the wider audience, curious about students from the other side of the world."

Assessing the individual's contribution to the collaborative process. All these sentiments are laudable, but there comes a point where a judgment is needed about how well a student has "gotten it." Obviously, students need to make such judgments themselves, but we also need to have objective measures so that potential employers can make decisions. How do you measure how well a student has collaborated with her peers?

One way of approaching this problem is to devise a rubric. A rubric consists of a number of statements or descriptors, and the idea is to see if the student's behavior is reflected in one of them. Rubrics have two main problems. The first is that they are open to subjective interpretation and may lack validity and reliability. Validity is the degree to which something actually assesses what it purports to assess; reliability is the degree to which similar results will be obtained by different classes.

Another problem is, does the rubric emphasize process at the expense of product? In educational information and communications technology, it's believed that it's the process that's important (see Cofino above). That is not entirely true. We do young people a grave disservice if we fail to tell them that product, as well as process, is important. Bottom line: Assessing collaboration is difficult per se, because it's hard to know how much a student contributed to the final outcome. What you can do is devise some sensible criteria and agree on how everyone will interpret them. Let students into the secret so that they can measure their own progress and achievement.

What collaboration tools are available? There is a large and growing range of tools available. Here is the list I used in the survey:

- Google Docs or similar web-based word processor
- Wildspaces or similar site
- SlideShare or similar tool
- Video service, such as YouTube
- Live video streaming, such as Ustream
- Instant messaging with webcam (could include Skype)
- Instant messaging without webcam (could include Skype)
- Voice over Internet Protocol, for example, using Skype
- Ordinary word processor and email
- Twitter or similar social messaging utility
- Facebook or similar social utility

If you are thinking of setting up an international collaborative project, you will need to consider issues such as whether a particular website is blocked at any of the participating schools. Facebook and YouTube are prime examples of sites that are frequently inaccessible within schools.

Unsurprisingly, around 50% of the respondents to my survey used Google Docs or Wikispaces, tools that lend themselves to collaboration without requiring people to be online at the same time. The rest used a mixture of instant messaging and video. Reasons for choosing wikis or similar applications included the following comment from Emily Huglin, a student in Australia: "Could talk with everyone and everyone could help with a problem or concern." Reasons for using instant messaging with a webcam included this observation from Anne Mirtschin, a technology coordinator in Australia: "Easy to use, minimal cost, accessible to all, video quality improving all the time, good to use in sharing classrooms, collaborating with staff involved, etc."

Factors to consider when setting up a social collaboration project. Think about the advantages of particular tools. You would be well-advised to try out the tools for yourself, or with a small group of colleagues, before basing an actual project on them.

All of the tools listed earlier are fairly robust, apart from some problems experienced by Twitter occasionally due to heavy traffic. However, because of potential problems, it is a good idea to have a Plan B in the form of another tool that could be used instead. However, as Maria Droujkova, a coach in the United States, advised in her response to the survey: "Don't count on users understanding any software without being walked through it step by step." In fact, the success of an online collaborative project depends very much on the preparation that goes into it. From my experience and that of others I would suggest the following are absolutely essential:

- A shared understanding of potential benefits of the project
- Knowledge on the part of both teachers and students of how to use the tools effectively
- A good block of time on the timetable in which to do the work
- Support from your principal and other staff, and from parents
- An infrastructure that will facilitate the project rather than create obstacles; for example, broadband connectivity is a must
- Good technical support

Difficulties will arise, but the advice of the respondents to my survey may be summarized as "keep talking, and be organized." Make sure that communication between all the parties is frequent and clear, and as Julie Lindsay, a veteran of such projects, said in her response to my survey: "Be organized, be consistent, and insist on a high level of engagement from all participants."

Kim Cofino has the last word. In her response to my survey she said, "Start small, with something achievable and let it grow from there. Find a partner that has close curricular goals—don't try to force a connection that doesn't match with jour learning needs."

Good luck!

SOURCE: Adapted from Terry Freedman, "Working Together Internationally," *Knowledge Quest* 37 (March/April 2009): 56–60. Used with permission.

COLLECTION DEVELOPMENT
CHAPTER TWO

Children's magazines and collection development

by Susan Patron

Magazines for kids pose one of the great conundrums in juvenile collection development in public libraries. Of all the material we provide, magazines are probably the most ephemeral, expensive, flimsy, difficult to shelve, attractive to steal, and inviting to mark up. Ignoring these magazines, with an estimated readership of 60 million, would be done at our peril. As with adults, kids enjoy the browsability, informality, topic-focused approach, and glossy look of magazines. A broad collection tells young patrons that the library is responsive to them.

Magazines can be key to converting a blasé reader into an avid one. For passions ranging from scouting to archeology, from oceanography to fashion, and from crafts to pets, there is a kid-friendly magazine and companion website devoted to the topic, with a noncurricular look and approach. These are fun to read, they fuel readers' interests, and they don't have the stigma of textbooks. That said, some of the best magazines for kids also bolster the school curriculum and provide timely, accessible, and current information on an ever-changing world.

Search engines and databases such as EBSCO's Primary Search and Gale's Kids InfoBits, designed for both elementary school libraries and public libraries, provide access to the rich contents of many children's magazines. Other databases offer full text for popular magazines as well as indexing and abstracts.

Examples of publications covered in Primary Search include: *Appleseeds, Boys' Life, Cobblestone, Cricket, Highlights for Children, Hopscotch, Jack & Jill, Ladybug, Ranger Rick, Science World, Spider, Superscience, Time for Kids,* and *Turtle.* Kids InfoBits is a database developed for beginning researchers in kindergarten through 5th grade. It features a developmentally appropriate, visually graphic interface. The curriculum-related, age-appropriate, full-text content covers geography, current events, the arts, science, health, people, government, history, sports, and more.

How do you select magazines that kids will flock to the library to read? My survey, "Miles of Magazines," *School Library Journal* 50, no. 3 (March 2004): 52–57, provides an annotated list of more than 50 English-language magazines for toddlers through 11-year-olds. The list is based on the magazine collection of the children's literature department of the Los Angeles Public Library.

If I had to choose only a dozen titles for preschoolers through 5th grade, assuming the collection would be for a branch library in a diverse city such as Los Angeles, I would include:

Ask. Carus/Cricket Magazine Group. How the world works and how discoveries are made. 9 issues, $33.95. *Website:* www.cricketmag.com.

Calliope: Exploring World History. Carus/Cobblestone. 9 issues, $33.95. *Website:* www.cobblestonepub.com.

ChickaDEE. Bayard. Animals, peoples, and places. 10 issues, $34.00. *Website:* www.owlkids.com.

CousteauKids. The Cousteau Society. Cousteau expeditions, sea creatures, and so on. Bimonthly, $20. *Website:* www.cousteau.org/media/cousteau-kids.

Creative Kids: The National Voice for Kids. Prufrock Press. Stories and artwork by and for kids. 4 issues, $19.95. *Website:* www.prufrock.com.

Cricket. Cricket Magazine Group. Folk tales, fiction, poetry, and so on. 9 issues, $33.95. *Website:* www.cricketmag.com.

Highlights: Fun with a Purpose. Highlights for Children. Human interest, science, culture, history, and so on. Monthly, $34.44. *Website:* www.highlights.com.

Kahani: A South Asian Literary Magazine for Children. Kahani. Stories, science, and so on. 4 issues, $20. *Website:* www.kahani.com.

National Geographic Kids. National Geographic Society. Nature themes. 10 issues, $15. *Website:* kids.nationalgeographic.com/kids/.

Ranger Rick. National Wildlife Federation. Nature themes. 10 issues, $19.95. *Website:* www.nwf.org.

Zootles. Wildlife Education Ltd. Animals. Bimonthly, $29.95. *Website:* www.zoobooks.com.

SOURCE: Adapted from Susan Patron, "Children's Magazines and Collection Development," *Children and Libraries* 4 (Winter 2006): 44. Used with permission.

Collaborating with teachers to empower students

by Eleanor B. Howe

Near the end of my first year as librarian at Pine-Richland High School in Gibsonia, Pennsylvania, an English teacher came to me and said he would like to continue a project begun with my predecessor. He wanted his honors students to make recommendations for the library collection. I leaped at the opportunity for collaboration and student input!

His goals were to have more nonfiction and reference books in the collection for his students' (grades 9 and 11) research papers and to improve their writing skills by submitting a written recommendation for a title to add to the collection. My immediate goals were to involve the students in their library and to develop a collection that would reflect their academic interests and needs.

As we collaborated on the project through subsequent years, my goals became more refined and extended: to improve student catalog search skills and to improve their evaluation of information resources, including those already in the collection and those recommended for purchase. Both of us wanted to show our students that they could have a positive input into and impact on their school through its library collection and that they would leave a legacy after graduation.

The project was quite successful. Even though there were no funds to purchase every student-suggested book, and the choices were subject to collection development policy, I was able to purchase more than 10 of their suggested titles a year. The recommendations were made not only by the teacher's students but also by those doing research for other classes in English and American history and culture. The students were happy to receive my thank-you letter confirming the purchase of their titles, and the success of the project led a second English teacher to use a similar process of student recommendations for the fiction collection.

Ultimately the project worked this way: The teacher began by taking a number of student-recommended titles already in the collection to class to show his students the results of the assignment in which they were to write a researched and reasoned recommendation memo on a title to add to the collection. In their memo, students would have to address the need for the topic, the specific book they had in mind, its value for students and teachers, and its strengths compared to other available titles—all supported by printouts of their searches. After the teacher graded the memos, he would give them to me.

Working in groups of two or three, students developed a list of three curriculum-related topics probably not covered in the collection and then spent three days in the library on the project. Some students used their own previous research on topics that they thought were not sufficiently supported in the collection. In some cases they found that they had not adequately searched the collection before, and in other cases the need was real.

On their first day in the library, I gave the students additional instruction on thorough searching of the catalog for books on or related to their topic. They used both subject heading and keyword search strategies, printed out lists of books, and went to the shelves to evaluate the existing books' usefulness, age, and coverage for course assignments. Such thorough searching would be helpful in doing research in college.

On the second day, I discussed the evaluation of information resources by authority (author and publisher), audience, scope, depth, purpose, objectivity, publication date, cost, and special features. I provided students with a checklist of these criteria that they could use in evaluating books to purchase and in writing their title recommendation.

The next step was to find the best title available on their topic. I demonstrated and shared my own collection of print selection tools, which contained age-appropriate, curriculum-related titles and a built-in professional review. The students could also use online resources, provided they found a professional review of the title.

In their project packet, students wrote a recommendation memo on the best of their three final title choices. They appended printouts from the catalog to establish need for coverage, described probable student use, and printed or copied book descriptions and professional reviews for each of their finalists. This enabled their teacher to evaluate their writing and rationale and enabled me to evaluate the best three titles each group selected on the topic of demonstrated need. In the process both the teacher and the students learned much more about the library collection and the evaluation of available resources.

The second English teacher wanted to develop a similar project to strengthen the fiction collection and to stimulate her students' interest in reading. I wanted to develop the collection to accommodate students' and teachers' reading preferences. Because her students were not in the honors program, we adapted the project. In order to justify curricular use and meet collection development criteria, her students were to select an author they had enjoyed reading, limiting their choice to authors in the English Department Year-Round Reading Program (grades 9–12). Both searching the collection and selecting a specific title to purchase were less involved for these students than for the honors students, but the students were also asked to write a recommendation memo, too, with supporting printouts of collection need and descriptions of recommended titles.

The student collection recommendation projects have been very successful. I enjoyed collaborating with both teachers on developing and refining the projects, working with the students, reading their memos, purchasing their recommended titles, and writing letters to those students whose titles were selected. In addition to a recommendation plate placed in the book, student names were included on the catalog record. The students, of course, were the ones who gained most: They improved their search, evaluation, and writing skills; they developed ownership and pride in their library by contributing to its collection; and they created a more relevant collection available for all students.

SOURCE: Adapted from Eleanor B. Howe, "Collaborating with Teachers to Empower Students @ Your Library ®: Building a Relevant Collections with Student Recommendations," *Learning and Media* 38 (Summer 2008): 8–9. Used with permission.

The International Children's Digital Library

by Ann Carlson Weeks

The International Children's Digital Library (ICDL) began as a research project funded primarily by the National Science Foundation, the Institute for Museum and Library Services, and Microsoft Research to create a digital library of outstanding children's books from all over the world (en.childrenslibrary.org). The project was introduced at an international celebration at the Library of Congress in Washington, D.C., in November 2002.

The collection focuses on materials that help children understand the world around them and the global society in which they live. The materials reflect similarities and differences in cultures, societies, interests, and lifestyles of peoples around the world. Its goal is to build an exemplary collection of historic and contemporary children's books from around the world and make them freely available to children and scholars of children's literature via the internet.

The ICDL was created by an interdisciplinary research team (computer scientists, librarians, educational technologists, graphic designers, and graduate students) at the University of Maryland. Other important contributors to the research are the members of the College Park Kidsteam, a group of six children ages 7–11 who work regularly with the adults in the Human-Computer Interaction Lab.

The ICDL collection has two primary audiences. The first audience is children ages 3–13, as well as the librarians, teachers, parents, and caregivers who work with them. The second audience is international scholars and researchers in the area of children's literature. Both contemporary children's books and significant historical works are included in the collection to meet the needs of both primary audiences.

Books are selected by experts in children's literature in the country or culture of origin. All books are presented in their entirety and in the original languages in which they were published, and in additional languages in translation if permission has been given. Only books that have been published in print form are included in the collection. The intent is to make children's books more accessible worldwide and preserve the best of children's literature through technology.

A history of success

ICDL has a history of success. Research practices, policies, and international relationships have fostered an environment in which creativity and enthusiasm flourish. The interdisciplinary team developing the ICDL collaborated with children in the design process to create child-friendly technology. Their input helps make the ICDL collection easy, exciting, and fun for children to use. Technology created with children results in technology that children want to use.

In addition to this partnership for interface development, the ICDL also established partnerships with national libraries, public library systems, professional associations, commercial publishers, authors, illustrators, and school districts around the world. These partnerships were critical to the ICDL's collection development efforts and helped the research team better understand the needs of users in library and school environments so that they could be adapted and improve the underlying technology. The collection, which now includes almost 4,500 books in 55 languages from 60 countries, continues to grow month by month. The search interface is available in 19 languages and many of the project's web pages have been translated into Spanish, Russian, and Mongolian.

In 2010, the ICDL received the American Library Association's President's Award for International Innovation and was selected as one of the 25 best websites for teaching and learning by ALA's American Association of School Librarians.

Unique characteristics

Categories for children's books—such as true or make-believe, book color, and genres that meet children's needs—make it easier for young children to find books they'll enjoy. The option to search by color is actually the result of the research team's collaboration with children. Often, children and adults are able to remember the physical characteristics of a book but not the specific bibliographic information. Librarians in public and school libraries have reported that children frequently remember a book by its physical characteristics and shelf location (the "big blue book that was at the end of the bottom shelf").

In addition to aiding in the recall of a book, many children simply enjoy searching by color as a means of browsing for books they haven't read before. This preference is particularly useful in searching for books in the ICDL collection. It is often difficult for children to search for topics in languages unfamiliar to them. Thus, searching by color simplifies the process when searching for books in a collection that includes such a wide variety of languages.

It is also true that children frequently choose books based on how attracted they are to the covers. This behavior is evident in bookstores and physical libraries, as well as in the ICDL. Other search categories unique to the ICDL include how a book makes a child feel (happy or sad); whether the book is short, medium, or long in length; and books with kids as the main characters. Like searching by color, these categories were developed as a result of the research team's partnership with children in the design of the ICDL.

Managing copyright

The ICDL includes a copyright policy agreement to protect the interests of the rights-holders of the books in the collection. In order to include a book still under copyright protection, the ICDL requires written permission from all individuals

or organizations who own rights to the book. Each book accepted for the collection must be accompanied by a copyright license signed by each rights-holder. In signing this license agreement, ICDL book contributors are not giving away all rights to their works.

Obtaining copyright permission is a very important and time-consuming part of the process in building the collection. The ICDL includes a copyright notice and an acknowledgment of the rights-holder's license with the University of Maryland in all displays and publications for each book in the collection. This license only gives the ICDL the nonexclusive right to reproduce digital versions of the books and make them freely available for public display on its website.

The ICDL also employs technological measures designed to prevent the downloading, printing, and unauthorized further display or distribution of the books. These security measures have been a major factor in the ICDL's success in gaining the trust of authors, illustrators, and publishers. With these security measures in place, many rights-holders around the world have come to recognize that participating in the ICDL project benefits them by providing greater global exposure for their books.

Ebook access

Three book readers (standard, comic, and spiral) were developed by the ICDL research team. The comic and spiral readers require installation of freely downloadable software in order to use, but the standard reader requires nothing more than a computer with internet access.

All materials in the public domain are accessible with ICDL's standard reader in HTML format. Any copyright-protected material is accessible according to the preferred security levels selected by the rights-holders. The security levels range from minimal security measures that

require no additional software to read the books to encrypted images that require the ICDL-developed Java readers. The security levels do not restrict access to the collection, but rather protect the interests of the rights holders by disallowing downloading or printing of the materials.

Funding

In early 2006, the ICDL Research Team created the International Children's Digital Library Foundation, a nonprofit corporation. The

ICDL Foundation is the oversight organization that continues to support the collection-building strategies, the creation of alliances worldwide, the promotion of the value of the ICDL, and the expansion of access to the digital collection. Funding is critical to the ICDL's growth and stability. Individuals, as well as corporate and philanthropic organizations, can contribute to the ICDL as members and sponsors to help build the library and support its many programs. Information about the foundation and its activities and on becoming a member or sponsor is available on the ICDL website.

Participation

The ICDL collection includes books both in and out of copyright from various sources around the globe. The goal is to reflect as many of the world's cultures as possible. The ICDL, therefore, relies on the international participation of libraries, publishers, authors, and illustrators to ensure that the collection remains as diverse as possible.

The research team makes every effort to follow up with any information that might help rights-holders make the decision about contributing their works to the ICDL collection. The ICDL also accepts contributions of public-domain materials from private collections that meet the ICDL selection criteria. A copy of the library's collection development policy can be found on its website.

While the ICDL continuously needs support to build the collection, there are other ways for individuals to contribute to the ICDL. One way to participate is by volunteering as a translator to translate the bibliographic information (metadata) for the books into different languages.

Another way to participate is by becoming an ICDL ambassador. Ambassadors advocate for the ICDL by sharing information about the project with rights-holders, showing children and adults how to use the library, testing new features, and submitting "featured books" reviews, which are highlighted on the homepage for visitors to read.

Logging on

You can visit the ICDL website and simply browse the collection or choose to create an account (which is optional). By creating an account, it is possible to set the interface to one of the 19 languages, including Arabic, Thai, Polish, and German. In addition, library account–holders can save favorite books to their virtual "book shelves." This wonderful resource can be shared with other library media specialists, teachers, students, and parents. The ICDL website is user-friendly and easy to navigate.

SOURCE: Adapted from Ann Carlson Weeks, "The International Children's Digital Library: Increasing Children's Access to Books through Technology," *School Library Media Activities Monthly* 23, no. 7 (March 2007): 27–30, including an update of this article by the author before publication.

Getting started with graphic novels
by Elizabeth Haynes

Graphic novels have become increasingly popular with young people over the last few years and are more prominent in popular culture in general. If you are not familiar with this combination word-and-picture art form, assistance is not hard to find to select titles that are appropriate for your library.

Background and terminology

A graphic novel is different from a comic book. Comic books are short, flimsy stapled books, little more than pamphlets and presenting one installment in an ongoing serial story. Graphic novels are longer. They usually contain a story with a beginning, middle, and end. Graphic novels may be part of a series, but each volume typically contains a complete story; and they are published in sturdy trade paperback format or in hardcover.

The graphic novel is a format, just as chapter books are formats. Graphic novels encompass many different genres: humor, fantasy, science fiction, romance, mystery, horror, realism, and even nonfiction. Superhero stories are far from being the only type of stories available in graphic format.

Most graphic novels are equally dependent on both pictures and text, although a few exceptions, such as *The Arrival* by Shaun Tan, are wordless or near-wordless. One feature of graphic novels is multiple panels or pictures on most pages.

A subset of graphic novels that is of particular interest to many young people is manga, or Japanese comics. The majority of titles are published in the original format as printed in Japan, which means they read from back to front and right to left. While most manga (at least those published in English) are aimed at teenagers and adults, a few titles can be considered suitable for all ages or for elementary students. The vast majority of manga come in multiple-volume series with continuing story lines, so if you start to purchase a series, you should be prepared to continue with it if popularity warrants.

Manga generally fall into either the shōnen or shōjo categories. Shōnen manga frequently have young male protagonists who often engage in martial arts or other forms of fighting or are involved in action-oriented adventures designed to appeal to boys and young men. *Naruto* (published by Viz Media), one of the best-selling manga titles in the United States, falls into this category as it deals with a young ninja-in-training. Shōjo manga may have both male and female protagonists and the emphasis is on relationships, although the storyline may be dramatic or mysterious. Another best-selling series, *Fruits Basket* (published by Tokyopop), is an example of shōjo manga, which are meant to appeal to girls. These classifications are not absolute as both genders read series that fall into both categories.

Selection issues

Graphic novels should be selected based on the suitability of that title for the age group(s) served by your collection, as well as its curriculum and entertainment value. Pay careful attention to information furnished by reviewers and publishers regarding the age range for a given title. Excellent graphic novels are available for every age group, but many are not suitable for elementary grades, and others are too juvenile for upper grades.

Compared to text-only books, graphic novels can be costly as pictures are more expensive to prepare and print than text. Many graphic novels are available only in trade-paperback binding or for purchase from rebinders or sent out to be rebound. If sending them out yourself, be sure that the gutter is wide enough for the book to be rebound without cutting off part of the pictures.

Selection problems arise with manga, notably with the violence and different cultural customs between Japan and the United States. Japanese tend to be more at ease with nudity, and while most manga for teens does not show detailed nudity, non-detailed nudity may be present. Some indulge in "fan-service" which includes exaggerated breasts, panty shots, and other images. U.S. publishers of manga put age ratings on their series. These ratings are not standard, but the company website can be consulted for interpretations of the publisher's ratings. A few manga titles are suitable for elementary grades, but the vast majority of titles are intended for teenagers. Major bookstores carry manga series, and librarians can review the series there or in library publications.

After the purchase

Perennial topics about graphic novels in libraries are cataloging and shelving. Pre-processed graphic novels are likely to come with a Dewey classification of 741.5. Shelving your graphic novels in that location keeps them together but they are not easily found by students. Graphic novels can be shelved in their own section in a similar fashion to fiction or easy books. They can be cataloged as fiction and shelved with those books. Decide what shelving and classification options will work best in your situation after considering the various options. Subject headings are more easily dealt with, as the latest edition of Sears Subject Headings has added a number of terms that are relevant for graphic novels.

Graphic novels are a great way to promote reading and provide enjoyment for your students. If you don't already have graphic novels in your collection, buy a few titles and see what happens. I believe you'll be very pleased with the results.

SOURCE: Adapted from Elizabeth Haynes, "Getting Started with Graphic Novels in School Libraries," Library Media Connection 27 (January/February 2009): 10–12. Used with permission.

More than just superheroes in tights

by Zahra M. Baird and Tracey Jackson

Either you get it, or you don't. Simply put, graphic novels get kids reading. Graphic novels use both words and pictures to appeal to readers of all ages; as the popularity of this format has grown, so has the genre's value, literary prowess, and role as a pathway to literacy.

Graphic novels are here to stay. We love graphic novels. A successful graphic novel starts with a stellar story told with words and pictures that augment the story, providing insight that text alone cannot do. Fans of the genre love graphic novels. Why? Because even before they pick them up, the covers capture their attention. Once opened, the story unfolds between the panels, steadily pulling readers in, quickly and completely. Like all good literature, the graphic novel moves readers to experience story.

The wide range of genres and themes that graphic novels explore include adventure, legends, fantasy, memoirs, comedy, horror, social issues, religion, and biography. Most graphic novels are original stories, though many classic works of literature have been adapted to the format.

History of the graphic novel

The graphic novel has had a colorful, shifting past and continues to evolve every day. Will Eisner, the modern godfather of graphic novels, wrote *A Contract with God* (Baronet, 1978), considered one of the first graphic novels. Art Spiegelman also helped set the cornerstone for graphic novels with his 1992 Pulitzer Prize–winning *Maus: A Survivor's Tale* (Scholastic, 1992). In 2005, Scholastic created an imprint called Graphix, launching it with a full-color version of Jeff Smith's *Bone: Out from Boneville* (Cartoon Books, 1995).

Definitions for graphic novels are rampant. The most straightforward comes from Allyson A. W. Lyga in *Graphic Novels in Your Media Center* (2004): "The graphic novel is usually a monographic work and has a storyline with a start and a finish. It is published on an independent schedule and is typically in bound book format (trade paperback) and has a higher quality."

Many books incorporate comic-style illustrations, such as dialogue balloons, and are sprinkled with panels while retaining the feel of the traditional chapter book. Differing from Western graphic novels, manga (Japanese comics) are a collection unto themselves; the characters have overstated features, and heavy emphasis is placed on the pictorial cues rather than on the text.

The graphic novel debate

Arguments exist among librarians against establishing a graphic novel collection. Age-unsuitable content (violence, sexuality, nudity, and stereotypes) can be dealt with by locating graphic novel collections in what the library deems an appropriate section. Weak bindings and difficulty ordering replacement titles are not unique to the graphic novel format. The pros seem to outweigh the cons, as graphic novels appeal to many children including visual learners, reluctant and struggling readers, budding artists, fun-seekers, and pleasure readers.

What trends will shape the future of graphic novels? Will librarians and publishers work together to set industry standards? Will more nonfiction subject matter be published in this format? The graphic novel has the appeal, popularity, and literary value to spark the imagination and motivate children to read. So the question the authors leave you with is this: "Got graphic?"

SOURCE: Zahra M. Baird and Tracey Jackson, "Got Graphic Novels? More Than Just Superheroes in Tights!" *Children and Libraries* 5, no. 1 (Spring 2007): 5–7.

What is manga?

by Gilles Poitras

In one definition, manga are simply Japanese comic books. The Japanese part of the definition is crucial, as these are products originally published by Japanese companies for a Japanese audience. That definition does not actually work well enough; manga is far more complex than the American comic book, which has been

2

dominated by superhero, underground, and what are termed "art" or "independent" comics for the past 50 years. Manga is published with every demographic and genre that one finds in prose, fiction, and nonfiction.

In the United States, the growth of the manga market has been stunning. A leading trade journal, the *ICv2 Guide to Manga* (2007), estimates that the North American manga market for 2002 was $60 million, and that by 2006 it had grown to an estimated $190–$205 million, with more than 5,000 paperbacks in print. This growth is partly explained by one factor: manga for girls. The U.S. comic industry has focused on boys, young men, and women, ignoring this demographic. It has also ignored another interesting genre: romance stories for boys. These are coming-of-age tales centering on boy-girl relationships that often deal with issues of mutual responsibility and the risks of young adulthood.

Putting aside the thematic, genre, and demographic elements in manga, illustrated narratives are approachable by many readers who may be reluctant to pick up regular prose. The imagery increases the reader's enjoyment of the stories as the complimentary blend of pictures and the written word tell a tale.

The visual structure of manga has significant differences when compared to comic books. First, for those who pick up a translated manga for the first time, they recognize that the cover opens from left to right. Images and individual elements, such as word balloons, are read from right to left, the opposite of European books. It is surprising how easy it is for most readers to adjust to Japanese-style reading.

Second, American comics are still largely done in a standard rectangular panel format, similar to comic strips in the Sunday newspapers. Manga creators bent and broke those conventions decades ago. While there is still a logical progression of images, they are not confined to simple rows of boxes. A panel may be a triangle, a polygon, or circle; it may even overlap and flow into an adjacent panel.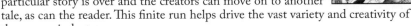

Finally, a less obvious but significant difference: Almost all manga are a single tale told over a series of volumes. American comics are still mainly thin pamphlets with one story per issue. A manga title can easily be 10–20 volumes in length, each volume with well over 100 pages, telling a single longer tale. This requires, and in fact encourages, a commitment on the part of the reader to spend the time and effort to read a longer tale. When the tale ends, unlike American comics that often run for decades, the particular story is over and the creators can move on to another tale, as can the reader. This finite run helps drive the vast variety and creativity of the manga industry.

All of the elements one finds in manga can draw readers of different ages and interests to a large number of works. In fact the variety of manga is important to consider in selection. Some of the adult manga may be action-oriented, with conflict played out on the page, or it may contain a few scenes with sexual content. These scenes may not appear in early volumes, only occurring as the relationships between characters change over time. One can find erotic manga in English, many written by and for women.

All in all, manga is a diverse source for material in a library and should be selected with all the care that prose works are given. For more information on manga and anime see *The Librarian's Guide to Anime and Manga* (www.koyagi. com/Libguide.html).

SOURCE: Adapted from Gilles Poitras, "What is Manga?" *Knowledge Quest* 36 (January/February 2008): 45. Used with permission.

EVALUATION
CHAPTER THREE

Getting it together

by Brian Kenney

In May 2007, I attended a symposium at Kent State University called "The Multiple Faces of Collaboration" on—you guessed it—collaboration between school librarians and classroom teachers (and, in a few instances, university librarians). Jointly sponsored by the Rutgers Center for International Scholarship in School Libraries (CISSL) and the Kent State University Institute for Library and Information Literacy Education (ILILE), the centerpiece of the conference was the release of the findings of a three-year ILILE study in which 130 school librarians and teachers worked together to create and implement programs in their schools.

"Collaboration is good" and "you must collaborate" are two of the mantras of school librarianship in this country. So it's always worth paying attention when someone pulls aside the veil to provide some fresh insights into how collaboration really works.

What did we learn in Ohio? That teachers primarily collaborated to build collegial relations, but librarians did it to market library services and increase their status in the school. Both groups felt they brought their own areas of expertise to the relationship; for teachers, it was curriculum knowledge, but for librarians it was technology and information skills. What each group hoped to gain through the experience also differed. Classroom teachers wanted to improve their pedagogy and content knowledge while, again, school librarians wanted to better integrate the library into the school.

Overall, the study, authored by CISSL Director Ross Todd, showed that collaboration is hard, and that the mandate to "go out and collaborate" needs sustained professional support (something this group was fortunate enough to have, thanks to ILILE). With plenty of impediments along the way (with time and scheduling leading the pack), in the end collaboration was seen as powerful, with many tangible benefits to the school as well as to the participants.

Allison Zmuda, in responding to the study, was quick to point out what was missing. "Shouldn't the point of collaboration be improvement in student learning?" she asked. As with any school or classroom activity, learning outcomes are the bottom line, Zmuda asserted, and not necessarily improved professional relationships or advocacy of the library program.

Now I have no doubt these collaborations had a positive impact on student learning, and in fact there was an exhibit of the wonderful portfolios that were created by kids who took part in these joint programs. Participants reported that they perceived that collaboration led to improved information literacy and increased

39

content knowledge among their students. Perceptions and portfolios are no longer enough. We live in a world where school librarians are having their jobs cut right and left, often to be replaced by other educators who are believed to have a greater, and measurable, impact on outcomes. Improved student outcomes are, after all, what every principal wants.

If there's a conundrum for the school library community to solve, it's this: What is our impact on student achievement? Neither better relations with our colleagues nor more preaching about the importance of information literacy will save our jobs. Data, that measurement of a library program's impact on student learning, isn't something we traditionally collect, or even know how to collect. If we are to survive, it's the information we desperately need.

SOURCE: Adapted from Brian Kenney, "Getting It Together," *School Library Journal* 53 (July 2007): 9. Used with permission.

The impact of school libraries on academic achievement

by Keith Curry Lance, Marcia J. Rodney, and Bill Schwarz

Where administrators value strong library programs and can see them doing their part for student success, students are more likely to thrive academically. This is the overarching conclusion that can be drawn from a 2009 study of the impact of school libraries, this one in Idaho. Survey responses from 176 principals and other administrators included:

- how much they value selected practices characteristic of strong library programs;
- how highly they evaluate the teaching of Information and Communication Technologies (ICT) standards in their schools; and
- how these beliefs relate to the performance of their students on the state test, the Idaho Student Achievement Tests (ISAT).

Data from the survey respondents as well as recommendations for action based on the study findings and sample success stories from those respondents is included.

Valued library-related practices

Principals and other administrators were asked to assess the value they place on various library-related practices, rating them as essential, desirable, acceptable, or unnecessary (see Table 1). More than half of administrators (56.9%) valued appointing the librarian to school committees as essential. Almost half (48.9%) placed a similar value on library access being scheduled based on instructional needs rather than a fixed schedule. Almost two out of five administrators (38.5%) considered regular meetings between librarians and their principals as essential. More than a quarter of administrators considered it essential for librarians to provide professional development opportunities to faculty (29.9%) and for librarians and teachers to design instructional units together (27.6%). Only about one out of five administrators considered it essential for the librarian's role in the school to be addressed in teacher hiring interviews.

Table 1. Library-Related Practices Valued by Principals and Other Administrators

Practice	Importance to Administrator of Activity Happening in School/District			
	Essential	Desirable	Acceptable	Unnecessary
Library access is scheduled based on instructional needs	85 (48.9%)	66 (37.9%)	19 (10.9%)	4 (2.3%)
Librarian and teacher design instructional units together	48 (27.6%)	107 (61.5%)	15 (8.6%)	4 (2.3%)
Librarian provides professional development to faculty	52 (29.9%)	93 (53.4%)	23 (13.2%)	6 (3.4%)
Librarian is appointed to school committees	99 (56.9%)	63 (36.2%)	11 (6.3%)	1 (0.6%)
Librarian and principal meet regularly	67 (38.5%)	74 (42.5%)	31 (17.8%)	2 (1.1%)
Librarian's role is addressed in teacher hiring	31 (17.8%)	73 (42/0%)	54 (31.0%)	16 (9.2%)

Self-assessment of ICT standards

Principals and other administrators were asked for self-assessments of how ICT standards were taught across their schools or districts (see Table 2). Responding principals and other administrators thought that their schools and districts did the best job teaching independent learning (40.1% rated excellent), followed by ICT literacy (30.8%) and social responsibility (24.3%).

When administrators highly valued a variety of library-related practices, they were often at least twice as likely to rate the teaching of ICT standards highly. Where administrators considered it essential or desirable for librarians and teachers to collaborate in the design and delivery of instruction, they were twice as likely to rate as excellent or good the teaching of ICT literacy and social responsibility. They were also more than half again as likely to rate the teaching of independent learning highly.

Similarly, administrators were consistently more likely to rate ICT standards teaching as excellent if they valued as essential several additional library-related practices including:

- librarians providing in-service professional development opportunities to teachers;
- librarians and principals meeting regularly;
- librarians serving on key school committees; and
- library access being scheduled flexibly.

In addition, where administrators considered it essential or desirable to address the librarian's role in teacher interviews, they were more than twice as likely to

Table 2. Administrator Self-Assessment of ICT Standards Teaching

Standard	Excellent	Good	Fair	Poor
ICT literacy	52 (30.8%)	64 (37.9%)	38 (22.5%)	15 (8.9%)
Independent learning	69 (40.1%)	71 (41.3%)	27 (15.7%)	5 (2.9%)
Social responsibility	41 (24.3%)	76 (45.0%)	42 (24.9%)	10 (5.9%)

rate as excellent the teaching of ICT literacy and social responsibility, and more than half again as likely to rate as excellent the teaching of independent learning.

Where principals and other administrators rated the teaching of ICT standards as excellent, students at all three grade levels—elementary, middle, and high school (represented by grades 3, 4 and 5; grades 7 and 8; and grade 10, respectively)—were consistently more likely to earn advanced scores on the ISAT reading and language arts tests. Notably, while the absolute differences between groups are usually single-digit percentages, the proportional differences between groups are consistently into double digits, as well as being higher at the high school than at the elementary level. For instance, at the elementary level, 48.6% of students in schools rated excellent at ICT literacy teaching scored advanced ratings on reading, compared to only 40.1% of students where ICT literacy teaching was rated lower. That is an absolute difference of more than 8%; but a proportional difference of more than 21% (48.6 ÷ 40.1 = 1.21). Similarly, at the high school level, 18.7% of students in schools rated excellent at ICT literacy teaching scored advanced ratings on language arts, compared to only 13.8% of students where ICT literacy teaching was rated lower. That is an absolute difference of less than 5%, but a proportional difference of more than 35% (18.7 ÷ 13.8 = 1.355).

Support of administrators

These findings underscore the importance of administrative support for strong school library programs. Administrators tended to assess the teaching of ICT standards more highly where they considered certain practices to be essential (or, in one case, at least desirable). Such practices include: flexibly scheduling access to the school library, instructional collaborating between librarians and teachers, librarians providing in-service opportunities to teachers, librarians serving on school committees, librarians and principals meeting regularly, and the librarian's role being addressed in teacher hiring interviews. In turn, where administrators self-assessed the teaching of ICT literacy as excellent, students were consistently more likely to earn advanced scores on the ISAT reading and language arts tests.

Recommendations

On the basis of the results for principals and other administrators, three major sets of recommendations can be offered:

- To encourage collaboration between librarians, teachers, and administrators, principals and other administrators should: (1) set the stage for effective collaborations by making it known that they expect it to be the norm; (2) meet regularly with the librarian; and (3) address the librarian's role with prospective new teachers during hiring interviews.
- To improve access to instructional resources, principals and other administrators should: (1) make it school policy to schedule library access as flexibly as possible, and (2) appoint librarians to school committees that will enable them to understand as fully as possible the instructional resource needs of their schools.
- To improve the skills of teachers, principals and other administrators should foster the creation of schedules, facilities, and librarian-teacher relationships that enable librarians to be "resident" providers of in-service professional development to teachers.

The bottom line

These recommendations are demonstrably easier to fulfill when the library is staffed by a school librarian. The full study report can be examined for detailed findings supporting this claim (libraries.idaho.gov/doc/idaho-school-library-impact-study-2009). School librarians are encouraged to continue their professional development so they can best fulfill these recommendations. Non-professionals working in school libraries, as well as the teachers and the administrators of the school, are also encouraged to pursue academic courses or professional development opportunities that will better equip them to ensure that their school libraries do as much as possible to foster student success.

ICT standards

The three ICT standards referenced in the surveys—ICT literacy, independent learning, and social responsibility—were defined as follows.

ICT literacy. Students are taught to identify information needs and to access, evaluate, manage, integrate, create, and communicate information.

Independent learning. Students are taught to pursue information related to their personal interests, to appreciate literature and other creative expression, and to generate knowledge.

Social responsibility. Students are taught to recognize the importance of information in a democratic society, practice ethical behavior in regard to information and technology, and to share information and collaborate in its use in groups.

SOURCE: Adapted from Keith Curry Lance, Marcia J. Rodney, and Bill Schwarz, "The Impact of School Libraries on Academic Achievement: A Research Study Based on Responses from Administrators in Idaho," *School Library Monthly* 26, no. 9 (May 2010): 14–17. Used with permission.

A new California study
by Douglas Achterman

Results of a 2008 study of California's public schools fall into a statistical dead heat with five other states with the lowest 4th- and 8th-grade reading scores nationwide. California's school libraries have the lowest (1 to 6,673) school librarian–to-student ratio in the country. In fact, the gap in this regard between California and the 49th state is greater than between the 49th and first state, according to the 2007 *Digest of Education Statistics*. The temptation to further decimate school library staffing appears to be too strong to resist during the current budget crisis. However, if school districts still value student performance on the California Standardized Testing and Reporting (STAR) tests, they may find such cuts foolhardy.

In this statewide study, results at the elementary, middle school, and high school levels consistently showed:

- The levels of certificated (school librarian) staffing and total staffing are strongly related to the level of services a school library program provides.
- Increases in the level of services school library program provide are significantly related to increases in STAR test scores.

The strength of the relationship between library services and test scores increased with grade level; the correlation at the elementary level between English Langu0000age Arts (ELA) scores and total library services was $r = .14$, $p < .001$; at the middle school the correlation with ELA scores was $r = .19$, $p < .001$; at the high school, the correlations with ELA scores jumped to $r = .49$, $p < .001$. These results remained significant when accounting for all school and community variables that were part of the study, including average parent education level, poverty level, ethnicity, percentage of language learners, percentage of teachers who are highly qualified, and average teacher salary.

The following trends are evident. The greater the staffing, both certificated and total staffing, the more service a library provides. The more services a school library provides, the higher the test scores. California's results, related to both certificated and total staffing, align with a host of studies that indicate staff levels are among the best predictors of student achievement among all library program variables.

Access to the school library

The California study also indicates that student access to the school library, measured by the number of hours the library is open, is significantly related to

test scores at all three levels. As library hours increase, there is a corresponding trend toward rising test scores. As with total library services, this correlation at the high school level persists when accounting for all school and community variables in the study. In a declining economy, the number of hours a school library remains open can be critical, especially for students without access to books or technology at home. Jeff McQuillan in *The Literacy Crisis* (1998) noted that children in low socioeconomic areas who have access to print materials and who like to read are successful in school. Given students' propensity to use the school library over the public library, the California study draws attention to the importance of access to the school library and its resources in addressing educational quality.

Instructional role of the teacher-librarian

This study also points to the instructional role of the school librarian as a critical element in student success. At the elementary, middle school, and high school levels, significant relationships were found between test scores and the following services regularly provided by school librarians:

- offering a program of curriculum-integrated information literacy instruction;
- providing instruction on internet searching and research;
- informally instructing students in the use of resources.

As with staffing, the correlations between these services and test scores remained significant when controlling for all school and community variables.

High schools lead the way

Without exception in the California study, the strongest correlations between test scores and library program elements were found at the high school level. On the

English Language Arts test, the library program was a stronger predictor of success than the other school variables. On the U.S. history test, the library program was, in fact, the best predictor of student performance and better than both other school variables and community variables including parent education and poverty levels.

Why are correlations between school libraries and test scores strongest at the high school level? A likely explanation is that a substantially greater percentage of high schools have full-time staffing as compared to the middle schools or elementary schools.

Both professional and paraprofessional staffing is critical for a school library program to be effective, a point borne out through much prior research. Most notably, Daniel Callison found in a 2004 statewide Indiana study that full-time school librarians at all grade levels were more likely to fulfill instructional roles than those who were employed part-time. In a pair of case studies in which the activities of school librarians were examined in detail, Christine McIntosh and Linda Jean Underwood noted the interdependence of the paraprofessional-professional team.

The implications from this study are clear: At the elementary, middle school, and high school levels, increases in school librarians and total staffing are significantly related to increases in the services library staff provides, and increases in those services correlate with higher STAR test scores. Schools that support their library programs with both professional and paraprofessional staffing give their students a better chance to succeed.

SOURCE: Adapted from Douglas Achterman, "A New California Study: School Libraries Give Students a Better Chance at Success," *CSLA Journal* 33 (Summer 2009): 26–27. Used with permission.

Staying the course:
Racing for Ohio's students

by Debra Kay Logan

Sometimes the race does not belong to the swiftest. Sometimes how fast you can run is not as important as how far you are willing to run and the willingness to persist in running, especially when winning seems like an impossible dream.

Coming from behind to win. In July 2009, Ohio's House Bill 1 became law. Under HB1's "licensed librarian and media specialist factor," $60,000 per organizational unit will be phased in over the next 10 years. Every Ohio school district will have funding for at least one licensed librarian/media specialist and many will have funding for at least one professional librarian/media specialist per building (www.oelma.org/Leg_update_7_15.htm).

As soon as the 2002 Operating Standards for Ohio Schools were announced, the Ohio Educational Library Media Association (OELMA) began advocating to preserve and restore school library services and learning opportunities for Ohio's schoolchildren. When the situation looked hopeless and as program after program was reduced or cut, OELMA never gave up. When an opportunity came in the form of education reform, OELMA was prepared, positioned, and present. This is a story of work and preparation coming together with opportunity. This is a story of teamwork and persistence.

A no-win situation. In the fall of 2000, OELMA leaders became aware of plans to revise Ohio's Operating Standards and to significantly reduce requirements for school libraries. OELMA testified to the State Board of Education, but it was too late; the standards were written and would not be changed. Ohio moved from requiring every library to be supervised by a professional school librarian to ambiguous requirements. Once the new Operating Standards went into effect on July 6, 2002, the only way school library positions could be required would be if the state would pay for them. That would be impossible given the state's financial issues.

Visualize the race. When the new standards were announced, school library leaders from OELMA, the State Library of Ohio, INFOhio, and the Ohio Department of Education (ODE) formed a group called Leadership for School Libraries or L4SL. This group's thinking and efforts informed and drove more than OELMA's advocacy efforts. They were behind the Ohio Research Study and OELMA's evidence-based practice training and modules. Although L4SL dissolved several years ago, its thinking and strategies persisted and provided the foundation for OELMA's ongoing advocacy efforts.

Get in the race. One priority of the renewed advocacy efforts was to make certain that the association is never again caught by surprise by major initiatives. School library leaders began to position OELMA as a member of the Ohio educational team. Its goal was to have school librarians represented on every Ohio Department of Education committee possible and representation at a variety of education functions such as state Board of Education meetings.

When Governor Ted Strickland began his education reform process, OELMA's president was invited to be part of his Governor's Institute on Creativity and Innovation in Education. The governor held a series of "Conversation on Education" meetings in the fall of 2008, and OELMA identified individuals who articulated how strong, professionally staffed school libraries and the 21st-century skills training those libraries offer align with the governor's educational goal.

Team building. OELMA built on that concept of mandated courses and worked for the inclusion of school librarians on each of

Gov. Ted Strickland   the standards-writing teams. This approach resulted in information-literacy standards being integrated into the other content standards.

Carla Southers, L4SL member and then–ODE's Library and Technology Consultant, promoted the writing of best practices guidelines for Ohio's school libraries. Because school library guidelines were not legally mandated, ODE did not have the funding for the school library guidelines that were made available for the mandated content standards. ODE gave the writing team one chance to meet. ODE was surprised by how the team's work connected to its own values and goals; the writing team was given permission to continue working on their own time.

Information literacy is a key component in Ohio's technology standards and school librarians were represented on the writing team. The library and technology standards clearly connect Ohio's school libraries and librarians to the priorities and agendas of Ohio's state and local educational systems. Even though the library standards are not legislatively mandated, they support and align with the state's educational priorities, ODE printed them and they are posted on the standards pages with all of the other state standards. School librarians are now part of Ohio's educational team.

Statistics: The Ohio Research Study. L4SL knew that while the second Colorado study and other research projects provided strong statistics, Ohio needed its own state-specific research. L4SL searched for an individual to develop a research study for Ohio that would build on the Keith Curry Lance team's exceptional work in other states. That led to Dr. Ross Todd's work on the LSTA-funded Ohio Research Study.

This study provides quantitative and qualitative evidence from constituents across the state. Since the voices are those of constituents, the data is relevant to every Ohio local, state, and national decision-maker. Collecting and analyzing the data led to L4SL working with Todd to develop the Model of the Ohio School Library as a Dynamic Agent of Learning. This changed the image of school libraries from a kind of "mall" where learners picked out resources to a laboratory where students are guided and encouraged to effectively select and utilize resources in order to construct an original information product. Ohio's strong school libraries are transformational and not simply informational. The findings positioned Ohio's school libraries to be key participants in the race to prepare Ohio's students for the future.

Evidence-based practice. Ohio needed to strengthen its school library programs. The strategy was to build strong programs both to advocate for and with. L4SL led OELMA's efforts to build the use of evidence-based practice (EBP) in Ohio's school libraries. The primary goal of EBP is to gather and use quantitative and qualitative data to improve practice and to provide evidence of student learning.

Evidence of student learning should be shared at every opportunity. When decision-makers are faced with cutting programs, it is imperative that school librarians have worked to educate decision-makers before those decisions are made. "Proactive" and "prevention" are key words. The time to deal with potential cuts is before they happen.

A few things learned along the way

OELMA's advocacy efforts supported the work of L4SL and persisted long after it dissolved. During the nearly 10 years that followed, OELMA has worked to preserve and restore school library services for Ohio's students, and new strategies have evolved.

Negative messages are frequently blocked or dismissed. One of the most consistent and persistent advocacy messages OELMA sends is the request for positive, constructive messages. Advocacy is more effective when messages build relationships rather than destroy them. Positive messages include expressing appreciation for past support and saying thank you for current support.

Decision-makers do not care about school libraries and librarians per se; however, they can be educated to care about what school librarians do for children. Weave positive, student-centered messages through grassroots efforts.

The day the Ohio legislature passed HB1, OELMA's leaders celebrated and began talking about next steps. OELMA urges members to reach out and thank state decision-makers for supporting learning for Ohio's students through strong school libraries. OELMA will continue to promote EBP. It has plans to promote visits by local, state, and national decision-makers to support strong school libraries; we want our leaders to know exactly what they are getting for students for their money.

SOURCE: Debra Kay Logan, "Staying the Course: Racing for Ohio's Students," *Library Media Connection* 28, no. 4 (January/February 2010): 12–13. Used with permission.

Survey your world
by Kathy Fredrick

Raise your hand if you've printed out surveys then spent hours sorting and collating the data manually. We know the importance of research and statistics in the current educational climate. Research-based teaching methods and test scores, as well as action research initiatives, are all reasons we gather data and use those results to show the effect of our role as school librarians. We can make use of Web 2.0 to focus our work on designing good surveys. What's involved in designing a good survey? How can we learn to use the survey tools found on the web?

We can start with a new set of names: SurveyGizmo, Response-O-Matic, FormSite, QuestionPro, Zoomerang, and SurveyMonkey, among many others. Most online survey tools have levels of access based on a subscription payment; but the most basic level is free. At the free level, you can do 10 questions per survey with 100 responses. You'll have access to 15 different types of questions, for example, fill-in-the-box, multiple choice, Likert scale, or short-answer responses. Try out a survey with your colleagues or with a set of students without worrying about cost. If you find this a viable tool and want to do more extensive surveys, subscription prices begin around $10–$20 per month for an individual account.

The mechanics of online surveys by using SurveyMonkey, as with most Web 2.0 tools, means setting up an account. Choose a username, password, and provide your email address. Once you've established this, you're free to create a survey. If it's your first time, you'll create one from scratch, add a survey title and click the "create survey" button to set up the questions. Once you've gotten one survey under your belt, you have the option to copy an existing survey as well.

The template for questions is easy to use. You can choose a background theme that sets the appearance of the survey, then click "add question here" to enter information. A pull-down menu lets you choose the kind of question, complete with a sample to show what it will look like. If you are worried that it won't turn out correctly, there's an "edit" button that allows you to go back and make changes. At any point during the design process, you can use the "preview survey" button to see what respondents will see when they go to answer the questions.

Once the survey is completed, you need to determine how responses will be collected. You can have SurveyMonkey collect responses from a web link placed on your website, or as an alternative, you can have an email sent from SurveyMonkey with your list of addresses. This option also gives you the ability to send messages for a new survey or to correspond with those who have responded and those who haven't, or you can set your own criteria. As in the survey question section, there are options to choose from as you go.

The beauty of online surveys is that the information is collected for you and the results are tallied. By going to the "analyze results" tab, SurveyMonkey will show the answers to survey questions. Depending on the question, you'll get percentages for particular responses, compilations of short answer questions, and so on. From there, the data is yours to use and interpret.

This is the mechanics of online surveys, using SurveyMonkey as an example. As you get started, check out the support resources provided by your chosen online survey site.

If you are new to surveys and to designing survey questions, you'll also want to do some reading on developing effective surveys. Some good resources are online and in professional journals. Here are a few key points to remember:

- Clearly define the purpose for the survey. Each question asked should connect to objectives.
- Make sure that the questions asked will garner the information wanted. Feel free to use a variety of question styles (multiple choice, short answer, scales) based on the kind of information being collected.
- Craft the questions carefully. Use neutral language and don't use leading words that might skew potential responses.
- Keep the survey as short as possible, and don't forget to include instructions for the survey respondents.
- Pretest the survey to get feedback about the survey before releasing it for the larger group. Check answers to test how well the questions have been designed to match survey goals.

Where will the research begin in your library media program? You may want to experiment with a simple survey on reading interests or a questionnaire at the end of a research project. Whatever you choose, an online survey tool can make the process easier. Armed with clear goals and great questions, you can reap the benefits of these great online utilities. You can focus on improving your practices, supporting student achievement, or documenting your impact in the learning process. Expand your horizons—survey your world.

SOURCE: Adapted from Kathy Fredrick, "Survey Your World," *School Library Media Activities Monthly* 25, no. 2 (October 2008): 43–44. Used with permission.

Evidence = assessment = advocacy
by Pamela Kramer and Linda Diekman

Powerful advocacy occurs at the local level when library stakeholders are given "the evidence," though it is most often perceived as the big splashy things such as the relentless pushing for a cause by talking to legislators and government officials.

Advocacy is about educating stakeholders using the best available evidence, and it is an ongoing process. It is a consistent message delivered in a variety of ways that demonstrates how the teacher-librarian contributes to student learning and has an effect on student achievement.

Teacher-librarians plan strategically, assess for learning, and document what they are doing and what students are learning. The message must then be about how we prepare students to function in the 21st century. For example, a principal tells a teacher-librarian that the library media center will be closed unless the librarian can show that what he does as he interacts with students increases their test scores on the annual achievement tests. If he cannot, funds for salaries, resources, and space might be reallocated to a classroom teacher.

A fairy tale? Hardly! Even administrators who normally support school library programs are putting teacher-librarians on notice. The flagging economy means there is less money going to districts. With high-stakes testing of students and data-driven decision-making by administrators, school boards, and parents, teacher-librarians must demonstrate how they contribute to student learning. It is no longer good enough to say "I taught all the 6th graders how to evaluate websites" or "Every senior had information literacy training from me." The essential question is not "how many," but "who learned."

Evidence

Most teacher-librarians know that what they do improves student achievement and the research supports this. Much national research, as well as the *Illinois Study: Powerful Libraries Make Powerful Learners* (Illinois School Library Media Association, 2005), the 15th of such studies done by Keith Curry Lance, have documented in aggregate the value of school libraries in relationship to test scores. Another excellent report is Ross J. Todd and Carol C. Kuhlthau's *Student Learning through Ohio School Libraries* (Ohio Educational Library Media Association, 2003), which was the first study conducted from the students' point of view.

However, it is easy for an administrator to dismiss these studies by saying, "I need evidence in my school." Many school administrators work in an environment where their jobs are dependent on test scores. They ask questions like: "Why do school libraries need access to databases?" "Why do they need print materials, since we can Google everything?" and "Why should I spend money on a certified teacher-librarian?" It is therefore incumbent on teacher-librarians to measure at the local level their contributions to student learning and to communicate to their stakeholders: other teachers, administrators, parents, community members, and legislators. The important question is, "What difference is made by specific library encounters?" Is it possible to identify specific actions and strategies that improve student achievement?

This is an incredible challenge. Teacher-librarians have the American Association of School Librarians' *Standards for the 21st Century Learner* (2007) that is embraced not only by the school library field, but by many educators. They complement the Partnership for 21st Century Skills' *Framework for 21st Century Learning*, which provides a well-rounded approach to teaching and learning to enable students to function in an increasingly complex world. At the same time, schools are being challenged to meet annual yearly progress (AYP) and improve students' test scores. Teacher-librarians often feel like their roles and content (information literacy) are outside the realm of the classroom teacher. In reality, teacher-librarians have a great deal to contribute to the standards that classroom teachers are struggling with. Teacher-librarians need to become a part of the school learning conversation.

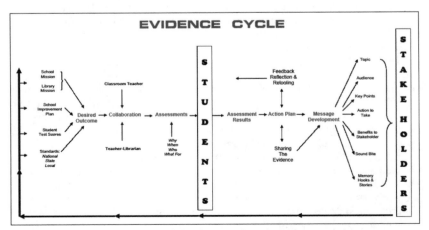

Here is a depiction of what happens along the evidence cycle—
when stakeholders are given the evidence.

Learning to gather evidence

In 2008, through a grant titled Here's the Evidence: Teacher-Librarians Help Students Achieve, a cohort of teacher-librarians from the DuPage and North Suburban Library Systems in Illinois entered training on how to plan strategically, use outcome-based lesson planning, and develop tools to measure the effect they have on student learning. In addition, cohort members learned communication and message-development skills, so once they had the evidence they could share it effectively with the stakeholders. The content of the project was based on Violet H. Harada and Joan M. Yoshina's book *Assessing Learning* (2005). The grant for the workshop was funded by the Illinois State Library, a division of the Office of the Secretary of State, using funds provided by the Institute of Museum and Library Services, under the federal Library Services and Technology Act.

Grant managers invited more than 30 individuals to participate in the project and 28 accepted the invitation. In general, individuals were invited because they met the criteria outlined in the grant application. However, some individuals asked to participate when they heard about the project because they were interested in the assessment issues.

Cohort participants were required to be certified teacher-librarians and to have at least two years experience, established collaborative relationships with teachers, and a letter from their administrators acknowledging they would attend the six days of training spread over the grant period. The teacher-librarians who formed the group evenly represented elementary, middle, and high schools.

An important grant component was to provide access to "academic partners." These were individuals who taught in graduate programs at Dominican University, National-Louis University, and Northern Illinois University. These partners and the grant managers participated in the training sessions and were available throughout the grant period by phone, email, and in person for consultation and support as the cohort moved through the training, project development, assessment, and reporting.

Overall, the biggest challenge for some of the cohort members was learning to plan strategically. According to presenter Violet Harada, professor in the Library and Information Science Program at the University of Hawaii at Manoa, who appeared via web conference, planning strategically means finding out what matters most to teachers and administrators. Therefore, the teacher-librarian in collaboration with a teacher looked at the subject area standards, reviewed test scores, and examined the school-improvement plan to see what students were expected to know and do. Then they focused on the classroom's standards to help students achieve the outcome.

After completing their collaborative lessons, cohort members filled out a reporting template and submitted electronic portfolios to the grant managers. One hundred percent of the projects undertaken by participants provided data to inform stakeholders. Twenty-three projects aligned directly with the local school improvement plans and 15 Illinois Learning Standards were used representing grades 1–12. One grant participant, Linda Diekman, explains her experience as a member of the cohort:

> I was nervous about which project to select for the assessment grant, so I decided to take the advice of the grant leaders and look for a small project. The fifth grade teacher I approached was enthusiastic about having me teach note-taking as part of a larger research project. I designed a checklist that focused on the areas we thought were important. We wanted to make sure students were putting the notes in their own words, putting one note

on a card, and correctly citing their sources. After the first pretest was given, the results were shared with the teacher. We were able to identify the students who needed additional coaching and in what areas. The teacher was thrilled. Within the week, the two other fifth grade teachers asked me to do the some lesson and assessment with their classes.

Students used the checklist as a self-assessment before turning in their note cards. I used the checklist for the final assessment and the teacher included the note-taking results in the grading rubric for the project.

How did the students do? On the note-taking mechanics, the teacher and I felt there was marked improvement on each measure.

- After 29% of the students copied information directly from the text in the pre-assessment, all students progressed to putting facts in their own words at least some of the time.
- Over half of the students wrote in full sentences in the pre-assessment, and at the end of the project that number had been reduced to only five students.
- Students improved in their use of note cards and source citation and all students were placing one fact on a card at least some of the time by the end of the research, with the vast majority of students using cards correctly all of the time.
- By the projects' end, only four students struggled with citing sources where 20 students had difficulty earlier in the process.

Now that's evidence!

Evidence does not need to be a formal pretest and posttest. It can be a simple KWL chart, an exit slip with a question such as "What one thing did you learn today?" or a check mark on a clipboard to record a verbal answer to a simple question such as "Did you find something you can use for your report?"

Education: Assessing the evidence

It was not enough just to collect and document the learning. Assessment and documentation led to a two-part action plan. First, cohort members reflected and retooled the lessons in order to improve student learning. Second, they communicated results to stakeholders through reports made at school board meetings, during informal conversations with parents and other teachers, and with written documents such as a newsletter. An essential component of the grant project was communications training.

Cohort members learned that they must consider the needs and interests of their audience, identify key points to make, and discuss the benefits to the stakeholder. They learned also to ask the audience to take some action. It might be as simple as coming into the library to see the classes in action or as complex as adjusting teachers' schedules so there is more collaborative planning time with the teacher-librarian. In addition, they developed such memory hooks as "School libraries don't cost—They pay!" and elevator speeches.

Over 90% of the cohort members reported their levels of communication with stakeholders had increased. Most reported their interactions were with other teachers and administrators, with some reporting they had communicated with parents, school board members, and members of the community. Additionally, in many schools the results were included in the annual report to the school board. Here is what happened after Linda Diekman's first experience gathering evidence:

I was able to take the results of the fifth grade note-taking project and share it with the fourth grade team. They were excited about having another teacher collaborate and assist with their upcoming state project. One teacher indicated she was doing a "warm-up" project and asked if I would do the note-taking instruction and assessment process on two research projects. I was delighted to be asked! This involvement allowed me to gather another set of data. Not only was I looking at student achievement on the task at hand, I could look at the data in a summative format. Those students who had two research projects, for the most part, transferred their note-taking abilities from one project to the next.

The state project involved higher-level vocabulary and made it more difficult for students to put notes in their own words. Terms like "transportation," "economy," and "tourism" proved to be stumbling blocks. This knowledge informed our practice as teachers, and we made notes to modify instruction for the next year's project.

Oh, that fifth grade team? They asked me to collaborate on a storytelling unit. I designed the unit and assessment rubric, and was the lead teacher on the project. I don't think that opportunity would have come about if it weren't for that initial note-taking project.

Advocacy

Advocacy links the evidence gathered with the education of the stakeholders to answer the essential question: How does the school library instructional program affect student achievement? It is not enough to collect data on circulation statistics, numbers of classes, and students who use the library, or how many collaborative projects or state goals were taught. Teaching the content to students is very different from students learning the content; it comes down to the issue of accountability. Assessment is an ongoing examination of learning and a shared responsibility with other teachers. For the library media specialist, documenting assessment results provides a compelling case for the value of the school library program, so when issues of funding and accountability arise and decision-makers have to identify priorities for staff and budget, teacher-librarians can produce student-focused data to support their requests. It is important to realize this kind of information should not be gathered only when there is an immediate threat. Teacher-librarians should be doing this kind of data gathering for nearly every instructional encounter they have. Linda Diekman put the evidence she had gathered and her communication training to work:

> When I initially asked for permission to join the grant cohort, my superintendent was skeptical. He wanted to be sure teachers were involved and that I wasn't acting in a solo role. At the end of the grant period, I reported to my principal with the documentation of how I had contributed to student achievement. She arranged for me to communicate the student successes to the superintendent, who was pleased at the depth of teacher collaboration and student impact.
>
> In addition, I put my communications training to work during a school board visit to the library. I had my "elevator speech" ready and while we discussed the advantages of the OPAC software, I filled them in on student successes. They were most impressed that these successes happened in the classroom and that I was assisting teachers meet learning standards.
>
> Now when someone asks, "How are things going in the library?" I

3

have my elevator speech all ready. My answer is "Just great! Did you know that 90% of the 5th graders attained 'master storyteller' status last week?" They can't help but stop and have a conversation and I am able to share the details of student success.

Evidence, assessment, advocacy = always

Cohort members began to speak the same language as other leaders and stakeholders. They gained new respect among their peers. One commented she got on the radar screen with the new principal. Another said she and her staff had gained more credibility: "I am not just an extra." They heard teachers who collaborated with teacher-librarians comment on how much learning had taken place and how they wanted to continue the relationships with their colleagues. Administrators realized that teacher-librarians had something to contribute to school improvement plans and curricula and appointed them to serve on school and district-wide committees. Even two years after the beginning of the grant program, cohort members were reporting that as the financial crisis loomed large in Illinois, the grant program prepared them to prove their value to student learning and that they were being taken more seriously as curriculum partners.

Other teachers, administrators, and stakeholders have seen the evidence, were educated about its value, and are now advocates for the school library program. In the high-stakes testing and standards-driven school environments all across the country, it is vital that teacher-librarians prove their value to the learning process. The survival of teacher-librarians may depend on just how much they affect student achievement. Assessment data needs to be reported regularly rather than only in times of threat. It is a constant stream of why we are at the center of teaching and learning.

Finally, the real winners in all of this are the students. Therefore, the message is: Here's the evidence; teacher-librarians improve student achievement. In this project, they did just that!

SOURCE: Pamela K. Kramer and Linda Diekman, "Evidence = Assessment = Advocacy," *Teacher Librarian* 37, no. 3 (February 2010): 27–30. Used with permission.

High stakes for school librarians
by Chris Lehmann

As school districts nationwide face budget cuts, the role of librarians and school libraries are being called into question like never before. While some argue that the digital age has made the librarian obsolete, librarians face a far more insidious threat—the growing reliance on high-stakes testing.

Certainly, the last 20 years has fundamentally changed the way we, as a society, think about and access information. We are perhaps much too slowly realizing that our schools must evolve to keep up with a changing world. While technology has fundamentally altered the role of every educator, it's a mistake to assume that these changes have made the librarian any less important. In fact, today's librarian, the information specialist, is more vital than ever before.

From an administrator's perspective, I consider librarians important for several reasons. First, we live in the information age, and our librarians have long functioned as the information specialists in our schools. Secondly, as schools change and traditional classrooms evolve so that more students have time to spend beyond the rows of desks, our libraries become even more essential. Finally, libraries provide a critical place for student-centered learning. For decades, librarians have helped students find books and topics that interested them. We need more of this in our schools, not less.

It is not the internet or the changing nature of information that threatens our school libraries, but the change we are seeing in our school value system. With the advent of current government mandates and the high-stakes test, the very values that make libraries so essential in schools are at risk because their measurement is messier.

Our school librarians are the keepers of the progressive flame, the "guides on the side," helping students to find information, make sense of it, and craft meaning from multiple sources. More and more schools are moving away from these values in favor of preparing students for the standardized assessment that No Child Left Behind (NCLB) demands.

As schools narrow and script the curriculum in "teaching to the test," the question becomes: What is the role of the school library in the era of NCLB? We need our libraries now more than ever. We need librarians to help students make sense of the blizzard of information at their fingertips. We need our librarians to continue to help students find the joy in learning something new.

Our librarians have always known that the vast store of information available to our students did not end at our walls. Helping the rest of us deal with that in our classrooms makes our librarian colleagues even more relevant today. Finally, we need our librarians to remind us each and every day that our students can learn more and do more than a high-stakes test could ever measure.

SOURCE: Adapted from Chris Lehmann, "High Stakes for School Librarians," *School Library Journal* 53 (July 2007): 20. Used with permission.

What does it really look like when students are learning in the library?
by Allison Zmuda

Walk into any library media center and you will see lots of students busily working on classroom assignments. While these students may be focused and industrious, the real questions are: What drives their work, and are they learning? Student learning comes from active efforts to construct knowledge that requires them to pursue inquiries, locate and evaluate evidence, make connections, analyze patterns, reconcile apparent discrepancies, deliberate about language, communicate thinking, and, finally, revise their work. The focus of this article is on the need to transform the passive learning found in student efforts to merely locate information to an active engagement in constructing knowledge. This transformation begins with the library media specialist's collaboration with colleagues.

Owning the problem

Many students regard the assignments they are given in the library media center as comparable to completing forms, little more than bureaucratic exercises that

are part of the daily drudgery of school. They may be committed to recording an answer to the question or a response to a prompt but remain uncommitted to the unavoidable struggle required in knowledge construction. They may become impatient with library media specialists for not telling them where they can find what they are looking for, or how to document their research the right way, or when they have enough information and can move on to the next part.

Such disengagement inhibits true learning; it prevents students from the responsibility as well as the opportunity to build their intelligence. Mel Levine, in a 2007 article in *Educational Leadership*, worried about the impact this disengagement has on the child's future success. He writes, "Many students emerge from high school as passive processors who simply sop up intellectual input without active response. Some passive learners, although able to scrape by academically, endure chronic boredom in school and later suffer career ennui. Their habit of cognitive inactivity can lead to mediocre performance in college and later on the job." The solution to this problem involves more than collaborating with classroom teachers to produce authentic research tasks; it also requires constant analysis of how students are working to ensure that they can learn something from the experience.

When I conducted a workshop in western New York, school librarians and their partner classroom teachers lamented that when students are given robust research-based assignments, they still behaved as if these assignments were low-level search-and-retrieval tasks. My challenge to them was to describe what these learners look like so that the school librarian and classroom teacher can more effectively design and facilitate research-based instructional experiences that will cause learning.

Not only do students misunderstand their job as learners, but they seldom get to experience a true sense of accomplishment that comes from constructing their own understanding and becoming steeped in knowledge. Eleanor Duckworth states:

> Of all the virtues related to intellectual functioning, the most passive is the virtue of knowing the right answer. Knowing the right answer requires no decisions, carries no risks, and makes no demands. It is automatic. It is thoughtless.... Knowing the right answer is overrated. It is a virtue—

Good and Bad Business Practices for Library Media Specialists	
Moving away from bad business where	**Moving toward good business where**
Success is defined by the number of staff who collaborate with the library media specialist.	Success is defined by the quality of the work completed in the library media center.
Success is defined by doing whatever is asked in order to be recognized as valuable or important.	Success is defined by investing resources only in those tasks that are central to the library mission.
Success is defined by helping students find what they are looking for.	Success is defined by engaging students in the construction of deep knowledge through the exploration of ideas and information, conducting of investigations, and communication and evaluation of findings.
Success is defined by the number of instructional sessions held in the library media center.	Success is defined by the student learning that resulted from completion of work centered on subject area and information literacy goals.

there is no debate about that—but in conventional views of intelligence it tends to be given far too much weight. (*The Having of Wonderful Ideas*, 1996, pp. 64–65).

Recently, when I was conducting an observation in the school library, I saw a group of students diligently recording information on a particular research topic of their choice. When I asked each of them what was most interesting in what they had found so far, I got blank stares. When I probed further, one student finally remarked, "I think you misunderstand the assignment. We don't have to find things interesting. We just have to find things."

The joy and pain of knowledge construction

When students are working to locate information to answer a question, they may be temporarily engaged in the hunt but find little intellectual satisfaction from their efforts. When students are really researching, however, the hunt is altogether different. Instead of being driven to find what they believe to be a predetermined answer, they are in the pursuit of truth. They work to find out what really happened, how something really works, or what really matters. They work to persuade an audience, to communicate information and ideas, to describe an event, object, or life. And this hunt is inevitably frustrating. They find sources that disagree with each other, point them in different directions, and challenge the validity of their original research question or thesis.

So what do students look and sound like when they are truly engaged in a research task that is

---

What does it looks like when students are working on a robust research task where little learning is likely to result?

They look for direct answers to indirect/complex inquiries.
They follow an orderly, linear process or execute a plan from start to finish without reflecting on whether it's working.
They copy what they find without thinking about it.
They work to complete the task as quickly as possible.
They confuse quantity of information with quality of research.
They view every published source as valid (both to the inquiry and as an authority on the subject).
They focus more on the "bells and whistles" of the task than the substance.
They operate with an overly narrow or broad inquiry that they are unable to refine.
They collect details without thinking about connections and areas of incongruence or information gaps.
They assume that if they find the "answer" in one source that they have "finished" looking.

If students are really researching, then . . .

How would they move around the library?
What kinds of questions would they ask teachers and the library media specialist?
What kinds of conversations would they have with their peers?
What would they find interesting?
How long would it take them to complete a task?
What would they find frustrating?
How would they work to overcome obstacles?
Who would they want to collaborate with?
How would they document what they found?
How would they work to organize and develop their ideas and information?

likely to cause learning? Collaborating with classroom teachers to describe these learners is a significant step in answering that question and elevating the quality of student work in the library. Indicators, developed by both classroom teachers and the school librarian, can be used to monitor student learning and appropriately scaffold instructional interventions so that students can successfully complete the task. Development of indicators can be based on the following reflective prompts:

Library Media Specialists As Learning Specialists		
K What do we know a learning specialist to be?	**W** What are we curious or concerned about if the library media specialist is reframed as a learning specialist?	**L** What have we learned about what reframing the library media specialist as a learning specialist will require?
• Someone who believes that all students can be successful learners. • Someone who is up on the latest trends in teaching and learning. • Someone who has work experience in both the classroom and the library media center. • Someone who uses assessment data to determine student strength and weaknesses to inform future instruction. • Someone who can diagnose learning problems and design ways to address them. • Someone with deep content expertise about how people learn. • Someone who works with staff and students. • Someone who constantly reflects on his/her own practice and how to improve. • Someone who is able to break things down into small, manageable pieces. • Someone who is fluent with the curriculum goals across grade levels and subject areas. • Someone who can coach performance (from staff and students) through the design of challenging and motivating tasks. • Someone who seeks out new learning experiences, tools, and resources because of what the learners need.	• How do we articulate our role in an effective way so the message is heard? • How do we use professional learning communities to facilitate work? • How much do we really know about how different types of learners learn in the library media center? • How can we earn respect of staff and the larger system as a learning specialist? • How does the learning specialist fit into the hierarchy of the school or district organization? • Who has the authority to make decisions about what instruction will look like in the library media center? • How do we increase the number of teachers who want to collaborate with us in the design, implementation, and evaluation of learning? • How do we hone our leadership skills so that we can improve the effectiveness of our collaborative work with staff? • How do we elevate the quality of instructional and assessment practices in the school/district? • Who are the other learning specialists in the school? What relationship do we have with one another? What relationship should we have?	• Just because it isn't happening in front of us doesn't mean it isn't happening—the teacher's classroom is an extension of the work in the library media center. • We will never be considered learning specialists without collecting evidence of student achievement in our classroom. • Because disengaged learners learn nothing, we have a responsibility to "fix" instructional designs that are low-level, information retrieval tasks. • A learning specialist, like any teacher leadership position, is an inherently precarious, messy job because it lives somewhere between the administrative ranks and the teaching ranks. • Without a clear job description (on paper and in practice), it is impossible to know whether we are doing the right things. • Staff think that we are what they see us do—if they only watch us organize, sort, manage, and support, they will not see us as learning specialists.

Note: Specific contributions to the KWL chart were made by audience participants at a breakout session facilitated by Allison Zmuda on November 15, 2007, including but not limited to the reflections of: Debra Kay Logan, Hilda Weisburg, Dee Giordan, Linda Piscione, Pat Slemmer, Diane Drayer Beler, Pat VanEs, Christine Lopey, and Dawn Henderson.

It is important to note that research is only one type of learning that takes place in the library. A similar process could be applied to other types of learning in the library such as communicating information and ideas to an audience and pursuing personal and aesthetic growth through reading (see AASL *Standards for the 21st-Century Learner*).

In addition to observing students as they work on a task, it also is of vital importance that the learning environment is conducive to knowledge construction. Violet Harada and I have delineated features of such learning environments in our book *Librarians as Learning Specialists* (Libraries Unlimited, 2008). These features include the following examples:

- Opportunities to pursue areas of interest and curiosity as part of the curriculum.
- Conferences between staff members and individuals or small groups of learners based on their current level of work or understanding of ideas.
- Student development of plans to achieve goals and a feedback cycle of planning, evaluation, and reflection to determine whether the plan is having the intended effect and make any necessary adjustments.
- Physical spaces conducive to the nature of the work—collaborative space to think and develop ideas together; quiet places to read, process, analyze, reflect, and create work; whiteboard or Smart Board space to visually illustrate concepts; and visual cues that provide vital information about procedures, protocols, and strategies.
- Assignments completed in a range of ways based on a combination of what the student needs, his or her preferred way of working, and the focus of the learning goal.
- Students measure current work (both their own and their peers) based on a set of established criteria and articulate adjustments that would improve the quality of the work.
- Students routinely explain both to one another and to staff how they arrived at a conclusion and are as curious about the process as the result.

Key actions to make this happen now

It is possible to create learners who are actively searching to make meaning, who are internally motivated to pursue an answer, who are evaluating information to determine its relevance and its credibility, and who are taking care to correctly document their findings. There are four key actions that library media specialists can begin to take today to make this more likely to happen:

1. Describe what it looks like when students are really doing the assignment and when they only appear to be doing it.
2. Develop instructional interventions that refocus passive efforts to active struggles.
3. Examine assignment directions, scoring tools, and revision opportunities to ensure that they communicate the value of making connections, analyzing evidence, developing ideas using information, drawing conclusions, and refining work.
4. Examine library practices and policies to ensure that they facilitate the unavoidable risk-taking, messiness, impulsiveness, analysis, frustration, and joy that come from the pursuit of a curiosity.

While this may seem like a solitary endeavor at times, library media specialists can consistently work to enlist others in envisioning what success looks like and strive to create the conditions (feedback and then space) necessary for others to reflect on the implementation of successful practices. Both students and teachers alike will begin to see that a true sense of accomplishment in the library media center comes from the genuine struggle to make meaning.

SOURCE: Allison Zmuda, "What Does It Really Look Like When Students Are Learning in the Library Media Center?" *School Library Media Activities Monthly* 25 (September 2008): 25–27. Used with permission.

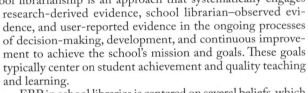

Evidence-based manifesto
by Ross Todd

Every fall, *School Library Journal* hosts a national Leadership Summit that brings together a mix of school librarians, administrators, other educators, researchers, and university professors, as well as policy-makers and elected officials. While the topics change, the summit always focuses on an issue of critical importance to school librarians.

The 2007 Leadership Summit, "Where's the Evidence? Understanding the Impact of School Libraries," dove headfirst into evidence-based practice (EBP). Evidence-based school librarianship is an approach that systematically engages  research-derived evidence, school librarian–observed evidence, and user-reported evidence in the ongoing processes of decision-making, development, and continuous improvement to achieve the school's mission and goals. These goals typically center on student achievement and quality teaching and learning.

EBP in school libraries is centered on several beliefs, which most school librarians already share:

The fusion of learning, information, and technology presents dynamic challenges for teachers, school librarians, administrators, and students in 21st-century schools. Providing the best opportunities for children to learn and achieve, and knowing that they've done well, is at the heart of quality teaching and learning, and is the driving force behind EBP.

School libraries as schools' information and knowledge centers are essential for addressing curriculum standards, the complexities of learning, and quality teaching in information-intensive 21st-century schools.

School librarianship derives its mandate from a diverse body of theoretical and empirical knowledge, and active engagement with this knowledge is what enables the profession to continuously transform and improve. Leading this transformation is the professional expertise of certified school librarians who possess expertise, insights, and skills based on the knowledge that they apply in practice.

All students can learn through engagement with school libraries. School libraries play a transformative role in the lives of students, not only by helping them develop intellectually, as measured by standardized test scores, but by encouraging students' intellectual, social, and cultural development.

The transformation of information into knowledge, and the development of attitudes, values, and beliefs are enabled through carefully designed instructional

interventions and reading literacy programs that guide and engage students.
The value of a school library can be measured. Learning outcomes, as well as
personal, social, and cultural growth, can be documented.

Evidence of the school library's crucial role in student achievement is not fully
understood, seen, or acknowledged by many stakeholders.

Accountability is an essential component of sustainable development of the
school library profession. Accountability is a commitment to growth through
examining progress and practices. It brings alignment, innovation, collaboration, introspection, and effectiveness.

Sustainable development through accountability requires a move from rhetoric
to evidence, from a "tell me" framework to a "show me" framework, and from
a process framework to an outcomes framework.

If we do not show value, we will not have a future. EBP is not about the survival
of school librarians, it's about the survival of our students. This is the social
justice and ethical imperative for evidence-based practice.

3

Multiple types of evidence

EBP recognizes multiple sources, types of evidence, and ways of gathering evidence. This facilitates triangulation, an approach to data analysis
that synthesizes data from multiple sources. By
using and comparing data from a number of
sources, you can develop stronger claims about
your practice's impact and outcomes.

Different sources and types of evidence might
include student interviews or portfolios, reflection
and process journals, formative and summative
assessment tasks, standards-based scoring guides
and rubrics, surveys of students and teachers,
pretest and posttest measures, student-generated products, statewide assessments,
skills measurements, ongoing performance-based assessments, general student
data, and systematically recorded observations.

What is EBP for school librarians?

Evidence-based school librarianship uses research-derived evidence to shape and
direct what we do. EBP combines professional wisdom, reflective experience, and
understanding of students' needs with the judicious use of research-derived evidence
to make decisions about how the school library can best meet the instructional
goals of the school.

In order to accomplish this, school librarians need to systematically collect
evidence that shows how their practices impact student achievement; the development of deep knowledge and understanding; and the competencies and skills for
thinking, living, and working.

This holistic approach to EBP in school libraries involves three dimensions:
evidence for practice, evidence in practice, and evidence of practice.

Evidence for practice focuses on examining and using empirical research to
form practices, inform actions, and identify best practices. This is the informational
dimension of school library practice.

Evidence in practice focuses on integrating the available research evidence with the deep knowledge and understanding derived from professional experience, and using local evidence to identify learning dilemmas and needs, and achievement gaps. This kind of reflective practice enables us to make informed decisions about how the school library can bring about optimal learning outcomes and actively contribute to fulfilling the school's mission and goals. This is the transformational dimension of school library practice.

Evidence of practice is derived from systematically measured, student-based data. It's about the real results of what school librarians actually do. Evidence of practice focuses on measured outcomes and impacts, going beyond process and activities as outputs. It establishes what has changed for learners as a result of inputs, interventions, activities, and processes.

None of these dimensions are linear or static. Taken together, they are a dynamic, ongoing, and integrative process that informs practice, generates new practices, and demonstrates a practice's impact on learning outcomes.

The central questions

EBP in school librarianship is driven by central questions that give school libraries their *raison d'être*. For school librarians, the big question regarding EBP is, "Why do school libraries matter today, particularly in the context of an educational world that increasingly relies on diverse, complex, and often conflicting sources of digital information?"

The answer to this question lies in student outcomes; specifically, what school librarians can do in their instructional practices to ensure those outcomes. This, in turn, raises some interesting questions:

- How do school libraries impact student learning? How do they help students learn?
- Do students who have been taught information skills perform better academically?
- How do we ensure that our school libraries are sustainable and accountable—in infrastructure, personnel, resources, and instructional processes—so that optimal student outcomes are achieved?
- How do we spread the word about the impact of school libraries on student achievement and demonstrate their educational, social, and cultural value?

EBP emphasizes the actual work of the school librarian, including the creation of focal initiatives that document and demonstrate the individual school library's impact on learning outcomes. Accordingly, EBP generates local versions of the above questions. For example, how does my school library impact student learning? How does my school library help students learn?

An emphasis on outcomes

By emphasizing outcomes, EBP shifts the focus from articulating what school librarians do to what students achieve. Accordingly, EBP validates that quality learning outcomes can be achieved through the school library and that the school librarian is an important instructional partner. While some see EBP as a theory of practice, fundamentally it's not about theory. Rather, it is an approach to best practice.

Evidence-based practice is action-oriented. It goes beyond an awareness of statewide studies and the evidence they provide about school libraries, and the assumption that sharing the results of a study is enough to ensure quality school libraries for all. It asks school librarians to take action, to engage in local initiatives, rather than simply keeping track of the number of books that are checked out.

This is not to disparage what has traditionally been at the center of school library practice, such as the number of classes in the library, the number of items borrowed, and the number of items purchased annually. However, these are evidence of inputs and processes, rather than evidences of outcomes. They do play a role in making decisions that will lead to optimum outcomes, and should not be overlooked. But they are not the centerpiece of evidence-based practice.

EBP means a shift in focus from information inputs to knowledge and skills outputs, such as mastery of curriculum content, critical thinking and knowledge-building competencies, mastery of complex technical skills for accessing and evaluating information, and using information to construct deep knowledge. EBP also includes outcomes that are related to reading comprehension and enrichment, as well as to the attitudes and values associated with information use and learning.

Outcomes and national standards

The 2007 American Association of School Librarians' *Standards for the 21st-Century Learner* emphasizes learning outcomes, underpinned by reading as interpretation and the development of new knowledge by students. These standards explicitly identify outcomes, using descriptions such as "inquire, think critically, and gain knowledge"; "draw conclusions, make informed decisions"; "apply knowledge to new situations, and create new knowledge"; "share knowledge and participate ethically and productively as members of our democratic society"; and "pursue personal and aesthetic growth."

The standards clearly provide a framework for the evidence that should be generated. They provide a structure for making evidence-based claims about the school library's contribution to learning, and give focus to specific evidence-collecting strategies. These strategies can lead to many claims such as:

- Students' final products showed improved ability to analyze and synthesize information.
- Students' research reports showed improved ability to draw conclusions and state implications of their findings.
- Students' presentations showed ability to present different viewpoints and a strong case for their own positions.
- Eighty-three percent of the class show improved ability in thoughtfully analyzing and evaluating major alternative points of view.
- Following instructional interventions that focused on establishing the quality of websites, 100% of the students' bibliographies showed use of high-quality sites.
- The analysis of the final bibliographies submitted by the students compared to their initial research plans showed a change from generalist background information to specialist, detailed information sources.

Such examples of knowledge-based outcomes, particularly expressed in the language of curriculum standards, are far more meaningful than library outcomes that track, for example, the number of users or the size of collections.

Key challenges of EBP

The following questions and even some answers emerged at the last summit.

How do we make research-based evidence more accessible and applicable so it can be integrated into practice? Often research is reported in the context of sophisticated methodological and statistical procedures. This is important to the quality of the research, but it can make some studies tough to understand. Research needs to be repackaged to make it more accessible and to establish its practical utility and applicability.

How do we build a stronger community of participatory research? This involves both knowing what educational research is occurring and having the opportunity to actively participate in it. There's a sense that research is not consulted because it doesn't address the real-world concerns of practicing librarians.

How do we share and accumulate locally generated evidence? We need structures and processes for storing data, as well as good examples that showcase the outcomes. For example, what might a portfolio of locally generated evidence look like? How can this evidence be accumulated across individual schools and districts, and be shared and built upon?

How do we deal with negative evidence arising out of research? What happens if research at a local, state, or national level shows that school librarians are not making a difference? How do we build a widespread commitment to evidence-based practice within the profession? And how do we address school librarians who fear being accountable for learning outcomes or who don't see the value or necessity of EBP? Resistance from colleagues, or branding such advances as passing fads, is not unique to our profession.

How do we provide professional training in EBP? For starters, by making the training developed in the Delaware and Ohio studies more widely available.

How do we address the perception that most librarians don't have enough time for EBP? Time is consistently presented as the key barrier to implementing evidence-based practice, and there's also the perception that more support staff are needed to undertake this "additional" work. But EBP is not about scrambling to find additional time. It's about establishing priorities and making choices based on your beliefs about the importance of school libraries and learning.

How do we persuade school administrators that EBP is a key component of the work of school librarians and garner their support? Some school administrators may resist EBP because the library is not perceived as a classroom and the school librarian not perceived as a teacher.

Does a school librarian need the authority of school administrators to engage in evidence-based practices? A profession without reflective practitioners who are willing to learn about relevant research is a blinkered profession—one that's disconnected from best practices and best thinking, and one which, by default, often resorts to advocacy rather than evidence to survive. EBP exists in other disciplines and it can be used in ours; but there is plenty left to do before EBP can become integral to school librarianship. This responsibility lies with all of us; it's time to get working!

SOURCE: Ross Todd, "The Evidence-Based Manifesto for School Librarians," *School Library Journal* 54 (April 2008): 38–43. Used with permission.

The first step in online learning

by Priscille Dando

Editor's note: Dando discusses the Blackboard content management system as a way to conduct library instruction and other library services. A variety of commercial content management systems are on the market that can do the various things discussed in this article. Interested readers should investigate systems supported in their schools and districts to take advantage of the many features that keep getting more sophisticated over time. A course management system along with the free and safe Google Apps for Education provides many opportunities to turn one-way communication with students and teachers into a giant conversation.—*B.W.*

For years I've maintained my high school library's website as a dynamic resource to assist more than 2,000 students with their research as well as to inform parents and the community about the library program, services, and resources. Library web pages have been extremely successful as a form of public communication, but they have too many limitations as a learning tool.

For instance, posting passwords for remote access to online databases would violate the subscription contract. Posting resources such as pathfinders and resource guides online is possible, but certain critical learning materials couldn't be published because putting them on the web would be considered a copyright violation. Then my district made Blackboard accounts available to all teachers and school librarians, and we had a powerful, interactive tool with greater freedom to provide exactly the resources and online assistance students—just when they need them—at school or at home.

What makes an online course management system like Blackboard unique is that it is a closed online community for the students, teachers, and parents. Each student has a password-protected account. When students log in, they see links to all their classes and, of course, a link to our library site. I administrator this site, and I can design and organize it any way I choose. Its many functions allow for more than just posting documents and links. I conduct assessments and surveys, post articles and resource guides that include passwords, hold discussion groups, and make announcements that reach every student in the school.

My first use of Blackboard was as an assessment tool. Every year I strive to improve the library orientation of our 9th graders. Introducing more than 500 students to the resources, services, and procedures of their school library is an important aspect of orientation, and I look for new ways to make this first meeting more interactive. Paper and pencil surveys, even with bubble sheets, were never practical to administer because of the cost of the materials and the time involved analyzing results. Online courseware provides the ideal solution.

A colleague at another high school and I decided to work together to develop an online information skills inventory for every 9th-grade student. Our first step was to determine what to measure. We developed and compared lists of the information we most wanted to assess. We pored over benchmarks and questions released by the state from our standardized tests. We analyzed information literacy skills assessments available online from universities and high schools.

We drafted our inventory together, but modified individual items to meet our library's program goals. I limited mine to about 20 items, such as

> Information that you find on the internet (choose one):
> (a) Is far more reliable than books and magazines;
> (b) Is factual because the internet is constantly monitored;
> (c) Should be evaluated by the user for reliability, or
> (d) Is accurate, timely, and appropriate for all research.

The next step was to create the inventory within the online courseware. I discovered that Blackboard contains test and survey functions that led me step-by-step through the process of creating the inventory. While mine was multiple choice, I could have just as easily added short-answer or true-or-false items. I was able to paste images into some questions. For example, on questions about our online catalog, I was able to incorporate screen shots to focus on the catalog's functions.

The first part of the library orientation was a typical introduction to the staff, services, procedures, and resources of our library media center. I then explained I wanted them to answer a questionnaire about their previous experiences conducting research in a school library. This would help in designing lessons based on their answers. The library's research lab was used to take the assessment. With only 20 questions, the entire procedure for logging on, accessing the assessment, and completing the questions took less than 15 minutes with logging on being the biggest obstacle to those who had never used Blackboard before.

A screenshot showing Blackboard's user-centric interface

In real time I can review a summary of all results: how many students have taken the assessment, their average score, and an item-by-item analysis. I can see which questions caused the most problems and also identify which wrong answers students chose. I was able to analyze the 9th graders' performance and identify strengths and weaknesses in their information skills and background in a matter of minutes.

With hard data illustrating gaps in student knowledge, this information was shared with teachers. Ninth-grade English teachers welcomed my suggestions on how to integrate specific information skills instruction throughout the year to address student weaknesses; it was a springboard for our collaborative efforts to meet student needs and increase their achievement. I administered the assessment again in the spring, hoping to measure improvement and gain additional data to show the impact of library instruction on student learning. The results showed significant overall improvement in areas I targeted. In fact, some students improved by as much as 50 percentage points—impressive evidence to share with my principal of the effectiveness of my library instruction.

Online courseware is more than just a testing tool; it provides access to important material that students are expected to use. As a collaborative effort the English and social studies teachers and I developed a writing and research handbook that is now used by every student and teacher. It consists of checklists, models, and explanations of every step of the research process, and includes bibliographic citation models along with sections on Boolean searching, validity of sources, parenthetical documentation, writing source cards and note cards, avoiding plagiarism, developing a thesis, and more.

The widespread adoption of this handbook has revolutionized our information-skills instruction and has become a model for other schools in my district. Teachers expect students to use their handbooks conscientiously, and students have learned to consult its contents for every research assignment. Since students sometimes leave their handbooks at school or lose them, we posted a PDF version of the handbook on Blackboard, giving students around-the-clock access.

The school library provides our community with 27 online databases, and the library web page contains links to and descriptions of each. I am contractually prevented from posting password information on the public website, so I post my handout with an overview of database instructions and passwords onto Blackboard. In a similar fashion, I develop and post pathfinders and resource guides for specific assignments. Teachers link from assignment sheets on their Blackboard sites to my customized library guides. Every handout, user's guide, brochure, newsletter, PowerPoint presentation, or other document I can produce can be made available to students and teachers.

Recently I have begun to create announcements that automatically appear when students log in to their school accounts. Even if they are just checking their homework assignment and don't access the library section, I can promote library programming and special events or alert them to important new information from the library.

To expand my use of Blackboard, I will create brief online assessments after particular projects or lessons. This will include teachers' evaluations of student performance on an assignment. Our current face-to-face student and teacher book clubs will be opened to virtual members who may not be able to attend the meetings but want to join the discussion. I plan to develop student and staff surveys about library resources, services, instruction, and programs.

While Blackboard is very versatile, the options and commands are not always intuitive. As a novice I am frustrated by some of the more advanced functions, but I like having control of basic functions. As the library's site administrator, I can easily modify students' accounts so that they may choose a new password when it has been forgotten. By using a closed online school community in conjunction with my library's open website, I can increase the effectiveness of my outreach, provide valuable learning tools for students to use, and gather information that ultimately makes the library program stronger and, most importantly, increases student achievement.

SOURCE: Adapted from Priscille M. Dando, "First Steps in Online Learning: Creating an Environment for Instructional Support and Assessment," *Knowledge Quest* 34 (September 2005): 23–24. Used with permission.

Testing the Web 2.0 waters

by Mark E. Funk

It's pretty difficult to avoid all the commotion about Web 2.0 nowadays. It seems to be always on the news, in magazines, and featured at conferences. You've been meaning to start playing around with this stuff, but you've been busy. You're certainly no Luddite (you can whip out a fancy Excel chart with the best of them), but you feel the need to catch up. Here, then, is a quick primer on some very useful Web 2.0 tools.

Even tech-savvy librarians can lag behind the curve. When the Medical Library Association offered an online course on basic Web 2.0 tools, more than 700 members signed up with requests for us to repeat it. Obviously if you're a Web 2.0 newbie, you are not alone.

What exactly is Web 2.0? You can find many definitions, but Web 2.0 is mostly conceptual. Wikipedia says "the term encapsulates the idea of the proliferation of interconnectivity and interactivity of web-delivered content." The old web (now retroactively dubbed Web 1.0) acted as a simple publication platform. It was pretty much one-way: Those who paid for a website and knew HTML programming could deliver content over the internet. Content didn't change until the programmer changed it.

Web 2.0 is a two-way platform. While content is still delivered over the internet, the process has become more participatory. Now people can easily put up content, add to others' content or make comments on it, and, in certain cases, change others' content. The emphasis in Web 2.0 technology is on two-way communication, low cost, and ease of use.

Unfortunately, one reason many librarians are not participating in Web 2.0 activities is that they haven't been given the official word from their administration to take a look at the technology. One of the coolest things about Web 2.0 is that it isn't delivered from on high. With most Web 2.0 tools, you can skip the bureaucracy that usually goes with adding new technology: you don't have to get budget approval for a large purchase, send out RFPs, schedule vendor presentations, award a contract, wait for installation, or go through weeks of training. You can use these tools, mostly for free, as long as you have internet access. You can start today.

Wading in

Just being introduced to Web 2.0 can be confusing. There are myriad tools that don't tell you what they do. Where to start? How do you choose? To make things easier and less intimidating, I have described a few basic, common tools, grouping them by what's important: how they can solve a problem. For additional explanations, Common Craft (www.commoncraft. com) has short, clear, amusing videos and explains the tools mentioned below, plus many others.

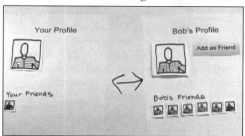

A screenshot from the Common Craft video on social networks

To keep in contact with friends and colleagues, you may remember the Rolodex. Today, more than 25 million professionals use LinkedIn for their personal database of connections. Here, you can create a profile of your professional accomplishments, then invite colleagues to connect to you. Colleagues of colleagues can even be found, so you can create a large personal network quickly and easily.

Other, more informal tools to stay in touch with friends and colleagues are social networks such as Facebook or Myspace. Again, the idea is to connect, but with these tools you can add photos, update what you're doing or planning, and let friends know what's going on in your life. The amount of information you want to share is totally up to you (www.commoncraft.com/video/social-networking).

Many librarians have created their own Facebook or Myspace pages for their libraries and themselves and encourage their users to friend them or become fans of their libraries. This is a great (and free) way to connect with younger library users, updating them on library activities and services, sharing photos of exhibits or speakers, and making the library feel more approachable. Take a look at Brooklyn College Library's Facebook and Myspace pages to see what can be done.

Are your bookmarks getting out of hand? It's difficult to manage a large number of browser bookmarks and favorites. Plus, those bookmarks are only on one computer. Social bookmarking tools come to the rescue. The main tool is Delicious. Simply sign up for a free account, install a bookmarking Tag button in your browser, and you're ready to go. When you find a useful site, click the Tag button, and the site is saved in your Delicious account. You can also import existing bookmarks from your browser. After you've saved a site, you can annotate it with descriptive tags that you choose, or include a note to remind yourself why you saved it. Even if you're on another computer, you can log into your account and see your saved sites.

4

Why is it called social bookmarking? Because not only can you see your sites, you can see what sites others have saved and add them to your own list. You can search your tags or everybody's tags. Rather not have anyone else see your bookmarks? You can make them viewable only to you.

Social bookmarking is particularly useful for reference librarians. Some reference departments maintain a network of Delicious accounts so their reference librarians can see each other's collections easily (www.commoncraft.com/video/social-bookmarking).

Is keeping current on your favorite sites taking too much time? It can take a lot of clicking and loading on blogs and websites, only to find nothing is new. Instead, subscribe to RSS (Real Simple Syndication) feeds, which automatically notify you of new posts by showing you a brief headline. Some web browsers have RSS-feed capabilities built in, but many people prefer to set up a free RSS account using Google Reader or Bloglines. The advantage of these is that you can check your personalized news from any computer just by logging in. There are also standalone, downloadable RSS reader applications.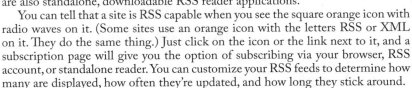

You can tell that a site is RSS capable when you see the square orange icon with radio waves on it. (Some sites use an orange icon with the letters RSS or XML on it. They do the same thing.) Just click on the icon or the link next to it, and a subscription page will give you the option of subscribing via your browser, RSS account, or standalone reader. You can customize your RSS feeds to determine how many are displayed, how often they're updated, and how long they stick around.

Many librarians are adding RSS-feed capabilities to their home pages or blogs so they can quickly and easily notify their users of upcoming library activities, new additions to the catalog, new issues of the library newsletter, and emergency closings (www.commoncraft.com/video/rss).

Making prints from your digital camera can be expensive, and emailing photos to everyone is a pain. Short of dragging your computer around to show your digital photos, photo-sharing websites such as Flickr, Kodak Gallery, or Picasa Web Albums are your best bet. Most of these sites offer a free version with limited storage and monthly upload limits, as well as a paid version with larger or unlimited storage and uploads. Paid versions for most sites are around $25 a year, although they vary. Once you've signed up, you can upload photos from your browser or with a special utility. Once uploaded, you can arrange photos into albums and tag them with searchable descriptive terms. You can choose to make your photos private, viewable only to you or invited friends; or public, viewable to everyone. If a site is public, anyone can see and even make comments on your photos, making the site part of the social web. Most sites allow you to order prints, and some offer the option of putting images on such items as greeting cards, shirts, calendars, or mugs.

Many libraries use Flickr to share library events with their communities; Google "libraries" and "Flickr" to see the wide variety of libraries participating in photo sharing. The Library of Congress is using Flickr to share its massive collection of photos, allowing the public to tag photos, which in many cases had minimal or no information, with identifying names or locations (www.commoncraft.com/video/online-photo-sharing).

Taking off the floaties

This has been just a dip in the shallow end of the big pool of Web 2.0. I intentionally left out commonly discussed Web 2.0 tools such as blogs and wikis. While they are terrific tools for group projects or institutions, it's rare that an individual needs them to solve a personal problem. The goal is to get you started using Web 2.0 tools that are useful to you today.

So, what do you do now? Play with the tools. Have fun. Learn their capabilities and limitations. After you're comfortable with them, start thinking how you could use them in your library. Look at how other librarians use them. Go to your administration and demonstrate what could be done quickly, easily, and cheaply. Borrow some ideas and adapt them to your needs.

Web 2.0 tools offer amazing ways to connect with your library users more easily. Isn't that what we all want to do? Trying these few basic tools may not turn you into the Mark Phelps of Web 2.0, but you can't swim with the big fish until you jump in. So come on in, the water's fine.

SOURCE: Mark E. Funk, "Testing the Web 2.0 Waters," *American Libraries* 40 (January/February 2009): 48–51. Used with permission.

Using social bookmarking to organize the web

by Kristin Fontichiaro

Have any of the following situations ever happened to you? If so, then social bookmarking may be a solution to your needs.

- You took a computer workshop but misplaced the list of URLs that the facilitator distributed. You mutter, "I visited all of the sites during the workshop. Why couldn't I just have an online record of where I went?"
- Your bookmarks or favorites list was wiped out when your computer was reimaged or replaced.

- You work at many computers and wish you could access the same list of bookmarked favorites from each.
- You'd like to make a pathfinder or list of recommended resources for a class, but it just takes too long to update the media center web page. Isn't there a faster way to save sites for classroom use?
- You and your friends share many mutual interests, and you'd like a way to be able for them to access the same websites you like. Is there an easy way for them to visit your updated list?
- Your students are using the web to research but haven't kept track of the sites they have visited.

What is social bookmarking?

Social bookmarking is the process of saving and sharing favorite URLs using online storage tools. When you use this technique, your favorite sites are saved to a website, not the browser, and you can access them from any computer. This makes them ideal for itinerant educators or for students and teachers who work at multiple work stations. Web-based bookmarking also protects your favorite sites if your hard drive fails, your computer is reimaged, or your district is upgrading its computer equipment.

The "social" in social bookmarking

The best-known social bookmarking sites are Delicious (www.delicious.com) and Diigo (www.diigo.com). These sites are referred to as social bookmarking because the user has the option of sharing his or her saved websites with other users. After registering and customizing account settings, users receive a unique URL, a web page where all of the saved URLs marked "public" appear.

delicious

The tastiest bookmarks on the web.
Save your own or see what's fresh now!

Learn More

In a school setting, social bookmarking can be a quick way for library media specialists to create and keep an updated web pathfinder, without any knowledge of HTML or web programming needed. Students working in collaborative groups will also find it useful to track one another's web resources via these public pages or to use Diigo's Groups feature to quickly share their preferred links with colleagues.

If you choose to create a single social bookmarking site to track sites for your personal and professional life, you may not want your students to have access to all of your links. In this case, you may wish to make your account private, meaning that the saved URLs can only be seen when you log in and will be hidden to the general public.

Getting started. Both Delicious and Diigo offer free accounts. Follow the onsite instructions to create an account. For personal safety reasons, avoid using student or school names for usernames.

If possible, install the site's buttons on your browser's toolbar so you can quickly add a site to your collection. If you have already accumulated a large number of bookmarked favorites on your internet browser, follow the instructions for downloading them to your computer and uploading them into your web account. Be sure to select the public/private settings that match your comfort level.

Describing what you're saving. Another feature of social bookmarking is that it allows the user to customize the descriptive information along with the URL. Depending on the web tool, users can assign keywords or tags (civilwar or crispusattucks), sort the saved site into a larger topic area (social studies, English, or science), add a descriptive phrase ("Shows how the new Food Pyramid differs from the previous one"), or save a quote from the site (perfect for student researchers). Adding descriptive information along with keywords drawn from their personal vocabulary helps users more quickly find a site among their saved sites. For example, Delicious lists all of the user's keywords and, by default, lists the newest saved posts first. Looking for all of the web addresses you've saved about blogging? Just click the "blogging" keyword, and all posts tagged with that word will be displayed.

Drawing on the collective knowledge of other users. While social bookmarking sites help users keep track of their own content, the sites also let users search for information. When a site is saved on a social bookmarking site, the site tracks how many others have saved the same site and displays that information next to the bookmarked information. As a result, users can search social bookmarking sites to find websites that have been identified by other users. This can be an indicator of the quality or effectiveness of the site's content.

An example would be a computer programmer who searches Delicious first when faced with a technology challenge. He or she types the question into the home page's search box, analyzes the search results, and then visits the sites that have been saved, with those most frequent first. He figures that if a site was saved by many others, it is probably useful. While this Google alternative is not foolproof, it can help students access relevant surface web information quickly.

Whether you like to share what you've found online or keep it to yourself, social bookmarking offers a wide range of options for helping educators and students navigate and organize online resources. Social bookmarking is an excellent way to make sense of the web.

Editor's note: Delicious was acquired from Yahoo! in July 2011 by Avos Systems, which has plans to continue it as a robust social bookmarking site.

SOURCE: Kristin Fontichiaro, "Using Social Bookmarking to Organize the Web," *School Library Media Activities Monthly* 24, no. 9 (May 2008): 27–28. Used with permission.

The web is alive with the sound of podcasts

by Kathy Fredrick

With apologies to Julie Andrews and anyone connected with *The Sound of Music*, podcasts can bring out the performer in all of us. Podcasts add another dimension to Library 2.0 and foster media literacy for students and teachers.

Just what is podcasting? The answer is the following equation: broadcasting + iPod = podcasting. Podcasting allows individuals to create digital audio content and post it on the web for others to hear, or save to a computer rather than on another medium like tape or CD. Is an iPod required? Not necessarily. A variety of other MP3 players will do the trick, and to start you don't even need to go beyond your computer. So just what do you need to create your podcast?

Equipment. You'll need a computer and a microphone. Either PC or Mac will do. You can use the microphone that came with your computer to start.

Software. If you have a Mac, GarageBand is a standard Apple software package included with your Mac. If you have a PC, you'll need to install digital recording software such as Audacity, an open source (free) software package. If you want to create MP3 files, add a plug-in called LAME, which partners with Audacity to produce files that can be heard on the internet.

Before you actually record, remember the rules for any good presentation: prepare, practice, and pare it down to what you really want to say. Do your homework for the podcast content. Is this a one-time show? Or, is this the first of a series, say a set of book-talks or a series of quick how-to lessons? If it's a how-to, make sure directions are clear and understandable. If you're reading a story, make sure you know the material before you record. Once you've determined what your content will be, script it.

PodCast

With your script all set and seated at your computer with the appropriate software opened and ready to go, take a look at your recording software. You'll see a toolbar that looks like the console for a CD or DVD player. Click the record button and start talking. If you're like me, you'll watch in fascination as the software shows the waveform patterns of your speech as it also monitors audio input and output. When you've finished, click the stop button. That's the very basic level of podcasting. Listen to what you've recorded. Did you hesitate or throw in a "you know" or "ummmm" that you'd like to get rid of? Using your mouse and clicking into the track at the point you want to change, highlight that portion, and use a right click/delete to eliminate that imperfection. Highlight the waveform, and you can use the program for such editing as adjusting volume levels, changing pitch, determining speed, and more.

Does your talk need background sounds or music? It's pretty simple to take it to the next level, adding special effects or background sounds and music. Find that digital clip, save it to your computer, and import it into the recording software using your menu options. Additional tracks will appear in your recording software. You'll have the same options for changing the effects that you had for your voice recording.

Once you've got your podcast completed, the last step in the recording process is to click "file" and choose the export option to save the file. In what is a surprisingly short amount of time, you're a recording engineer as well as a recording star!

Podcasts beg for an audience. If you're ready to go beyond your workstation, check with your school's technology staff to see if there's already a place for podcasts on your network. A number of online sites offer space for educators to post podcasts. If you're already a blogger, you can post podcasts as a part of your blog. Do you have to post your podcast to the web? Not necessarily; anyone who sits down at your computer can hear the podcast you create.

Don't forget copyright, however, in creating your podcasts. For example, you'll want to make sure any books being read aloud are in the public domain. If students are your narrators or content creators, get signed permission from them to use their work. You can model the concept of intellectual property for students, and they'll remember the thrill of being recognized for their work.

Like all good Web 2.0 tools, podcasting serves all users: students, teachers, parents, administrators. The list goes on! From a pedagogical view, you're using audio, another learning modality that's definitely a part of the MP-iPod learners we see today. You'll fill the web with wonders—explanations of how to research, library tour dialogues, booktalks—all saved for posterity and available 24/7. The web will be alive with the sound of your podcasts.

Podcast resources

Apple GarageBand. *Website:* www.apple.com/ilife/.

Audacity. *Website:* audacity.sourceforge.net/. Use with LAME MP3 Encoder. *Website:* audacity.sourceforge.net/help/faq?s=install&item=lame-mp3.

Creative Commons (copyright-free audio). *Website:* creativecommons.org/audio.

Creative Commons, "Podcasting Legal Guide." *Website:* wiki.creativecommons .org/Welcome_To_The_Podcasting_Legal_Guide.

Free Music Archive. *Website:* freemusicarchive.org.

iTunes Podcasts Directory (requires iTunes to be loaded on your computer; see education/K12 section). *Website:* www.apple.com/itunes/podcasts/.

Learning in Hand with Tony Vincent, "Podcasting." *Website:* learninginhand. com/podcasting/.

Podcast Directory for Educators, Schools, and Colleges. *Website:* recap.ltd.uk/ podcasting/index.php.

Podomatic (free space to post podcasts). *Website:* www.podomatic.com.

Schrock, Kathy. "What Makes a Good Podcast?" *Website:* school.discoveryeducation. com/schrockguide/evalpodcast.html.

SOURCE: Kathy Fredrick, "The Web Is Alive with the Sound of . . . Podcasts," *School Library Media Activities Monthly* 24, no. 6 (February 2008):46–47. Used with permission.

To Kindle or just burst into flame?

by C. D. McLean

Editor's note: Since this article was published, a number of other handheld devices are being sold, and students are now able to download books onto their cellphones.—*B. W.*

A January 11, 2008, *Newsweek* article on Amazon.com CEO Jeff Bezos and the Kindle, Amazon's e-reader, says that the device was "named to evoke the crackling ignition of knowledge."

An Amazon Kindle 3,
showing text from the novel
Moby-Dick

Independent school librarians generally have a greater measure of freedom than their public school colleagues when it comes to their budgets. Not having layers of red tape and administrative input is very desirable, especially for librarian technophiles who love to live on the bleeding edge. However, is the Kindle worth the price (plus shipping)?

Several independent school librarians purchased the Kindle with the intent of using it for required reading and textbooks. Anyone who has ever seen the alarming size of students' backpacks today (how 60-pound girls carry 80-pound backpacks is a science conundrum) would find the idea of students carrying Kindles containing all their textbooks very appealing.

Librarians have been criticized for not jumping on the Amazon.com-style catalog sooner. Its Whispernet technology is fabulous, allowing the Kindle always to be on, perpetually available for the owner to buy a book and have it, a few seconds later, on his device, ready to read. Losing a Kindle is certainly something to consider, but library laptops and expensive books also go astray, as do students' purses, cellphones, and iPods.

How could this tool be used in mass quantities by students, and how would the library's budget be protected from unauthorized charges? Perhaps Bezos could create a Kindle that is specifically designed to contain only classroom texts and required reading. Students must purchase all those books anyway. Why not sell the Kindles at a reduced rate to schools in place of textbooks and ship them with the texts already downloaded? Amazon sells textbooks and books? If Bezos could put a Kindle in the hand of every school-aged child, one that contained all textbooks and leisure reading, and figure out a way for parents to control the account, Kindle would become a flaming ball of success. Until then, school librarians will continue to burn with hope.

SOURCE: Adapted from C.D. McLean, "To Kindle or Just Burst into Flame?" *Young Adult Library Services* 6 (Spring 2008): 9. Used with permission.

Facebook as a virtual literature circle
by Paulette Stewart

4

Social networks have given rise to a reading activity called an online literature circle. Generally from four to six students meet together in an online chat room to discuss the same reading. In this environment, students engage in critical thinking and reflection as they read, discuss, and respond to books. Collaboration is at the heart of this approach as students reshape and add to their understanding while they construct meaning with other readers. Through structured discussion and extending written and artistic response, students are guided by a school librarian into a deeper understanding of what they are reading. Online literature circles can be flexible in size, length of time, roles, content, objectives, and assessment. This virtual circle is an emerging example of networked social scholarship.

Facebook

Jessie, a high school librarian, has been reading about the educational and social benefits that social scholarship can provide for her students and decides to experiment with a virtual literature circle using Facebook. Jessie decides that she will begin with one literature circle composed of a small number of students who work as library volunteers. These students are generally avid readers but, since they are in different classes and grades, rarely interact over their reading.

At an after-school meeting with the volunteers she describes her idea and invites participants and outlines the objectives of the project: to design social literacy activities that will stimulate critical thinking and animated discussion. They will be reading a book a month, and using the features and applications of Facebook to respond to tasks and collaborate with members of their group. Some students are unable to make the time commitment, but six students excitedly volunteer.

Structure and organization

Jessie meets with these six students, the members of the virtual literature circle. She discusses thoroughly the following features and applications of Facebook that she will be using.

Discussion board. Jessie explains that she would post her comments here for them to respond.

Posted items. Here students will post their final work for Jessie and their peers to review and give feedback.

The Wall. Students will use this feature to ask questions.

Chat. Jessie and her students will use this feature to interact with each other and to express any thoughts, concerns, or interests about the novel.

A structure will help them focus their discussions. Every member, on a rotating basis, assumes certain roles adapted from *Literature Circles: Voice and Choice in Book Clubs and Reading Groups* (2002) by Harvey Daniels to practice and master some key literacy skills. As the students become more experienced members of the virtual literature circle, these six roles will fade into more naturalistic discussions.

Leader. The team leader of the group ensures that the group's assignments meet the required standard, manages the group, and mediates differences when they arise.

Literary Luminary. This student's job is to choose a paragraph or sentences from the book to discuss with the group, helping other students by spotlighting something interesting, powerful, funny, puzzling, or important from the text. The student explains why those selections were chosen and provides page numbers so that other readers can locate them in the text.

Vocabulary Enricher. This role involves identifying a few important words in the selection. For words that are puzzling or unfamiliar, the student provides dictionary definitions for the group, and identifies where the words appear in the book. Words important to the story will be discussed using the Facebook Chat feature.

Connector. This job entails finding connections between the book being read and the outside world, connecting what is read with the reader's own life, to what happens at school or in the community, to similar events at other times and places, or to other people or problems. Once the Connector has shared, each member of the group will be invited to identify their own text-to-life connection, which, of course, may refer to a different passage.

Recorder. The recorder types the assignment in the Notes feature of Facebook if the task requires written work. If a summary is required, the recorder will be assigned to do this task.

Clarifier. This individual is responsible for giving examples or for suggesting alternatives when a consensus is reached by the group.

Jessie's role to the virtual literature circle members is a guide who is critical to ensuring that specific literacy skills are developed. She allows them to make choices, ask questions, and wrestle with collaborative discussion so that they will develop as independent thinkers and explore an academic use of Facebook, an environment that they know well as a social networking tool.

At this point Jessie includes her students in the selection of the novel they all would be reading. She now logs onto Facebook.com and joins, and creates a group profile in which she inserts the following details: Name: Virtual Literature Circle; Type of group: Books and literature; Description: To develop and improve students' literacy skills while experimenting with an academic use of a social networking tool; Access: Closed group; Related groups: None. Because the group is closed, students are not to invite friends.

Group members create a new Facebook profile not connected to one that they have for personal use. At this juncture Jessie customizes the privacy settings from the Privacy page so that only the virtual literature circle group members can view each other's activities. (Go to the Privacy page and click the word "Profile" to customize the Privacy page.)

The virtual literature circle members have one more thing to do: Place the book they are about to read on their Facebook Bookshelf. The instructions:

1. Click the "Shelfari" link on your profile page at the bottom left-hand corner or search it from the Applications Directory.
2. On the new page, select "Shelfari books" then click on "Go to this Application." In the Search Box field, enter the book title or the International Standard Book Number (ISBN), and then click "Enter."
3. Next click on "Add to Your Book Shelf," and then go to the top of the page and click "Go to Your Book Shelf." The book will appear on your Facebook bookshelf.

Jessie now goes to the Discussion Board and places a log showing when each task is to be posted and discussed. She also sets the times when all members can log on and use the Chat feature to converse with her.

Beginning discussion

Social skills are taught before students begin working because these skills facilitate successful interactions among people. According to Kay Burke, "teaching these skills will ensure that conflicts are minimized or do not occur." As students begin to read the book, they also begin posting responses related to their assigned task on the Discussion Board. The Connector finds a link between the book and something that happened in the school community. He posts this on the Discussion Board and, once shared, each member of the group responds, some commenting on the Connector's post, others making their own personal connections.

Likewise, the Literary Luminary proposes a paragraph to be discussed. They use the Chat feature to do this. The Leader encourages members who hang back and enriches discussions by pointing out differences and similarities, and by moderating disagreements. Group members who desire help may post their requests for assistance on the Discussion Board. Jessie views the postings before school and once in the late afternoon or early evening, makes comments, and offers feedback to guide students as they work with each other. At the end of the project Jessie goes to the Facebook Gift section, selects a gift for each student, and sends it them to acknowledge their accomplishments. Group members are willing to participate in an evaluation of the project along with Jessie to find out the impact it has made on them.

Evaluation of the program

Jessie asks group members to evaluate a number of elements: their individual participation, the group's effectiveness, the merits (or difficulties) encountered in using Facebook for a virtual literature circle, and the products or tasks they completed. She will use this data to make changes when this activity is repeated. Jessie also evaluates the products and processes. She focuses on three main areas:

Cognitive. What evidence does she have that students developed the literacy skills she identified as objectives?

Affective. What evidence does she have that students' social skills, attitudes, and emotions have changed or matured?

Psychomotor. Did students report improved practical skills related to using Facebook?

Students' responses and her own notes encourage Jessie to continue the project using different books and changing the roles so that her students can learn new skills. When group members tell friends from another high school in the district about their project, those students approach their own librarian about starting a virtual literature circle. Jessie's experience and advice persuades this librarian to begin a discussion group parallel to hers. Jessie adds the second literature circle under Facebook's "Related Groups." The project begins again with these two virtual literature circles reading another novel. Jessie is pleased with the progress of her idea, and recognizes that social learning theory and the cooperative learning design played a major role in its success.

Background to Jessie's success

Jessie's virtual literature circle was successful because it aligned with the theoretical basis of social learning. Russian psychologist Lev Vygotsky's social learning theory points out that social scholarship plays an important role in cognitive development because students are able to interact, share experiences, and learn from one another. Albert Bandura's social learning theory highlights the fact that people learn from one another via observation, imitation, and modeling. The addition of technology provides the opportunity to improve human cognition, interaction, and even social relations as teacher and students are able to effectively communicate educational content that students are able to grasp and share with each another. It has become evident "that sharing one's own ideas and responding to others' reactions sharpens thinking and deepens understanding," as Craig Zywicki puts it.

Jessie's success was also the result of her knowledge of cooperative learning design. This theoretical framework consists of five elements: positive interdependence, individual accountability, group processing, face-to-face interaction, and social skills. By creating a small heterogeneous group of students with a genuine interest in working together, the group would function collaboratively. As a cooperative learning group, students demonstrated positive interdependence asking each other for assistance when experiencing difficulty. To guarantee individual accountability, the features of Facebook were used to view the progress of each student and inter-ject support if necessary, because if any group member's task was incomplete, the group's work would be incomplete. Jessie designed the structure to ensure group processing; individuals were expected to evaluate final work and make suggested changes from other group members before they posted the assignment to the Notes area of Facebook. Since these students volunteered in the library during different periods making it unlikely they could often meet in a classroom setting, the Chat feature of Facebook substituted for face-to-face interaction. Adding these elements of cooperative learning design ensured the quality completion of the group's as-signed tasks and substantial individuals' participation.

The Facebook virtual literature circle was an excellent teaching environment for social and group work. The development of group dynamics and the application of cooperative structures encouraged equal and shared responsibility from all, includ-ing even the quietest students. Participants in the virtual literature circle were able to gain social value by developing mutual respect and, as a result, felt comfortable sharing ideas with each other. Respect for other people's ideas and learning from other perspectives are crucial skills both in the classroom and later life.

Undoubtedly, Facebook is a popular social utility that is widely used among students in high schools, colleges, and universities. With an understanding of social learning theory, the school librarian can use affordances in Facebook to turn a predominantly social experience into a successful academic learning environment and, in the process, scaffold the development of students' literacy skills.

Meredith Farkas supports using popular social networks for library programs. "It makes sense to look at what social networking sites our patrons frequent and how we can provide services there" (*American Libraries,* April 2007, p. 27). Librarians report that they gain credibility from using social networks. It is clear from this case study that Facebook can be beneficial to both students and librarians, positioning school librarians as innovative, interesting, and influential, as well as supporting engaging and relevant learning among students.

SOURCE: Adapted from Paulette Stewart, "Facebook and Virtual Literature Circle Partnership in Building a Community of Readers," *Knowledge Quest* 37, no. 4 (March/April 2009): 28–33. Used with permission.

The accidental technology steward
by Nancy White

4

If technology opportunity is knocking you down at your school, rather than simply knocking on your door, you have probably become an accidental technology steward (ATS). Technology stewards are people with enough experience of the workings of a community to understand its technology needs and enough interest in (and experience with) technology to become leaders in addressing those needs. Stewardship typically includes selecting and configuring technology as well as supporting its use. In other words, it's not just about technology itself. It is using that technology effectively in the context of your community.

Technology stewardship is important in learning communities, where technology is not a primary focus and there is much second-wave adoption. In schools, the students are usually first-wave adopters, experimenting and figuring out things faster than the weather changes in Seattle. Teachers, parents, and administrators are often the second wave—less comfortable with, interested in, or adept at technology adoption. Stewarding technology use for and between these two groups can ensure that its use is generative, rather than a force that threatens to divide the community.

What if you did not ask for this job? Are you an ATS? Or do you want it, but are not sure how to move into the role? Are you one of those people with some natural leadership in your community and enough fearlessness to experiment with technology, fooling those around you into thinking you know what you are doing?

You know you are an ATS when everyone asks you about the latest social networking tool they hear kids talking about, or how to download the latest thing from the web. Not knowing what they are talking about, you look at the person asking as if he is from another planet. Even if you are a wizard at internet searching, that doesn't mean you can also tell him why his email box is messed up. However, he continues to ask and, because you're curious, you look up the words you've never heard of and try to help. It turns out that you enjoy experimenting with new tools for nonschool reasons and start to see how they might be useful at school, but you aren't sure how to introduce them. You have learned informally, through trial and error, but may not totally understand what's beneath the hood of the tools you use.

When did you become your school's ATS? What was the turning point? More important: Why you? Do you like the role or is it becoming the bane of your existence? Do you feel valued and loved, or abused? Is it distracting from your work and your interest, or opening up a whole new world? Do you want to dive deeper into it?

Or, what if you are not an ATS? Why is it worth your time and effort to become one?

Benefits to your school

Community technology stewards are bridge-builders between learning and technology and among various community groups. Today there are an overwhelming set of technology options, many of which hold promise; but unless there is someone scanning the horizon, connecting with others who are experimenting, the benefits are hard to capture. It is easy to get left behind but hard to lead by yourself. The ATS is a lynchpin who invites others to join in the work and share in the effort.

The rise of Library 2.0 has begun to articulate how new web technologies are changing the role of the librarian and the library. Jack M. Maness has proposed that the essential elements of such a theory are:

- It is user-centered. Users participate in the creation of the content and services within the library's web presence or OPAC. The consumption and creation of content is dynamic, and thus the roles of librarian and user are not always clear.
- It provides a multimedia experience. Both the collections and services of Library 2.0 contain video and audio components. While this is not often cited as a function of Library 2.0, it is here suggested that it should be.
- It is socially rich. The library's web presence includes users' presences. There are both synchronous (IM) and asynchronous (wikis) ways for users to communicate with one another and with librarians.
- It is communally innovative. This is perhaps the single most important aspect of Library 2.0. It rests on the foundation of libraries as a community service, but understands that as communities change, libraries must not only change with them, they must allow users to change the library. It seeks to continually change its services, to find new ways to allow communities, not just individuals, to seek, find, and utilize information.

The key for a technology steward is "communally innovative." All the participants, including the patrons, must understand how to participate. Much of that will have a technological aspect. Tools such as tagging and social network systems will facilitate social search. Multimedia applications will allow production and consumption of audio, video, and images as well as text.

Benefits to you

The primary benefit of self-identifying with the ATS role is to connect with other stewards. No one can understand the technology landscape and still fulfill the role of librarian alone. Just as it takes a village to raise a child, it takes a community to steward technology. As you self-identify, you find others. Convene informal sessions when you go to conferences, and lobby for tech offerings on the formal agenda. Don't leave it to the geeks. Add your voice.

Technology competence is as much a state of mind as a set of skills. It is useful to reflect on what mindsets can make stewarding technology easier and more useful to you and others. Like a jazz violinist who loves and embraces his violin even though he cannot build one, technology stewards benefit from a positive state of mind about technology.

Create a technology stewardship team. Technology stewardship is not a solo pursuit. In fact, it doesn't lend itself to doing it alone. A great ATS strategy is to engage others in developing the community's technology practice and skills. Let's say your school community consists of 40 teachers, three administrators, 10 other staff members, and 1,000 students. Create a technology stewardship team. Imagine six to eight people, each investing a small amount of time. That might include four teachers, two students, and a couple of parent or community volunteers with an interest in technology.

The team can act informally, using experimental technology to work together. You don't need many meetings: maybe one to get to know each other and get started, and another when something comes up that requires a decision or major action. Best of all, you can work informally to think about how to usefully select and implement technology at school in small, incremental ways.

The stewardship role is about the daily tasks of your learning community. The focus is not on instituting a laptop program, or making major decisions on filtering policies in the school district. This is not to say that your stewardship group cannot be an important and influential player in technology decisions, if that is what you want; but the primary role is ongoing learning and usefulness. Here are some responsibilities that your group might take on:

- Scan the market. Hundreds of new technologies are offered each week, from the sublime to the ridiculous. While you don't need to master them all, it is important to scan for things that might be useful to your context. Scanning the market is a great team practice.
- Scan the education field. What is often most useful is noting where others are experimenting with technology in schools and learning from them. What worked? What didn't?
- Participate in other communities of interest and practice. Scanning brings in information, but participation in communities of practice helps us make sense *and* helps leapfrog us more quickly to useful tools and practices. In other words, we use the network's intelligence. This can include user communities focused on a particular technology, such as the Moodle, or loose affiliations of bloggers.
- Make sense of the harvest. Scanners are usually people who can spot bits quickly, harvesting somewhat randomly. Other team members need to be good at synthesis. They pick the diamonds out of the rock pile.
- Test stuff. The group should play with new tools and practices and that means you need enthusiasts and skeptics, a range of users from the technologically adept (often our students) to the technologically reticent.
- Weave the bits together. If you are not as interested in the technology, consider how you can support the flow of information and learning in your team and out to your school community. Pass along information to people and introduce people who may be useful to each other.

Serve yourself. Technology stewardship is the proverbial journey, not the destination. Therefore you need to make it pay off for you every step of the way. You can grow into this role, particularly if you look beyond the to-do's of the job and explore how can it be useful in your real life. There are only so many hours in a day—it's not just your work day, it's your after-hours day, your errands day, your chat-with-friends-and-family day, and so on. Some of the same technologies that people are using in schools can help us organize our life, connect with families and friends, and corral needed information.

As with anything you do to enhance your life or work, there's an on/off switch. We build knowledge incrementally. So take a tiny sliver of your time each day, each week and gamble with it. Odds are good you will become more comfortable as a technology steward, and I'm willing to bet you may actually even start to enjoy it.

SOURCE: Adapted from Nancy White, "The Accidental Technology Steward: Or, How You Can Gamble Very Little and Gain a Lot," *Knowledge Quest* 35, no. 4 (March/April 2007): 32–35. Used with permission.

The Access Pennsylvania Database project

by Mardy McGaw

The Access Pennsylvania Database is a project of the Pennsylvania Department of Education, Office of Commonwealth Libraries, Division of School Library Services. Access Pennsylvania is a statewide library union database containing the holdings of approximately 3,018 school, public, special, and academic libraries in Pennsylvania. 100% of school districts in the state currently participate. This is the largest database of its kind in North America and contains over 15 million titles and 67 million holdings. The Health Sciences and Libraries Consortium (HSLC) maintains the database and provides technical support and training sessions to all member libraries.

In 1986, the first 100 libraries joined the project. Libraries may either apply to be considered for state funding for the retrospective conversion of their holding records or submit them in the correct MARC format directly to HSLC. Each library must endorse the state interlibrary loan code and agree to participate in statewide resource sharing.

In *Access Pennsylvania: An Agenda for Knowledge and Information through Libraries,* Gov. Dick Thornburgh outlined the goals of the state library agenda in September 1984. In 1981, a library planning committee "under the direction of the State Librarian, Elliot Shelkrot, and composed of 95 leading citizens was convened to examine the problems and potential of libraries of all types." The findings of this committee contained 19 recommendations, but the three main goals were:

1. Developing a statewide library card system that will allow all Pennsylvanians to use any publicly supported library.
2. Expanding the use of technology to more effectively share our library and information resources.
3. Improving local financial support of public libraries and providing state assistance for the support of libraries in low-income communities.

The development of this technological change project and the ability to empower change is the story of the school librarians of Pennsylvania for the past two decades. The original project called for requests for proposals from vendors to facilitate the database management and dissemination of information of the holdings of the library records. The vendors offered means to share the MARC records so that the items could be requested from the library that had the item. What was needed were ways that would allow for the creation of a statewide database of holdings that could be produced cost-effectively.

The lead innovators for the Access Pennsylvania Project were Doris Epler, director of the School Library Media Services Division; Richard Cassel, technology coordinator; Larry Nesbit, director of the Mansfield University Library; and James Fogarty from Intermediate Unit 29. The winning vendor offered to produce a database of holdings in a CD-ROM format. This CD would be pressed once a year and disseminated during fall training sessions that each participating library was required to attend. An intermediate unit was chosen to provide training sessions on how to use the CD-ROM resources and how to make a request. The physical process of shipping books and record-keeping was also included in training sessions. Prior to using the internet to borrow resources, requests were made by fax.

The division also called for requests for applications from all types of libraries to have their library shelflists, the source of the library holdings information, retrospectively converted into MARC. This prospect was not without a good deal of stress on the part of librarians. The entire record of the collection would be packed into boxes and shipped to the retrospective conversion vendor (Brodart), processed, and returned at some later date. The libraries were ranked in order by the RFA qualifications to determine which holdings would be converted using state funding during each year that funding was available. The conversion costs were 40 cents per record for each holding. If a library had 15,000 items, the cost would be $6,000 for the conversion alone. Libraries also needed to commit to sending at least one staff person to attend a yearly training session and were required to install a fax with a phone line in the library. Library staff also needed to maintain records of the items borrowed and lent. The shelflist cards were turned into MARC records that could then be used by the librarian in an automated library circulation and cataloging system.

The online public access catalog (OPAC) was the other feature that was exciting for librarians. The cataloging software would allow the updating of one MARC record to create the several subject-access points, keywords, and title and author access, all through one record.

School librarians needed to purchase a computer as a file server and at least three more stations: one for circulation, one for cataloging, and one for the OPAC. Multiple OPAC stations often came later for most libraries at this early-adopter stage and would include three or four stations for patrons to access the new card catalog. These hardware and software purchases did not include the retrospective conversion of records, which would have doubled the price of the process. This ability to reduce the budget by 50% for this potential upgrade in services by participation in the database project was the biggest tipping factor in the decision to participate.

The next major development for this project came as the internet began to be better used through a graphical user interface like Mosaic or Netscape. The ability to access information via the web soon became a reality for schools. Libraries invested in a project known as Pennsylvania Online World of Electronic Resources (POWER) Library. Any school district that had one or more libraries participating in the Access Pennsylvania project could have the resources provided by the POWER Library project for free. The POWER Library is offered by Commonwealth Libraries to all public libraries and to school districts that participate in the Access Pennsylvania project.

Commonwealth Libraries reviews proposals from various vendors to promote the online resource database to all Pennsylvania library patrons. Patrons need to visit a public library or have a library card to access the databases from home. Commonwealth Libraries weighs the products with the public library and school library patrons' needs against the budget allocations for that year. These selected online vendors and their products have enabled access to valuable resources at a fair pricing. All of this is provided by state tax dollars to all Pennsylvanians.

The online resources included in this project vary depending upon the contracts with the state, but they include some of the same resources that school libraries could barely afford to offer but desperately wanted to use with students. Databases are expensive, and school librarians working with small budgets need to make difficult decisions as to which of the online resources they offer. This was just one of the several online resources that were available through the POWER Library. This was another incentive to move more school libraries into the database. It offered early adopters an engaging incentive to negotiate with school administrators over the need for this Access Pennsylvania service in their districts.

As the number of holdings and MARC records grew, so did the need for a more robust means of storing the data, and the database moved online. Requests are now generated through an email system that prioritizes the requests and moves the request through a queue of responders until the request is filled. This is called the Rota. Records of numbers of loaned materials and number of requests are generated by the database and these statistics are now maintained by the Access Pennsylvania database and accessible to each librarian and administrator.

The issues committee and the Commonwealth Libraries keep their eyes on the future. As the database continues to reconstruct to better meet patron's needs, it expands to encompass more special and academic libraries. The focus of technology changes once again to digital recourses. Recently ebooks have been offered through NetLibrary as part of the POWER Library and several special libraries are digitizing their archive collections that make them available statewide. These ideas have all come about due to the social conversations about needs and the current developments in technology that make them financially possible.

The success of Access Pennsylvania was due to funding, leadership, and librarians. The Statewide Library Card and the Access Pennsylvania POWER databases have been funded for more than 25 years. The leadership at the State Library Bureau has created the political means to keep Pennsylvania libraries at the forefront of the governor's agenda. The united support for the project from Barbara Cole, retired director of the Bureau of Commonwealth Libraries, and John Emerick, retired director of the Library Services Division, has fashioned the current success of Access Pennsylvania and POWER Library. The school, public, academic, intermediate unit, and special librarians have found common ground in this project and have worked toward the common goal of resource sharing.

The resources in the POWER Library database that have been made accessible to all school districts in the Commonwealth of Pennsylvania and to the patrons of the public libraries have made a wealth of knowledge free. Much in the same way Benjamin Franklin helped start lending libraries in Philadelphia, so have these library projects brought knowledge to the public.

SOURCE: Adapted from Mardy McGaw, "Access PA Database Project: 22 Years of Innovation," *Learning and Media* 37 (Spring 2008): 5–7. Used with permission.

OPERATIONS
CHAPTER FIVE

From library to learning commons
by Valerie Diggs

Recently the Chelmsford (Mass.) High School Library underwent a transformation that was not only long overdue, but it was also a metamorphosis that was to have tremendous effect on the students, administrators, teachers, and community members. Although the physical transformation of our facility was important and would certainly have a positive effect on the school, I did not expect the response it received from the community. The new space was unveiled in a special celebration that drew the press and Ross Todd, associate professor of library and information science at Rutgers University, and David Loertscher, professor at San Jose State University, who came to see what we had done.

This is a story of transformation in the truest sense, from the traditional school library to the not-so-traditional learning commons now occupying the third floor of Chelmsford High School where the library used to be. This transformation is much more than just a name change, new paint, carpeting, and furnishings. Numerous environmental factors were involved in the decision to renovate the library, but the condition of the physical facility was subordinate to the programmatic changes that made this transformation one of substance and meaning.

Transformation of the program

Hired to be the high school librarian in 2002, I began to look at what we were offering students as they entered the library. Study halls were eliminated with the introduction of block scheduling, and teachers were free to bring classes into the library at any time. Then the district received a grant of 60 desktop computers, 40 of which were placed in the high school library, bringing more teachers and students into the library.

All about the program

On my arrival, I began to work more closely with teachers. They became familiar with my questions and requests for assignments, as well as requests to look closely at assignments to determine how I could help. Thanks to two new courses in the English Department, "Writing for High School" and "Writing for College,"

Valerie Diggs in the Chelmsford learning commons

and a deliberate movement by all departments to require more writing, I became more and more involved with the curriculum and instruction. Student learning became the focus behind everything we did. The library began to play a key role in students' literary lives and was central to their learning experiences.

With one small step at a time, I started to build an assortment of events, ideas, and ways of doing things into our program. One of the first changes we made was to serve coffee one day each week in the library. Donated coffee, tea, hot chocolate, and trays of pastries and bagels beckoned the hungry students and staff members. The lines were long, the laughter loud, and soon the gathered students were enticed by the books on display to browse and check out while they waited for their hot drinks. Students also sat and talked while teachers and adminsitrators readied themselves for a day of teaching and instruction.

Almost at the same time, the Chelmsford Public School community began a professional development initiative to introduce the concept of professional learning communities (PLCs) into all seven of its schools. The theory behind PLCs is a perfect fit for any library program. Simply, a PLC encourages teachers to work together collaboratively. I began to think of ways in which different departments might work together.

Socialize the library?

Drawing on the talents of the art department meant offering these students a venue to showcase these talents in a positive way. This led to the birth of the Listening Lunches program. On Listening Lunches day, students have the opportunity to lunch in the library while listening to their peers read poetry, sing songs, perform skits, or play musical instruments. For two and a half hours the library is filled with the sounds of student talent. Students and teachers sit, stand, eat, listen, and socialize in the space called the library.

The school library should give students the space to work with each other. It is a place to go that offered technology, some privacy, and the atmosphere conducive to learning experiences with someone nearby to answer questions could also help.

Transformation of the facility

The school district began a $31-million renovation plan, which included plans for a new performing arts center and a new science wing with sparkling new labs, technology classrooms, and instructional spaces. Two middle schools received new libraries: 5,000 square-foot wonders. Through all those renovations and building projects, the high school library remained as is: a tired, 34-year-old space, with duct-taped carpet, bright-yellow shelving and walls, and desks with broken drawers and peeling façades.

Chelmsford hired a new town manager, Paul Cohen, who had been taken on a tour of the town's buildings and facilities by the search committee during the interview process. He saw the high school and its new science wing, the new performing arts center, and the two beautiful new middle school libraries. The search committee did not dare bring him near the high school library. Cohen was invited for a special visit to the library. He saw for himself the entire, sorry mess. That fall, the capital budget was announced and it included more than $200,000 for a renovation of the high school library. Our new learning commons was on its way.

Teaching and learning

A Spanish honors class is investigating the current immigration policy in the United States. What do they need to know about United States policies and why should they even want to know? These senior students came to the learning commons with their classroom teacher to find out, interested and ready to ask questions. This came about because, prior to coming into the learning commons, the students spent time with their classroom teacher discussing their own roots as a way of making the lesson personal. This discussion got them hooked and interested.

Organizing inquiry-based units around question development is a practice described by Grant Wiggins and Jay McTighe in *Understanding by Design* (2005) as essential to providing "teacher and students with a sharper focus and better direction for inquiry." They go on to tell us that developing personally meaningful questions "render[s] the unit design more coherent and make[s] the students' role more appropriately intellectual."

Collaboration makes this happen. It is sitting down with teachers and saying, "How can *we* improve on this unit so our students can learn not only more, but better?" It is the "*we*" in this equation that is important. Students will do only what is required of them; they will think thoughts only as deeply as we require of them. It is our job, alongside the classroom teacher, to offer our students the opportunity to think critically and develop questions that they really want to answer—questions that will lead them to turning information into knowledge and that knowledge into wisdom for a lifetime.

Above our central information desk are the words "Ask, Ask, Ask" and in the café area, the words "Think" and "Create" appear above the countertop seating. Learning becomes meaningful and lasting, and students come away with a wonderful skill: the ability to think for themselves.

Community support

The new learning commons has been the recipient of continuous support from community members both within and outside the school. Our grand-opening event was held with huge attendance, a long list of speakers, and a virtual landslide of donations of food, time, money, and wishes for success. Our learning commons was launched, speeches were made, and the general consensus was that we had created a space that had become the center of learning. Our impact on the culture of Chelmsford High School, the teaching staff, and our students, was beginning to be felt by all. The learning commons is a community pride, an electric sense of excellence, and opportunity to pay tribute both to a visionary teacher-librarian and to everyone who had participated in its creation.

The learning commons provides CHS students and staff members the opportunity to ask questions, think about answers, and create new meanings. We have become central to teaching and learning because our mission is tied to the mission and ideals of our school and district, and we are committed to offering our services and space to all of our constituents.

My advice is to build your program first. This may take years to accomplish, as it did for us at CHS. However, remember a strong program is the foundation for a true learning commons. For more information on the project, visit www.chelmsford.k12.ma.us/chs/library/.

SOURCE: Adapted from Valerie Diggs, "From Library to Learning Commons: A Metamorphosis," *Teacher Librarian* 36, no. 4 (April 2009): 32–38. Used with permission.

12 steps to a winning first year

by Karen Hodges

Congratulations! You have just landed your first job as a school librarian. Being the information specialist will be both challenging and rewarding as you undertake myriad activities. This article may serve as a short course to jumpstart your career and make your first year successful.

1. Good customer service is your goal. You are here to serve the faculty, staff, and students. Smile, smile, smile! Get to know those who frequently visit the library. If you don't know the answer to a patron's question, locate the answer as soon as possible. Teachers and students will see you as a caring person, and you will earn their trust.

2. Meet the people who can help you and remember their names: the principal, the assistant principals, the library administrator for the district, and your library aide or assistant. Make friends with the school secretary, an invaluable source of information who usually arranges for a substitute if you are absent and handles your paycheck. Get to know the person who answers the telephone for the school and the accounting clerk who helps you purchase books, supplies, and equipment. Meet the head custodian who assists you by getting chairs set up for an event and coordinating the clean-up afterwards, the school technologist, the person in charge of computer maintenance, and those who repair audiovisual equipment and computers. Don't forget to write thank-you's and give small gifts in appreciation for special favors. Cookies and brownies are always appreciated.

3. The school librarian should be a leader in the school. Speak with your principal about joining the school leadership team. You get to know the department heads and can point out ways the library can contribute to programs and school projects. Join the school technology committee. You will learn much and your being there may determine whether your library is included in the list of rooms to get the new computers or that new printer you need. You will meet the tech-savvy teachers in the school. Visit departmental meetings to learn what books and resources students and teachers will be using, and you can add your librarian-honed skills in the creation of research projects.

4. Learn your collection. One of the best ways to do this is to shelve books. Shelving will familiarize you with books your library has on a particular subject. You will notice outdated books in need of removal and areas where books need to be ordered to update your collection. If you are fortunate, you will have access to databases on the internet, such as magazine or encyclopedia databases. Practice using these so that you can demonstrate them to patrons. Create an attractive flyer to list the databases with the passwords to give to students, teachers, and parents.

5. Make enforceable rules and follow them. A school with student handbooks with a page of library information will give you an idea of previous library expectations: how many books a student may check out, and so on. The students will respect you if you adhere to the rules, but occasionally bending them

in specific instances may be needed. Make your rules student-centered. If you will bend every time a student asks, change the rule.

6. Be visible. Walk frequently around the library and talk to your patrons. Besides watching for problems, such as eating in the stacks or accessing inappropriate websites, you will be making yourself available to answer questions. Most schools conduct a "Back-to-School Night" at the first of the school year to give parents an opportunity to visit the classrooms. Open the library and greet the parents as they walk through. You may want to create a brochure about the library. Give them a copy of this as well as the flyer with the databases and passwords on it.

7. Learn how to order books and supplies. Pay attention to the district's deadlines. Begin reading book reviews now in preparation for your first book order.

8. Value your volunteers. Both student and adult volunteers can provide helpful manpower. Parents can check books in and out, shelve books, process magazines, and cover new books. Take time to talk to these valuable people so they will feel welcome. Student volunteers can shelve books, run errands to the office or classrooms, and straighten the shelves.

9. Network, network, network! Attending librarians' meetings will provide you with necessary information concerning district, state, and national programs. Go to your annual state library conference. You will learn new ways to serve your patrons, create useful friendships with other librarians, and get loads of freebies from bookmarks to pre-pub books. Teachers will appreciate your passing on new posters to them, and you may want to update the posters in your library. You will return energized for the rest of the school year.

10. Add excitement to your library. Author or storyteller visits, book fairs, and student presentations attract patrons to the library. Other ways are through bulletin boards and eye-catching displays. Often art teachers are delighted to have a place to showcase their students' work, and they fit well on the top of bookshelves to give the library pizzazz.

11. Practice using the audiovisual equipment. Even if there is a technologist in your building, teachers will be checking out these items from you and asking you questions concerning their use. Both you and your library assistant should understand how to use the equipment and be able to solve simple problems, such as replacing bulbs in the overhead projectors. You will want to know how to set up a data projector and laptop when your principal dashes in and requests one for a last-minute meeting. Be prepared.

12. Pace yourself. Don't do too much at once and burn yourself out. You are a valuable resource, and you need to be able to begin each day with enthusiasm. Keep a notepad on your desk with a list of teachers' and students' questions and tasks to be completed. Highlight the most important ones and work to complete these items first. As you go home, don't dwell on the unfinished list, but upon the highlights of the day. Congratulations! You have chosen an excellent career in which you can grow while serving others.

SOURCE: Adapted from Karen Hodges, "Twelve Steps to a Winning First Year," *Library Media Connection* 28 (August/September 2009): 18–19. Used with permission.

Children, teens, and the construction of information spaces

by David Loertscher

The school district's poll was over. It asked what students' favorite source of information was for schoolwork and for personal use from that digital world known as the internet. The votes were tallied. To no one's surprise, Google won hands down. Over the past several years, the best of school librarians have made inroads into the popularity of Google by constructing excellent digital school libraries, some using the format of web pages and others using a variety of tools, such as blogs or wikis.

School librarians have made a valiant attempt to attract young users on the basis that quality information online is a paramount issue. Yet our students continue to trust Google even in the face of the overwhelming numbers of documents retrieved for them by this ubiquitous search engine.

Let us take the student's point of view, which is probably very similar to our own. When we all sit down at the computer to do our work, we expect the organizations and services behind that screen will provide us with what we want and need instantaneously. Few care where the information comes from as long as it is what we need when we need it.

Suppose we turn the tables and accept the notion that students should be in command of their own information spaces on the computing devices they have access to, and that our role as school librarians is to help students build the kind of information space that will benefit their needs rather than say to them, "You need to use the information space as we have designed it for you." Such a switch in perspective challenges us to have a completely new view of the digital world.

The following model assumes that each individual student, teacher, and even ourselves as the information professionals would construct a "home page" or access interface to the world of information: a secure place, a safe place, a work space, a personal digital assistant that could be accessed 24/7/365 from any location.

This model demonstrates the creation of three parts of "my" information space: personal workspace, group workspace, and outer space (the full world of the internet). Each of these spaces has a function to allow users access, but designing such

My Information Work Spaces

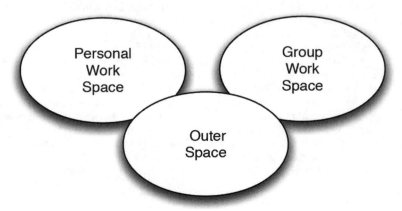

an engine requires that users learn to manage that space and manage themselves responsibly in that space.

Why should students be encouraged to construct their own information space? The fact is they already do, but probably not very well. It is reasonably safe to assume that most have a cluttered mess on their opening screen, and they seem to muck through with a few bookmarks and by searching for the source, folder, or document around the screen. Yes, operating systems encourage organization of the desktop, but it would be interesting to hold a discussion with children and teens about the status of their home pages. We should look at our own desktops, as information professionals, for a clue about how we organize our own information spaces. Perhaps the chorus of voices would unanimously state: "Well, it's quite messy, but I seem to manage." I would say this is not good enough.

Let us start with the basics as we consider the reasons, the whys, the wherefores, and the implementation of this turnaround idea.

Why should children and teens build their own information spaces? For many good reasons, children and teens should have lots of control under adult guidance:

- The world of the internet is getting larger, more complex, and overwhelmed with information. Children, teens, and adults increasingly need skills to manage that space because it can overwhelm any of us at any time. Since it is not going away, we either manage it or are overwhelmed by it.
- It is the nature of digital space, as it is currently constructed, to vie for our attention, the major currency of this generation. Psychologically, all of us need to manage rather than be managed.
- To survive in a flat world, children and teens need to realize the advantages of learning and knowing the major tools of productivity, both as individuals and collaboratively in groups. We usually think of productivity in terms of output of goods and services, but the same concept applies in digital space. Those who are well connected are proficient and productive. For example,

5

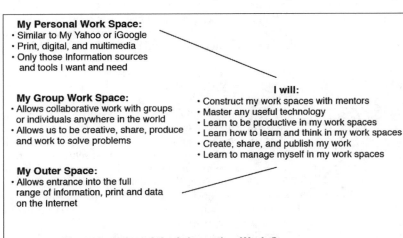

My Personal Work Space:
- Similar to My Yahoo or iGoogle
- Print, digital, and multimedia
- Only those Information sources and tools I want and need

My Group Work Space:
- Allows collaborative work with groups or individuals anywhere in the world
- Allows us to be creative, share, produce and work to solve problems

My Outer Space:
- Allows entrance into the full range of information, print and data on the Internet

I will:
- Construct my work spaces with mentors
- Master any useful technology
- Learn to be productive in my work spaces
- Learn how to learn and think in my work spaces
- Create, share, and publish my work
- Learn to manage myself in my work spaces

Characteristics of the Information Work Spaces:
- Under my control and safe
- Accessible on any device or from any location
- Utilizes both commercial and open source software
- Elastic in nature; that is, my spaces grow or decrease in size and complexity as my needs and interests grow and develop

a teacher's assignment, along with help from the school librarian, comes instantly to our desktop, is available 24/7, and connects us to the tools we need in order to accomplish that assignment. Those not in the loop suffer.

- In constructivist theory, if children and teens build their own space rather than have others build it for them, they will acquire management skills, both of the space itself and, more importantly, management of themselves within that space. We teach children how to manage themselves as they cross the street, even though streets are a very dangerous place. The same care needs to be taken in the digital world. Adults need to assist children in developing management skills because the adults cannot be there every moment.

In the world of differentiation, varying abilities, differing learning styles, and individual skill levels (novice to expert), children can construct basic spaces to manage their work and then construct more complex systems as they develop the management skills to handle those spaces and themselves. For example, from the digital school library, students can pull onto their own pages a subset of tools and information sources rather than have everything—much of it irrelevant to them at any given time.

What are the essential elements of a personally constructed information space? The model illustrates three elements of information spaces: the personal space, the group or collaborative space, and outer space (the whole world of the internet). Each requires some elaboration.

Personal work space. Here we construct the tools, the information sources, our school or work assignments, our calendars to keep us on track, and the personal safeguards needed to function well. Some parts of this space are pull technology—information or tools I purposely pull onto my page from elsewhere and can use when I need them. Other features are push technology—information and tools that automatically appear on a desktop for attention. Assignments pushed to me from my teachers and school librarians are good examples of things I want to be informed about as soon as they are available. My personal space is my productivity space where I do much of my work, have the information conveniently at hand, and have constructed safeguards so I am not bothered by outside influences I don't care to encounter.

Group or collaborative work space. The advent of Web 2.0 technologies allows for collaborative communication, collaborative construction, and collaborative presentation spaces. As a student, I may be in a number of groups from different classes—some of these are classes at my school, outside the school, outside the school district, or anywhere in the world. Examples of collaborative spaces develop, it seems, almost every day. The most well known ones are YouTube, Wikipedia, and Facebook. They are admired and feared at the same time. We think of Skype to talk with small groups around the world for free. There are Ning Networks that are closed communities where everyone has a personal blog that can be read and commented on by all those in the Ning. Ning Networks also have a discussion forum to work on planning or discussing issues. We think of wikis as places to do collaborative information-gathering, writing, updating projects, joint planning, and a host of other group work. We think of Google Docs and Spreadsheets as perfect places for group writing and planning. The nice thing is that many of these tools are free. Whole courses can be taught using the open-source program Moodle. Others, such as Elluminate Live or Blackboard, require a considerable investment. In such group spaces, we go in and out of the groups we belong to as projects are completed or our personal interests and skills evolve.

Outer space. The third world on our desktop is the ability to interact with and pull from the totality of the internet, whether open or invisible. This is where the most crucial management skills are needed to protect ourselves, our privacy, and our work while taking advantage of the global information system. Can we, for example, subscribe to a major newsfeed without opening ourselves to a barrage of advertising? Can I connect to groups, information sources, libraries, organizations, activist groups, and global movements, as well as begin to build my own entrepreneurial forays into the global marketplace? Outer space is full of opportunity as well as dangers. How do I manage both?

What do you mean by students managing their information space and managing themselves in that space? Computer operating systems have become much better at assisting users to manage their systems and the information on them. But in the Web 2.0 world, many new tools have emerged to handle large sets of information. For example, Delicious helps us manage favorite websites, and RSS (Really Simple Syndication) feeds make us aware of changes in our favorite websites. iGoogle turns the computer welcome screen into one's own centralized organizational system of the three different information spaces. Imagine both an information-system–building workshop and a tune-up shop where young people constantly learn new techniques for updating their own skills and pushing out their own frontiers as they juggle the millions of entities trying to get their attention, take their money, or even abuse them or steal their identity. Since there is not a foolproof safety net and there will not likely ever be one, students need to learn safety rules for managing their own behavior in digital space. We already have some concerns in this area, but users need to discover some important guidelines:

- Decide whom to trust in digital space.
- Have a work ethic and know how to be productive.
- Work ethically in collaborative spaces, contributing rather than destroying.
- Learn to discern harmful elements and know how to control them so they don't control the user.
- Discern when I am caught in addictive online behavior and know how to break it.

At present, schools often try to control bad behavior or lock down systems that threaten children and teens. Wouldn't it be better to equip students with self-defense strategies? A famous person once said, "Teach them correct principles and let them govern themselves." Such an optimistic goal may not work for some children, but it will work for many, many others, and it will become a lifelong skill.

What about content on these self-designed systems? In the marketplace today, textbook companies are trying to capture the market of both printed and digital textbooks. Other companies have content-rich topical information systems they sell for a fee. Libraries subscribe to online databases for student research. In a student-run system, we need to have elastic content systems that children flow in and out of as their needs change. If I am exploring a topic, for example, I may want to enter a content system at an apprentice level, and I would then want to push my expertise toward the expert level. In other systems, I might need specialized knowledge for one project that requires me to use a database for only a half hour. Content providers try to maximize both usefulness and profits. If they saw more flexible, user-controlled systems emerging, they would design their systems to be useful across different platforms.

Would we abandon the construction of the digital school library or the public library information system? No. We would continue to build these systems but instead think of them in terms of a grocery store where our students can come and select apples, oranges, or cereal to drag to their own home pages to nourish their information use. We will soon find them pawing through our wares and picking what they want and need but not picking the spoiled apple or the yucky broccoli. Yes, that broccoli software might be good for them, but they have probably already found something that works better and faster for their individual needs.

One of the best uses of Web 2.0 tools is to have students construct their own content as they learn together, do projects, read, write, and solve problems. Best of all, their content and writing can be shared with the world through blogs, YouTube, wikis, and Flickr albums. There seems to be no end to the self-publishing opportunities using technologies that engage and motivate. Learning has never been so exciting.

Who would teach children and teens to create and constantly improve their information spaces? Certainly the school librarian, the district technology coordinator, and the building-level technology personnel need to collaborate to plan and develop systems and the needed channels to get students started and to provide the needed support. Instead of locking out all Web 2.0 applications, technology leaders need to find ways to include them. Much can be outsourced safely. For example, in a Ning Network, each member of a collaborative community must be invited, and no one from the outside can see any content. Thus, students and teachers can blog, add comments, show videos, discuss issues, and do other things without interference. Once the channel is opened up, the software and storage of information on the Ning is free, maintained off-site, and available from any connected computer throughout the world. The owner of the Ning receives all comments posted to the Ning and can review and monitor what everyone is doing if mischievous behavior begins to develop.

At the beginning of the school year, a construction session can be sponsored by the technology staff, school librarian, and interested teachers. Certified students can assist individuals and their friends to build, monitor, extend, and manage their information spaces. It is a community opportunity to share, help, and encourage. It already happens in the social networking world of children and teens. We just need to extend the influence in another direction.

So what? For years we have built computer information systems on the idea that "if you build it, they will come." Well, they came, but instead of staying, they did a work-around because of their needs in social networking. Instead, we propose that: "If they build it, they will learn." Learn what? Children and teens will not only learn how to construct a learning space, but in doing so will surround themselves with tools that help them learn. The fishing pole of the technology world, as opposed to giving them a fish, requires students to begin to take command of their information spaces and their own learning within that space. It is a gift of a lifetime.

Some might panic with this proposal against the centralized, one-fits-all system, assuming that outsourced systems won't work for children. The fact is they already do work. We are already at odds with the current generation, who see school as irrelevant and boring. Technology is one place to build a bridge that crosses the chasm between students' seeming boredom and the exciting world of learning.

SOURCE: David V. Loertscher, "Children, Teens, and the Construction of Information Spaces," *CSLA Journal* 31, no. 1 (Fall 2007): 32–35.

Proposal writing

by Blanche Woolls

Many school library media specialists would like to expand their services. One way to do this is to develop a carefully thought-out and documented proposal. The information you collect helps explain your need to the persons you are asking. This may be parents, the principal, or the school board. Proposals might stay in the school district, with the administration and school board accepting the proposals and funding the projects with local funds. At other times, the school district budget may be inadequate, and the school library media specialist, with school board approval, may seek outside funding. Whether a project remains in the district or is sent to an outside agency, a proposal must be developed.

The remainder of this section discusses writing proposals for the school district or agencies that fund proposals directly related to school library media center programs. However, sometimes school library media specialists are invited to join other, perhaps larger, agencies to develop a broader proposal. For some agencies, collaboration is either encouraged or required. Because many agencies ask for matching funds, it can be helpful to have more than your school or even the district involved in the proposal. The expertise, experience, or other resources of a cowriter's group can also add value to your proposal.

A project proposal should include the following elements: statement of needs and of goals and objectives, a plan of action or activities and procedures, an evaluation plan, comments about facilities and other resources available, and a carefully planned budget. Additional items, such as employment opportunity regulations, may be required if the proposal goes beyond the school district. You will also need to send vitae of staff and consultants for your project.

Developing the statement of needs

Few funders are willing to allocate money without a needs statement. As children we learn to justify additional allowance requests from our parents. As adults, personal budget decisions to make major purchases are based on a needs assessment. School library media specialists cannot expect additional funding from their school budgets without presenting a strong case of need. Needs are defined in a variety of ways. One is to read research studies that address the problem in your school. You can ask for funds to implement the program that addressed the problem.

Another effective way is to compare the resources available in your school with those in a similar school in the district or a nearby district where the student body is similar but achievement levels are higher. The difference in resources available could be suggested as a reason for the difference in achievement levels and would give you the opportunity to test the result of adding materials and equipment for student use.

The process will be much more effective if the input comes from the group rather than the media specialist as a single individual suggesting the needs. The composition of the group is very important. Funding agencies want to know if those to be served by the project helped identify needs and if those identified needs were used to help set the priorities. Proposal writers should cite the persons involved in the needs-assessment process. In this case, administrators, teachers, and parents are most likely to be those who helped establish the needs because they know when students have problems with reading.

Although a media specialist can say that the collection is inadequate, the statement is more powerful if teachers review the collection in their areas and find it inadequate, or if students write lists of missing or inadequate materials for assignments they have researched. It is important that the assessment of needs involves those directly or indirectly affected by the proposed project. It would be foolhardy to ask for an expanded collection of art books if the art teacher did not plan to use the books or make assignments that require students to use them. To confirm the participation of others in establishing needs, the proposal writer should list all meetings held and who attended, tests that were administered and the results, and any other relevant details. Participation may also be confirmed by letters of support, which are appended to the body of the proposal. Once the need has been established, a goal should be stated and objectives for the project developed.

LETTER OF SUPPORT

CLICK HERE

Preparing goals and objectives

A goal is a broad, general statement and is not measurable. Because a goal is such a broad statement, it is not always required for a project proposal. When a goal is required, it should be realistic. Consider reading materials as an example of a goal. Trying to overcome reading problems in an elementary school in a single year might be an unrealistic goal. If children are reading below grade level, if reading at all, a few books and magazines added to the library media collection will not alleviate the problem, and the goal cannot be met.

Objectives, conversely, must be measurable. They are designed to help solve the needs that have been determined, and they should state the precise level of achievement anticipated and the length of time expected to achieve them. Objectives must be an outgrowth of the stated needs. They should describe where the school library program should be in this time frame in relation to where the program is currently, and who or what is involved in the project. The better the objectives are written, the easier it will be to prepare the evaluation later. An attempt to increase reading scores will need to include the number of students, how much increase will occur, and in what time frame. This becomes the objective.

Goals and objectives themselves may be evaluated. Context evaluation is the assessment of goals and objectives to see whether they are written in terms of the intended constituency of the project. This evaluation reviews the number of students who will benefit from the project, for they should be part of the stated objectives. For the reading project, you might choose to work only with 3rd-grade students for one year and suggest that each student would raise reading scores by two years.

Objectives are often confused with activities. Rather than state the expected outcome, novice proposal writers often list the methods to achieve an outcome. These methods are activities rather than stated objectives, and they are a part of the plan of action.

Establishing the plan of action

The section of the proposal that states the plan of action, or proposed activities, describes the methods to be employed to meet the stated objective and alleviate the needs. A general statement of the overall design of the project includes the population to be served, how the population will be selected, and how the project will be managed. But the activities themselves must be directed to the objectives, and that relationship must be clear. Procedures to attain the objectives must follow from the objectives. If the relationship between objective and activity is ambiguous, those reading the proposal may reject it. Funding agencies and school administrators prefer projects with a step-by-step plan of realistic activities to meet the objectives and alleviate the need. The activity for 3rd-graders might be to give them books to read that they will want to read and allow them unlimited access to these books.

When a project planner is unsure that proposed activities will meet objectives in the anticipated time frame, alternative plans of action may be presented. A rationale for each alternative may include a brief statement about why the first plan of action was proposed and how, when, or why it will be decided to use the alternative plan. If providing a large collection of reading materials does not seem to be encouraging their reading, providing more reading opportunities during the school day and asking parents to help children read more at night at home could be an alternative plan of action or even a second activity. Whenever possible, proposal writers should include relevant research supporting their choice from the array of possible activities.

As the project activities are stated, a time line for each of the activities may be presented. The time line shows the sequence of separate activities that have gone before, what is in progress, and what will be done. This helps the reviewers understand how the activities relate—that is, if and when the initiation of one activity depends on the completion of another, when activities overlap, and the progress necessary for project completion.

Planning for evaluation

After the activities have been designed, proposal writers must then determine the best methods to evaluate the activities to see whether they are, indeed, meeting stated objectives. To do this, two kinds of evaluation are helpful: formative and summative. Formative evaluation processes occur throughout the life of the project. At each step, an evaluation may be made to see if the activities are accomplishing the planned improvements. If the project does not appear to be successful, an alternate plan of action may be put into place. Progress using the new activity will then be evaluated to see if it demonstrates more success than the previous plan. Formative evaluation further determines whether project progress is within the anticipated time period.

At the close of any project, a final, or summative, evaluation is conducted. At this time, each activity is evaluated to determine the degrees of progress made to meet the stated objectives. Proposal writers must detail the means by which they or their agency will verify for the funding source that the project has accomplished the objectives as stated and the degree to which the objectives have been met. Information to be collected must be described, methods to analyze the information must be outlined, and the degree of success that should be expected must be stated. With this example proposal, the obvious summative evaluation would be a reading test to see whether test scores have increased.

This is often not an easy task, and many proposal writers seek help from persons in tests and measurements offices in colleges and universities and in local or state agencies to help define the evaluation procedures to be used after the project begins. Many funding agencies prefer the summative evaluation be conducted by an outside evaluator to eliminate or modify the possibility of bias and add validity to the evaluation statements. When seeking project funding from outside agencies, choosing an outside evaluator—especially one highly regarded by the funding agency—may increase the likelihood of the project's approval. Someone not directly related to the project may be better able to measure the degree of success. Certainly the evaluation is one of the most important aspects of project planning and should be given full attention.

Deciding the dissemination

Although outside funding agencies may not ask about any presentation of the project and its outcome to the general public, the school library media specialist should be prepared to share the results of any project with the appropriate audience. Just as government agencies and foundation staffs need to know the degree of success of their investment, they anticipate credit for the contribution they made to the project. For locally funded projects, the school library media specialist reports project success to the superintendent and principal. They should be given material they can use for publicizing a successful project. It is no virtue to hide project success.

Funding agencies need good publicity to continue awarding money for projects; likewise, the school library media center is more likely to receive additional funds when successful projects are reported in the news media. Therefore, the media specialist must consider carefully how to present information to appropriate audiences beyond the project. It may be letters sent home to parents or full coverage in the news media, both newspapers and television. The school district may have a public relations director to handle this, or the library media specialist may need to send out press releases to reporters.

Information presented for publication must be well written, accurate, and complete. If photographs of students are submitted, permission for publication must be obtained from parents.

Finally, successful school library projects should be reported to the school library community through activities in professional journals and presentations at conferences and workshops. The media specialist must share the outcomes of projects with other professionals so that successful activities can be replicated in other school library media centers.

School library media specialists may be reluctant to make presentations. If you are the person in charge of the project, in developing the proposal with all its parts, the needs assessment, preparation of objectives, activities, evaluation, dissemination, you are the best person to share how this happened and the results of the project. Even if the project didn't meet its objectives, you will have some idea of how things could have been done differently. You need to share your expertise with your colleagues, and your professional associations may be the best place to do this. As you write the proposal, you will need to list all the ways information will be disseminated about the proposal.

Describing local resources

Project proposals should also describe the facilities where the project will be conducted. If the school or school district has excellent facilities in place to support project activities, there is a greater chance for success. Conversely, if an elaborate program is described but the school does not have adequate space for it, there is a greater likelihood for failure. Describing facilities and additional resources available, human and material, will help the funding agency realize that the school library media specialist has a better chance of conducting a successful project. If special equipment is needed for the project, the equipment must become part of the project proposal, or the method of securing the equipment must be shown in the project narrative and budget as in-kind equipment.

Proposal writers should list all resources that add credibility to what, or who, is being proposed. If a school library media specialist lacks long experience in the library media world, assistance may be available from a district coordinator. The community may be supporting the school library media specialist in some unique or special way, and this should be explained. Additional funding may be available for the project from other sources—the community, individuals, or the state department of education. This support should also be cited.

Personnel who work on the project must be listed. If they are available as in-kind contributions to the project, this means their salaries will be paid by the school district and will not be part of the cost charged to the project budget. All personnel to be added must be listed. Job titles, job descriptions, qualifications expected, and length of time assigned to the project must all be described. Resumes should be attached for all persons who are identified as part of the project staff. This includes project director, coordinator, consultants, clerical and technical staff, teachers, and evaluators. These resumes must be brief, and the activities and positions described in their backgrounds should be only those showing skills related directly to the project.

Before submitting a person's name as part of any project staff, proposal writers must secure permission from that individual. Most people are annoyed if their name is submitted without permission. Often, an implication exists that these proposed project consultants or staff have approved the proposal in principle, even if they did not actually participate in writing it. Also, there is the danger of including someone's name in a proposal when that person is writing a proposal in response to the same request for proposals.

When competing for limited funds, the proposal writer should try to find out whether project staff under consideration are known to the funding agency. The agency may be more willing to fund a project if they recognize the capabilities of those directly involved. Also, the funding agency may insist on approval of the categories of persons to be hired, such as researchers, technicians, media practitioners, or clerical staff. Finally, many funding agencies are reluctant to approve the hiring of new persons for a project if there is no indication of how this staff will be continued after the project is completed. School district administrators may find themselves obligated for any unemployment benefits for furloughed staff unless they can be placed in other positions.

Building the budget

The final part of project planning, the budget, includes the anticipated costs of the project, item by item. Government agencies provide a form to be completed. These items can be used to verify that the information usually required is included in the project budget.

Two budget items that may cause unexpected problems are fringe benefits and overhead. Fringe benefits are part of salary statistics. The percentage figure used to calculate fringe benefits for proposed project personnel will be the same used for all school district salaried staff. Fringe benefits for a district employee are determined by the monthly salary, percentage of time and length of time of the project. That is, if a school library specialist with a $2,000 monthly salary is to be employed half-time for six months, the project would show $1,000 times six, or $6,000 for the project. If the school district has a fringe benefit package of 27%, $1,620 must be added to the project costs.

Overhead percentage may be set by school districts, universities, and private agencies. Overhead is an assessment of the use of staff, equipment, and facilities that will not be specifically included in the proposal budget. Examples of overhead are the preparation of purchase orders, checks for payment, bookkeeping, use of office furniture and equipment, heat and lighting, and computer use. The overhead costs are then added to the total costs for the project. This is sometimes discouraging to a proposal writer when the overhead costs add another charge to the project. It sometimes means cutting other parts of the project that seemed essential in order to submit a proposal that has a reasonable budget.

Some agencies such as state departments of education may limit or prohibit assessment of overhead percentages or limit the amount that can be added. This needs to be determined before you begin the project proposal so that it is not an unexpected cost to the planning. If your district has a contract with the agency to which you are submitting the proposal, you will need to put a copy of that contract with your proposal.

If space or equipment is to be rented, those costs must be calculated. Consultant or contracted services also must be listed. Consultants may be paid a per diem amount rather than a salary, in which case fringe benefits need not be calculated. School library media specialists should keep in mind that telephone charges, mailing costs, duplicating fees, online database searches, and office supplies should be added to the budget if the school budget cannot absorb these additional charges. Finally, if the staff or consultants require travel funds, these must be included.

Additional considerations

When planning the project, proposal writers should check to see if evaluation points have been assigned to each part of the proposal. The number of points assigned is the highest score that proposal readers can give each part of the proposal. Careful attention must be placed on all parts of a proposal, but special attention should be given to the sections that have been assigned the most points.

Throughout project planning and proposal preparation, school district administrators must indicate their support. It is heartbreaking to complete a project proposal and have the principal or superintendent refuse to send it to the funding agency. It is even more difficult when an agency awards funding and the school board refuses to permit the school district to accept the funds. Not all administrators or school boards welcome funding from an outside source, especially if they perceive that strings are attached. This is especially true when personnel must be added, because, as stated earlier, these persons may expect to become permanent employees at the close of the project. A successful project may encourage other administrators to demand similar materials, staff, or services from already overextended district funds.

Convincing administrators of the value of the project and the potential benefit to the school building and school district is important. This is better accomplished when the school library media specialist provides an honest, realistic assessment of the regulations and requirements for the school district at the close of the funding, the probable level of enthusiasm for similar projects in other schools, and the funds required to continue even a small portion of the project.

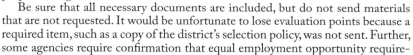

After preparing the proposal, the writer should reread it to make sure it is written without jargon, to be sure the plan of action is logical and will achieve the objectives, to eliminate extraneous words and unnecessary materials, and to correct any spelling or grammatical errors. Finally, the proposal should be neatly typed in an easy-to-read format or in conformity with the format outlined in the request for proposal. Format instructions might include spacing requirements, number of pages for each section of the proposal, length of abstract, and other details.

Be sure that all necessary documents are included, but do not send materials that are not requested. It would be unfortunate to lose evaluation points because a required item, such as a copy of the district's selection policy, was not sent. Further, some agencies require confirmation that equal employment opportunity requirements are met and other legal regulations are in place.

Most funding agencies are interested in what will happen to the project at the close of the outside funding. If parts of the project will be continued with school district funding, the project may have a better chance for outside funding. If administrators are involved in planning throughout, they can help determine how to continue the project.

Those who are required to sign the proposal must be available to do so. If the proposal requires school board approval, copies must be distributed to members prior to the board meeting, and someone from the proposal preparation team must be ready to answer questions at the meeting. It may not be possible to call a special meeting of the board, so the school library media specialist must pay attention to the closing dates of all requests for proposal, to allow time to secure board approval and all appropriate signatures.

Proposals must be submitted on time. If a deadline exists, this date must be met. Proposals that arrive after the deadline are usually returned unopened.

Writing proposals is a way of life in many situations. In others, it may be a way to get additional funds, expand a program to meet a specific need, add equipment, add materials, or try a different way to provide materials to help teach students.

Most persons who have had one proposal funded are very willing to write another. They have been given an opportunity to improve their school library media center, test a new method, offer a new service, or provide more materials for students and teachers.

To write a proposal is to enter a competition, and the process is similar to any other competitive endeavor; sometimes you win, sometimes you lose. Sometimes it may seem better to lose. One gains all the applause for the effort to establish needs, develop objectives and plans of action, and write and submit the proposal. It is an opportunity to meet new colleagues and reestablish communication with old acquaintances. Sometimes you win, and then you have to work to see that the project succeeds.

SOURCE: Adapted from Blanche Woolls, "Writing Proposals to Expand Programs," in *The School Library Media Manager,* 4th ed. (Westport, Conn.: Libraries Unlimited, 2008), 152–160. Used with permission.

PROGRAMMING
CHAPTER SIX

Don't hesitate, just collaborate
by Lynne F. Burk

The overriding goals of a quality school library program are to collaborate with teachers, administrators, parents, and students; to support building and district initiatives; and to integrate the teaching of literature, information literacy, and technology skills into the subject-area curricula. Numerous studies since the 1990s confirm a belief that collaboration with classroom teachers supports active and engaged learning, differentiates instruction, facilitates the use of a variety of resources, and ultimately influences student achievement. Professional literature and organizations emphasize the importance of collaboration.

It may seem to be a challenge to develop these collaborative projects. Budget cuts and fixed schedules, especially at the elementary level, are an all-too-common reality. Standards-based education and high-stakes testing have put increasing demands on classroom teachers and their time. However, effective school librarians can demonstrate that they understand these challenges, know the curriculum, and are familiar with the benchmark objectives students must master.

Help teachers move away from the "once a year" model of a special-research or library-based project and develop a seamless pattern of collaboration with the classroom teachers across a variety of curriculum areas, an ongoing and integral component of curriculum delivery. The emphasis becomes student learning. Here are the steps.

Talk the talk, and walk the walk. To be viewed as a teacher, act like one. Review curriculum guides and textbooks; know the units; review standards, benchmarks, and high-stakes tests. Develop rubrics and other assessments for library projects. Return the work to the classroom teachers with comments.

Advertise, advertise, advertise. During faculty meetings share books, websites, and other resources to support the classroom curriculum. Put materials on a web page, in teachers' mailboxes, and post them in the staff lounge.

Display student library work. Use library display areas, and even the hallway, to display student projects from regularly scheduled library class or from a collaborative lesson. Make sure the parents know as well. A "Library Project" stamp placed on completed projects being taken home helps parents understand that student learning takes place in the library media center.

Make it simple. Because teachers feel overwhelmed, collaboration, if it sounds like more work, will be difficult. Make it easy; spell out exactly what you will do, how long it will take, what objectives will be addressed, and how student learning will be assessed. Prepare any resources needed, from graphic organizers, to website links, to suggested assessment rubrics. Share these materials with your principal and with teachers at staff meetings.

Be the solution. When teachers are concerned about new content areas added to their curriculum or the new principal identifies a goal of integrating technology into the curriculum, come forward with concrete suggestions that will help solve their problems. Increased funding may come your way.

Focus on yourself, but keep the teacher in your sights. School librarians are educated about the importance of a quality library program and the value of developing information-literacy skills that integrate with the curriculum rather than exist in isolation. Classroom teachers are not. It is your responsibility to reach out and find out about your staff and their needs.

Frequency often matters more than complexity. When teachers are reluctant to engage in time-consuming library collaborations, develop a one-period WebQuest, create a booktalk to accompany an author study, or design a lesson that reviews literature vocabulary for the state reading assessment.

Allow time for trust to develop. Once the initial contact has been made and a successful collaboration accomplished, the trust developed between the librarian and the classroom teacher can lead to other opportunities.

Share, share, share. Share your success with your principal, teachers, and other school librarians in your district. Use shared folders on your network or on a website to make lesson plans and resources available.

Don't focus on your library tasks. Very few people care whether the call numbers are perfect or the MARC records complete. Make student learning the priority. Spending time with students and teachers is your most important assignment. We must demonstrate that school-library programs support the academic achievement and educational goals of the district.

So don't hesitate, just collaborate!

SOURCE: Adapted from Lynne F. Burk, "Don't Hesitate, Just Collaborate!" *Library Media Connection* 26, no. 3 (November/December 2007): 40–41. Used with permission.

Do you really want boys in your library?
by Helen Cox

Classes don't start for at least 25 minutes, but the library is already jam-packed with kids, mostly boys. Students are sitting at tables, browsing bookshelves, standing and chatting. Three untimed games of chess are going full tilt, and a long line has formed in front of the circulation desk.

But things weren't always that way. When I arrived four years ago, not many kids were rushing to the library. Who could blame them? Although there was a new circulation desk and a bank of 16 student computers, almost everything was dirty and disorganized. Storage rooms were crammed with old junk and most of the collection was in sad shape. New books were kept in a separate place for teachers only. And the room itself was one big unimaginative square with a 50-foot wall that housed four heaters and two air conditioners. Overall, the library looked like it belonged in a neighborhood that had low expectations because it didn't see an alternative.

Transforming this library into an irresistible place for boys begins with vision, energy, and a lot of hard work. Boys respond well to a scholarly environment. It's one of the ways librarians can encourage them to seek higher education and become lifelong learners. In addition to the hours spent scrubbing, sorting, and ruthlessly tossing out junk, our library also offered comfortable places to sit and read, places for privacy and quiet, and a large, beautiful wall mural. If you give boys the best and teach them how to take care of things, they respect their environment and begin to value themselves.

Think of your library as a place to market reading material. Carve out small sections (a "guys read" section) with large boy-friendly signs that make it much easier for a reluctant or emerging reader who may feel overwhelmed by too many choices.

Whether or not you approve of graphic novels, comics, pop-ups, 3-D illusions, and jokes, the bottom line is that boys are crazy about them, so make sure you stock them in your library. Add to the list the gross and the gory, the horrific, toilet humor, and action-packed adventures, short stories, comics, sports, and world records, as well as titles on drawing and calligraphy, origami, and paper airplanes. Add biographies of wrestlers and evil rulers, and titles on gangs and the military.

Ready for some action?

When it comes to active young boys, noise and energy are part of the package. Don't make them sit at desks six hours each day or learn from textbooks when hands-on application and movement are how they learn best.

Chess. If you do nothing else, provide chess sets. If you want to get fancy, try offering a chess institute. Set aside a Saturday, with training in the morning, a buffet-style lunch, and a tournament in the afternoon. Invite another school to the event to make it even more exciting.

Library club. It's an ideal place for students to generate ideas and help make policy decisions. Extend the sense of ownership throughout the entire school. Students determine how many books can be checked out and for how long.

Bug club. While the entire school loved this one, it soon became clear that boys were mostly interested in spiders that devoured bugs. Students purchased containers, caught spiders, and fed them each day with flies and crickets that they caught themselves. We watched caterpillars become moths.

Reading contests. Our reluctant readers read for six hours without talking. We upped it to seven, then eight. More than 95% of the participants continued to complete the contest, which resulted in a raffle for prizes, including home computers.

Homemade videos and DVDs. Library orientations can get old really fast, especially when you have more than 30 English classes and it takes two orientations per class to cover the basics. To preserve my sanity, I recruited some high school students and middle school teacher aides to create an orientation video. Orientation videos are unusual and fun, and they hold students' interest. Plus, they're far from polished, which is part of their appeal. Best of all, they cover all the rules and regs as only teens can do—by breaking every single one of them. Mock battles illustrate both why you don't play around in the library and how to take care of the furniture and share materials. Thanks to that video, every class got a complete tour of the library and our circulation increased. And all of the books that appeared in the video were checked out repeatedly for months.

It's all about attitude

If your library isn't a boy magnet, you need to check your attitude. Do you really want boys in your library? Those chess games they love aren't quiet one-on-one games. Do you smile and welcome boys with genuine warmth when they enter? The surprised look on their faces alone makes it worth it. Many boys are fearful and insecure most of the time. It's hard to be a boy these days. Do you use empathy and negotiation? Give them two appropriate choices. And just say no if they ask if they can do something other than the two choices that were offered. Do you give unconditional love? Boys are accountable for their actions, but don't take it personally when they jump over the couch or giggle over your last name. Discipline should be used to provide structure, not punishment, so five-minute time-outs still work. Do you laugh at their jokes? Trying to joke boys out of inappropriate behaviors goes much further than venting frustration or responding with condescending admonishment. Gentle teasing is more effective than punishment. Have consistent expectations and it's not about you.

The payoff

If you put these suggestions into action, you'll have more boys than you know what to do with, and girls too. It took a while for girls to start coming to the library on their own. One girl would stick her head in and say, "Why are there all boys here?" and leave. The braver ones finally started coming with groups of girlfriends, and now we have a friendly mix.

Some days I can barely keep up with checkout, and unbeknownst to the kids, they're not supervised at all. When the bell rings and they race off to class, I look around the library in amazement. It still stands and it's not trashed. Sure, there may be a few books on the tables or one or two shelves in disarray, even a paper or two on the floor; but considering how many students were just in here with little ol' me, that's great.

SOURCE: Adapted from Helen Cox, "Boy Story: Do You Really Want Guys in Your Library?" *School Library Journal* 56, no. 9 (September 2010): 26–29. Used with permission.

What libraries and kids can learn about gaming

by the Association for Library Service to Children Children and Technology Committee

In the closing keynote of the second annual ALA TechSource Gaming, Learning, and Libraries Symposium, held November 2–4, 2008, Jon-Paul Dyson quoted 17th-century British philosopher John Locke (left), who believed that required play is no longer play.

None of the things they are to learn should ever be made a burthen to them, or impos'd on them as a task. Whatever is so propos'd presently becomes irksome; the mind takes an aversion to it, though before it were a thing of delight or indifferency. Let a child but be order'd to whip his top at a certain time every day, whether he has or has not a mind to it; let this be but requir'd of him as a duty, wherein he must spend so many hours morning and afternoon, and see whether he will not soon be weary of any play at this rate.

Dyson (left), vice president for exhibit research and development and associate curator of electronic games at the Strong museum in Rochester, New York, discussed the power of play today and defined play as "fun, voluntary, its own reward, and taking place in a magic circle." A "magic circle" separates the play world from the real world. Dyson listed the benefits of play as refreshing us, relaxing us, increasing our flexibility to life's challenges, promoting learning, and sharpening us mentally and physically, as well as making us happier.

Games produce learning engagement

While few would argue that play isn't important for young children, there often is a perceived disconnect between learning and the majority's view of game play in

our lives. As Marc Prensky (left), author of *Don't Bother Me Mom— I'm Learning!*, stressed, "People play games not because they are games but because they're the most engaging intellectual thing we have." With digital games, many adults have a knee-jerk reaction, determining that a game is a waste of time, money, and brain cells without ever engaging with the game or seeking to have an open dialogue about gaming.

Prensky remarked, "If there's a concern about a book, we read it and talk about it. Movie? See it and talk about it. A game?" He implored librarians to gauge their own reactions, to remain open-minded, to discuss game play. Prensky encouraged librarians who are not game players to have gamers write synopses and reviews of games, to ask questions such as "Why do you like it?" and "Is there reason for concern about the content?"

Prensky recommended *Got Game: How the Gamer Generation Is Reshaping Business Forever* by John C. Beck and Mitchell Wade, stating, "Lots of people in their 20s and 30s attribute success directly to game play." Prensky noted that "complex games produce learning engagement," defining these games as being not trivial and lasting between eight to 100 hours. Multiplayer role-playing games allow players to cooperate, collaborate, and work in teams, and such game play promotes effective decision-making under stress. Complex games offer players the opportunity to make ethical and moral decisions, to apply new skills and information, to persist and solve problems, to think laterally and strategically, and to adapt to foreign environments. Games can be a bridge to solving real-life problems.

Three presenters looked at the younger gamer. One aspect of a study showed that 54% of 12- to 14-year-old respondents play digital games daily, and this group is most likely to use portable game devices. Massively multiplayer online games (MMOGs) involve a quest and a goal, while virtual worlds are typically areas of free play. Two virtual worlds, Whyville (www.whyville.net) and Disney's Club Penguin (www.clubpenguin.com), were mentioned by 13% of the 12- to 14-year-olds interviewed for the study.

In a Pokemon Primer session, the speaker made the case for Pokemon, stating, "It is a complex system of knowledge to learn for fun." Achieving level 100 represents "hours of toil," and Pokemon is a positive moral example of being kind to the environment and to others as one improves oneself, one's Pokemon, and the world.

Keynote speaker Andrew S. Bub (right) is a gamer and parent who reviews for the parent audience under the name GamerDad (www.gamerdad.com). The reviews are appropriate for librarians as well. Bub said that in most games "rash actions usually fail, so games can help some kids slow down and think." The love of a game can also be a child's motivator for reading. He explained to his daughter, "I told her, 'I'm not going to read [the text of the game] that to you anymore. If you want to play that game, you need to learn to read.'"

Learning to read is among the most complex endeavors any of us has undertaken. Some children learn to read by what seems like osmosis. They are keen observers of their environments and by the age 2–4 have become fluent readers.

Others come from print-rich environments and understand that the squiggles and lines go together somehow, making meaning. Still, there are many children who need the building blocks of the process of learning to read set before them. That is where games really come into play. And play they are. As we all know, children's play is children's work. These beginning games include memory games, matching games, sequencing card games, bingo games, board games, phonetic awareness games—which can be in a visual or in an electronic format—and more.

Some of the newest games are being developed for and played on the Wii system, which can support up to four players and offers the opportunity to move in all three dimensions. The Wii offers positive gaming experiences

for various types of learners. (Note: Other platforms are PlayStation, Xbox, other Nintendo platforms, PCs, and more.) Younger children can play early-literacy games where pattern, shape, and sequencing are key elements. The children learn in a group while laughing together to a game that highlights core preliteracy skills.

Matching learning objectives of games to state learning standards makes the foundation for gaming in libraries even stronger. For example, *Endless Ocean* meets the New York State Learning Standards in the divisions of math, science, and technology, and social studies. The New York State Standard 4 in science reads, "Students will understand and apply scientific concepts, principles, and theories pertaining to the physical setting and living environment and recognize the historical development of ideas in science." *Endless Ocean* also meets New York State Social Studies Standard 3, geography: "Students will use a variety of intellectual skills to demonstrate their understanding of the geography of the interdependent world in which we live, local, national, and global, including the distribution of people, places, and environment over the Earth's surface."

In a world where technology is advancing at record-breaking speeds, we must learn from others in a social environment. The perfect social environment is the library. Games are entryways that introduce us to new technologies, incorporate various learning styles, and simultaneously increase intellectual curiosity and growth.

Games are fun to play, and we learn in the process. Card games, board games, string games, electronic games, and virtual games are in a variety of formats and game durations, and there is a game for anyone and everyone. To reap the rewards of games, games must be played, and the earlier the better. A child's brain development is assisted by play, including games. First introduced in 1956 and well known among educators, Bloom's Taxonomy effectively states the six stages of cognitive development and advancement as: knowledge, comprehension, application, analysis, synthesis, and evaluation. Games often require a player to use many areas of the cognitive domain.

Our society wants and demands greater thinkers, and the 21st-century learner must have a set of skills that gives the opportunity for success at every turn. How do we get there from here? The most basic and simple answer: games. Games are central to learning, and we can easily put them in our libraries. Our libraries are the most social and intellectual edifices in our society. As we all know, library use goes up during tough economic times. This is our opportunity, our call to arms, to develop a national gaming program for libraries. We must get games into libraries and invite our patrons to play them. Take the opportunity to bring games into your library, play them, and judge for yourself the success.

SOURCE: ALSC Children and Technology Committee, "Going for Games: What Libraries, and Kids, Can Learn about Gaming," *Children and Libraries* 7, no. 1 (Spring 2009): 48–50. Used with permission.

Partnerships for Teen Tech Week
by Stephanie Iser

The Young Adult Library Services Association's Teen Tech Week initiative urges librarians serving teens to act as qualified, trusted professionals in the field of information technology. Teen librarians, although knowledgeable, often lack financial support, which can block quality teen tech programs and services. To address this financial issue, look outside the library for a potential partner. By partnering with local businesses and organizations with access to new technologies, you will gain resources to run a successful technology-based program.

Benefits of partnering

Along with the potential gain in resources for programs and services comes the opportunity to draw on the expertise of the partners. Store representatives probably know quite a bit about gaming systems, and they can make qualified recommendations to teens.

Another benefit is community-building. Through partnerships, the teen librarian can raise the visibility of their programs, and a new resource that wouldn't otherwise be available creates the possibility of recruiting new teen patrons.

Despite all the benefits of partnering, there are a few drawbacks. Partnerships require time and effort on behalf of both parties. There may be several meetings to plan and finalize the programs; plans may need to be approved by several levels of management. With careful planning and advanced preparation, however, these drawbacks have less impact.

Tips for partnering

If you are considering a tech partnership, here are a few tips:

Think locally. Start at the local level when approaching community organizations and businesses. For example, a call to central headquarters might not get you very far, but a visit to the local store is more personable and will likely receive better results.

Be flexible. There may be a few policies that make it impossible to get the donations you would really like. Find out what is available, and be sure to send a thank-you note.

Share a common goal. Be sure that the partnership actually benefits the teens in your community. Don't waste time with partners that want to take without giving anything in return.

Plan ahead. Begin developing the partnership at least two months before the service or program is scheduled. It could take a handful of meetings to make larger partnerships come to fruition, and there may be more than one level of management involved in the approval process.

Try, and try again. What works for one person will not work for the next, as policy tends to vary from region to region and store to store. For example, in one community, the GameStop might be more than willing to set up a monthly gaming event for teens. In another, the business may be understaffed and unable to donate time.

Be positive. Remember, you are representing the library and the needs of teens in your community. Every potential partner is worth the effort, because the request for support raises visibility of teen services in the eyes of community organizations and local businesses.

Through teen tech partnerships, libraries can gain the support and resources they wouldn't otherwise have to run successful Teen Tech Week events. Relationships with organizations and businesses also raise the visibility of teen library services within the community.

More partnership and program ideas for Teen Tech Week can be found on the YALSA wiki at wikis.ala.org/yalsa/index.php/Teen_Tech_Week.

SOURCE: Adapted from Stephanie Iser, "Partnerships for Teen Tech Week," *Young Adult Library Services* 6 (Winter 2008): 24–26. Used with permission.

The games people play

by Jenny Levine

Playing video games in libraries has become a hot topic recently, but gaming in libraries has been around much, much longer. As far back as the 1930s, New York Public Library was luring in kids using chess and board games, and many public and school libraries still have chess sets and other tabletop games for kids to play within the building. Libraries have always been in the business of content, and offering content inside a video game container isn't that a big a leap from offering Candy Land or Monopoly.

Even as we update the container, though, many of us haven't noticed that the content has changed, too, and that modern board games are very different from the ones we grew up with. The games I played as a kid usually involved rolling the dice, and a my fate depended on the square on which I landed or the card I drew.

The outcome in modern board games such as Carcassonne, Numbers League, or Ticket to Ride is determined more by strategic moves than luck of the dice or draw. If we can agree that titles such as Candy Land, checkers, chess, and Scrabble are okay for the library to provide to patrons, then surely newer games that require just as much critical thinking and strategic planning are as well. Both public and school librarians are already beginning to explore the learning that takes place in and around

Ticket to Ride teaches flexibility and persistence. Photo: Brian Mayer.

these games through collection development and in-house play.

Clearly there is a recreational (and very fun) element to these games, but there is also a lot of learning going on, even in many video games, a fact many nongamers may not realize. What kind of learning? To find out, just turn to the Association of College and Research Libraries' *Information Literacy Competency Standards for Higher Education,* which have been mapped to such popular video games as *Final Fantasy, Madden NFL,* and *Halo.* School librarians are also taking advantage of these new games, having tied many board game titles to the American Association of School Librarians' *Standards for the 21st-Century Learner* (see gaming.ala. org/resources/).

Another type of gaming that might be appropriate for some libraries is called "big games." These are games that take place in the real world, in which everyday objects become the pieces of the game. In some cases, libraries could be the perfect institution to create social interactions around community-based big games. As described by big game designer Greg Trefry, libraries are ideal places for big games, as we have tools (photocopiers, computers), secret codes (DDC, LCSH), a building for the game's headquarters (sometimes multiple buildings if there are branches), and referees (librarians).

Still other libraries are experimenting with adding gaming content to existing services, whether it's part of a school reading club (Pocahontas Middle School in Virginia), an information literacy class (University of Dubuque in Iowa or Arizona State University's West campus), or a career fair (Orange County Library System in Florida). The Old Bridge (N.J.) Public Library is even using video games as an introduction to computers and technology for seniors. These examples illustrate other models for thinking differently about gaming in libraries.

Services like these provide librarians with the chance to broaden our user base with updated services that are intellectually and socially meaningful to patrons. They also allow us to re-energize our roles as community centers, "third place," and informal learning hubs while providing a safe, noncommercialized, and information-rich environment staffed with knowledgeable experts as guides.

SOURCE: Adapted from Jenny Levine, "The Games People Play," *American Libraries* 39 (August 2008): 38. Used with permission.

6

LAN party, anyone?

by Jim Peterson

In the old days (more than five years ago in computer time), a Local Area Network (LAN) party was simply all the school's computer geeks getting together with their own PCs to play video games against each other on a network. Someone would bring a machine to act as a game server that would keep track of scores (also known as kills, frags, mad lewt, or pwnage), who was logged in, and serve the games. Usually, lots of munchies, pizzas, and beverages were consumed. But LAN parties quickly became very popular and grew in size so that groups were renting conference centers for these events that, sometimes, could go on for an entire week.

What is a LAN party?

Most games being released across all platforms can be played online. For instance, the Madden NFL series is available for the PC, Xbox, PlayStation 2 and 3, and Wii.

And you know what? This game allows someone playing on a PS3 to play against someone else, somewhere else on a PC, Xbox 360, or Wii, creating an instant online LAN party.

Do your older teens play *RuneScape*? Chances are that a group of friends are playing against each other over the internet. Public libraries can easily host an instant LAN party after school.

LAN tournaments and skill building

LAN games are a great tool for teaching good sportsmanship and building social interaction skills, since most of them allow you to chat with other players. The setup of a LAN gaming session can teach basic computer networking skills and, if it's a tournament setup, management skills. Managing time and resources are essential to a great LAN party, and planning carefully only makes it better.

Equipment

Most of the equipment for a LAN party can be brought to the session by players or purchased without a tremendous outlay of money. Almost any modern computer with a single-core processor and a gigabyte of memory will suffice as a server, and most games have their own server software built into the installation packages. Since the server doesn't have to render any graphics, it doesn't need to have a high-end graphics card. These game servers, depending on the number of players, can even run on a player's computer while the user is playing the game.

Another needed piece of equipment is a network switch. If your IT department doesn't have one, a good 16-port switch, capable of at least 100Mbs transfer rates, can be bought online for less than $100. This is the piece of equipment that creates the network for your game. The faster it can operate, the better; but you pay for speed, and a gigabit switch will likely run more than $150. Cabling is important also. A Category 5 cable will work, but a Cat5e or Cat6 are better. If your switch is gigabit-rated, a Cat5 cable won't be able to take advantage of the speed. It's like replacing a funnel with a sieve in terms of how fast the information flows through.

People who use a dedicated PC for LAN parties typically have a custom-built setup that either they or someone else has put together. Most people who have held a LAN party, as gamer or host, understand this unwritten rule: Bring your own machine. If you are hosting a LAN party, you will definitely see some powerful machines. Lots of gaming machines are now water-cooled.

Security

Security is a touchy subject. It is possible that someone could bring in a virus with their computer. You will have to make sure that all participants know they are plugging in at their own risk, and that they should run a virus/malware scan as a precaution. It is rare that someone would purposely infect everyone on the LAN while in-game, but it has happened. You will want to make clear that this behavior will not be tolerated, and that the activity is illegal and will be prosecuted. You could require that everyone use antivirus software while there, but that could slow things down for individual users. Most public LAN parties won't allow connection to the internet because it opens up too many liability doors in illegal downloads and other things. Besides, it's called a Local Area Network for a reason.

Planning a party

If you have one, get your IT department involved. You probably will have an in-house source of gamers to help you set up and provide the equipment. No IT department? No problem. Here is where you get your teens involved. When you start advertising the event, ask around and see if anyone has a switch that might be up to the task, extra cabling, or even a computer that has been used as a game server. You might want to think about setting up teams or brackets, or limiting participation based on the capability of your switch. For instance, you wouldn't want 48 people showing up if all you have is a 16-port switch.

LAN parties must have massive quantities of soft drinks and munchies. Refreshments are almost mandatory, but you could require that players bring their own, as long as they are within guidelines.

You can complete your LAN party in as little as an hour. It will take a few minutes to set up the switch and run the cables, and then get your participants plugged into the network and start playing. If you want to make this a monthly program, you can encourage the players to start a video game club. Make time for a weekend tournament. Get the young people together for an end-of-school-year all-nighter. It will be fun, and you'll be seen in a whole new light by your young patrons!

Many other games can be played online. Nearly any game produced these days will do. To find out more about game and software ratings, go to esrb.com. For additional information on hosting a LAN party, visit www.wikihow.com/Host-a-LAN-Party—and get ready to host one in your library.

SOURCE: Adapted from Jim Peterson, "LAN Party, Anyone?" *School Library Journal* 55 (March 2009): 26–27. Used with permission.

Teen Tech Week on a budget

by Jami Schwarzwalder

6

Editor's note: Although this is written for the public library's youth librarian, these ideas can be useful for school librarians and encourage cooperative efforts between the youth professionals in both types of libraries.—*B. W.*

Here are a few ideas on how your library can participate in Teen Tech Week, without giving you a nervous breakdown.

Hold a contest. Let teens recommend and then vote for the best video game, movie, TV show, YouTube video, and website.

Pro: Great for teen input; reaches teens who do not come to regular programs; can recommend books and other media teens might like on the basis of what they voted for.

Con: Many teens complained that the "best book" was left off the list.

Poster tag clouds and comments. Put blank poster boards on the end panels of your stacks asking the teens a general question, for example: Was a book character in a popular book "honest"? What is your favorite manga?

Pro: Great for teen input and reaches teens who do not come to regular programs.

Con: Provide pencils, not markers, to write on poster boards; this medium is anonymous. Teens who disagree write bigger or cross out others, and others will have a chance to correct.

After-hours alternative. To use all of the public internet computers, reserve computers at the library just for teens for a specified hour. Ask the teens to post reviews on a blog or teenreads.com, or compile of list of best online game websites.

Pro: Uses equipment you already have and gives teens without the internet at home more time to engage online.

Con: Do this during nonpeak hours so younger or older internet users are not displaced.

Buy a video camera or use a smartphone. A video camera can be used to record impromptu actions of teens like book and media reviews, and you can easily copy videos to your PC or email them to the teens.

Pro: Gives teens a chance to comment and discuss their favorite media without being in one place, documents for staff what you do and the positive effect it has on teens, and it is easy to use, even if you don't know a lot about computers.

Con: Encourage teens to not say their names when being recorded, and before you post on YouTube or another public website, get the teens' parents to sign a photo or video release form.

Have a DS meetup. A DS (left) is the handheld gaming console made by Nintendo. Consider inviting teens and tweens who have a DS to come to the library to play together.

Pro: Gives gamers a chance to socialize and if you advertise at game stores and movie theatres, you may get new teens in the library doors.

Con: Gamers bring the games themselves so they may not bring multiplayer versions. Teens may share equipment, so provide masking tape and markers for everyone to put their name on the games and the DS before they start playing.

Nintendo DSi game system

Equipment is pocket-size, so make sure that everyone understands the risks in sharing or leaving games unattended.

Borrow equipment. Sometimes local game and computer stores have tech-savvy adults who can come to your library to offer a program.

Pro: Gives teens a place to socialize and play games with their friends.

Con: Equipment could get damaged. If you are using older monitors, make sure they have a port for the red, yellow, and white AV cables, and make sure you have the right games for teen appeal and the console you are borrowing.

SOURCE: Adapted from Jami Schwarzwalder, "Teen Tech Week on a Budget," *Young Adult Library Services* 7 (Winter 2009): 37–38. Used with permission.

50 ways to promote reading in your library
by C. D. McLean

When I want to know how to promote reading to teens, I go to the fount of school library knowledge: independent school librarians.

First step: Be adventurous

1. Step out of your comfort zone and promote something other than fiction.

Many teens (boys especially) are not fiction readers; they may be more interested in your magazine collection.

2. Remember those reluctant readers. Promote YALSA's Quick Picks for Reluctant Young Adult Readers as fast reads. Have a spinner filled with fast reads and label it as such.
3. Get graphic. Many times they appeal to students who wouldn't ordinarily pick up a book.
4. Think outside the book club box. An anime club can lead to a manga or graphic novel club; strategic games or MMORPGs (massively multiplayer online role-playing games) can lead to a fantasy book club; and a writing or author club can lead to reading about writing or reading a particular writer's work.
5. Create some library leaders. Make the library in your school a place for young leaders to develop their skills.
6. Sponsor a poetry slam contest or partner with your school's literary magazine to host an event.

Read or Die anime

7. Have a "book love" session once a month. Serve cookies and ask teachers and students to talk about a book they have recently read and liked.
8. Consider reviewing for a young adult magazine and have your students review as well.
9. If you have all boys or have very competitive students, have a word-reading club and stand back and watch the numbers grow.

Second step: Be bold

10. Put your cool stuff up front. Use that high-traffic area to promote.
11. Books don't have to stay on the shelves. Put high-interest books next to your computers.
12. Use the lure of the forbidden. Tell them a book is banned or controversial.
13. Tie the book to a movie.
14. Have a book-related contest such as a Harry Potter contest.
15. Target your contest prizes. Book gift certificates are great.
16. Make your prize match your audience.
17. Mix it up. Instead of holding separate book clubs for students and faculty, mix it up and have them both at one meeting.

Marketing your materials:
18. Participate in any convocation when students meet for announcements. Place a slide of a new book in the slideshow of announcements.
19. Make your booktalks a blast.
20. Use props for your booktalks.
21. Use your teen actors to do your booktalks.
22. Podcast or vodcast your booktalks. Don't just present to a class; make or have your students make a vodcast and keep it on your library's website.
23. Move 'em out. Prepare a book truck with brightly colored graphics indicating the genre and filled with popular books; take it out to the cafeteria, study halls, or anywhere the kids gather.
24. Create short films to promote the library using faculty and student actors.
25. Celebrate Teen Read Week.

6

Third step: Be organized

26. Make it a point to promote your new books.
27. Print out posters of newly acquired books and post them all over campus.
28. Change your bulletin boards frequently and make them interesting.
29. Have your students and faculty contribute reviews and make those reviews into bookmarks.
30. Update your signature file on your email account with a "What I'm Reading Now" tag.
31. If you go to ALA Midwinter Meetings or Annual Conferences, bring back the advance reader copies and give them out to your students.
32. If your budget permits, be willing to buy books for your book club members.
33. Let your book club kids get first crack at the new books.

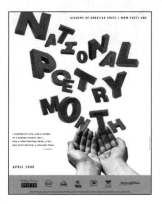

Fourth step: Be welcoming

34. Make the library a welcoming place by hosting parties designed to attract readers.
35. Remember that teens gravitate to online social activities, so by hosting a Dance Dance Revolution night, gaming night, or Guitar Hero night you may attract kids who might not normally come to the library.
36. Host an eat'n'speak or poetry slam. Teens are always writing; have them read their own works.
37. Bring in authors. An author visit may spark interest in reading.
38. Celebrate Banned Books Week.
39. Celebrate National Poetry Month or bring in a poet to speak.
40. Provide food.
41. Host a summer book fair before school ends to encourage reading over the summer.
42. If you charge late fines, be willing to take money off if they come into the library and read.

Fifth step: Be willing to ask for help

43. Have your students lead the book club discussion or have them pick the book.
44. Have your students run your book discussion blog.
45. Have a faculty or student pick of the week or month. Display it all over campus.
46. Ask your students or tech department for help creating a Facebook or Myspace page and list what you are reading or what books you recommend.
47. Ask your students what titles they think are missing from the library; then buy them.
48. Take your students to the bookstore with you.
49. Ask your faculty to sponsor a book for summer reading. Many students will want to read what their favorite teacher is reading.
50. Get your students to do the displays and bulletin boards.

SOURCE: C. D. McLean, "Fifty Ways to Promote Teen Reading in Your School Library," *Young Adult Library Services* 6 (Fall 2007): 8–10. Used with permission.

Give 'em something to talk about

by Michael Nailor

Collaboration between a high school English teacher and a librarian is never easy to pull off. Hopefully our report of this collaboration begins to answer the question of how to make literature from long ago a bit more relevant and interesting to 21st-century high school students. We used social networking technology to enhance this unit; but more importantly we used quality contemporary fiction to get our students talking.

Emily Dickinson

An English teacher and I were looking for a way to make the study of Emily Dickinson more interesting to her students. We wanted to engage students in a conversation with Emily Dickinson to illustrate to them that she is more than a dusty remnant of intellectual life of 19th-century America. We decided that it would also be interesting to engage Emily in conversation with writers of contemporary America. I also wanted these Honors English students who do not read much for fun during the school year to enjoy some of the high-quality fiction written in the last ten years.

Teenagers have some pretty strong preconceived ideas about the nature of poetry and about the poet Emily Dickinson. Their previous training has led them to believe that poetry is for the most part irrelevant. Their previous exposure to Emily Dickinson has focused on her oddity, personally and poetically, and her remoteness from contemporary readers. They have no understanding of the radically modern nature of her poetry, in part because they have no point of comparison.

We decided to take advantage of some of the features of the virtual classroom tool Moodle, introducing students to the discussion forums there. We wanted to engage all students in this conversation, so we accessed our students' prior learning about Emily Dickinson. As a starter, we gave students a copy of the only existing portrait of Emily Dickinson and asked them to post a discussion entry on Moodle on the topic of Emily Dickinson. What did they know about her life? What did they know about her poetry? The results of this "pre-test" revealed that these students had fairly stereotypical knowledge of the poet: how odd her life was, how odd her poetry was.

We chose two Dickinson poems, "'Hope' is the thing with feathers" and "I dwell in Possibility," because all five of the young adult novels in our unit start with ideas about hope and possibility in their first chapters. This instruction was focused on understanding or unpacking the language of the two Dickinson poems by making inferences about the multiple meanings of the language. Students should be able to paraphrase the poems, to make conclusions based on the evidence contained in the poetry about who each speaker is and what the situation of each poem is.

After the initial lesson, I presented booktalks on each of the five young adult novels: *Flight* by Sherman Alexie (2007), *The Christopher Killer* by Alane Ferguson (2006), *A Northern Light* by Jennifer Donnelly (2003), *Girl with a Pearl Earring* by Tracy Chevalier (1999), and *The Bean Trees* by Barbara Kingsolver (1988), all current novels with teens as strong main characters. Their themes could relate easily to Emily Dickinson's main ideas.

Students used Moodle to access links to reviews of each of the five books. After the booktalks and their brief research, they selected their books. Two sections of Honors English were involved in this project. Approximately 10 students chose

6

each book. Their first online discussion assignment was to relate the ideas of hope and possibility from Emily Dickinson to the first 25 pages of their novel and to make a response to another student's posting. We designed a rubric for a "four-star" response and published that online with the assignment. Four additional online discussion assignments focusing on character and theme followed over the next several weeks. The English teacher and I both participated in these online forums.

The culminating project of this six-week unit was a scripted conversation between Emily Dickinson and the main character of the novel that the student read. The format of each conversation was left up to the individual student but it had to include words and evidence from the texts. These projects were submitted in a variety of formats, both in print and in digital formats.

This particular unit had two main instructional goals. First, the content area goal was a deeper understanding of Emily Dickinson as a poet and as a representative of 19th-century American thought. This is appropriate because a familiarity with Emily Dickinson and a familiarity with a pattern for poetry analysis will be helpful to the students in their remaining English courses that they take in high school and in any English courses that they take in college.

> "HOPE is the thing with feathers
> That perches in the soul,
> And sings the tune without the words,
> And never stops at all"

Second, the English teacher and I wanted to engage students in contemporary young adult literature. We envisioned this unit as a conversation between a woman writing 150 years ago and the contemporary authors. A basic understanding of meaning, speaker, and situation was needed to start the conversation.

We knew that students are familiar with social networking sites on the internet and many have conversations online on a daily basis. We were certain that this could translate into an effective learning tool if we employed it in the cause of appreciation of literature. We knew that these students had the ability to make inferences about the poetry and the novels if the lesson and the unit were structured in a way that forced them to do original thinking in a step-by-step process. We knew some students were uncomfortable with instant analysis and needed time to reflect. The asynchronous nature of the discussions in Moodle gave them an opportunity to take time in their reflection and analysis if needed.

This element of choice in selecting which novel to read promotes fairness, equity, and access for all learners in the classroom as well as increasing student interest in the assignment. The student discussions of the five contemporary novels happened in Moodle, a virtual classroom. Each student was required to participate in five discussion assignments forums that we created. The magic of virtual discussions is that each student must participate. Students who are reticent to express their ideas have a medium of expression that seems a little more casual to them; the pressure of the classroom expression is mitigated somewhat by their facility with social networking sites like Facebook and Myspace. All students had in-class time to work on their postings and the ability to sign out a laptop from the library to work on their posts at home. Since the discussions were conducted online they were not confined to just one set time period. This asynchronous element of the discussion allowed students to contribute whenever they had something to say.

We wanted to encourage our students to make inferences or interpretations. We decided to always have two pieces of literature in front of the students at one time. Students, particularly in analyzing poetry, do better work in inference and interpretation if there are easy comparisons at hand. Rather than referring to their memories of other literature, the basic literature assignment should ideally be two works: two poems, or a novel and a poem. These comparisons between works make inference and interpretation easier for students. Our instruction was set up to reward inferences and interpretations. Bringing two works into a conversation with each other fosters deeper student thinking.

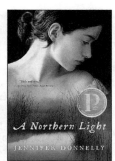

The goals for the unit were met. The ideas from Emily Dickinson were sufficiently understood by the students so that they could begin their conversations about the young adult novels that they selected. Evidence of this understanding can be drawn from the students' online postings about the first 25 pages of their novel. Student excitement about the young adult novels was evident in many of the posts. The enthusiasm about these books is just what we were looking to create.

Finally, we believe the lesson was a success because the online forums provided an avenue for every student in the class to think and to contribute. In response to the first two online assignments there have been a total of 188 postings of student thought. This is a stark contrast to the typical classroom session where so few people get the opportunity to participate in a thoughtful way.

Even though everyone participated in the online discussions and everyone seemed enthusiastic about the literature that they selected, we need to create more opportunities for students to speak in the poetry analysis lesson by doing a little pre-writing so that everyone would have something to contribute when called on. After my initial reading of the poems, I could have asked the students who did not speak to read selected lines. Both the English teacher and I look forward to teaching this unit again so we can create even more opportunities for students to begin their conversations with Emily Dickinson and with contemporary fiction.

SOURCE: Michael Nailor, "Let's Give 'em Something to Talk About: Contemporary Fiction and Nineteenth-Century Poetry," *Learning and Media* 37 (Winter 2009): 8–12. Used with permission.

Building a community of high school readers

by Julia Roberts

"Yo, miss, I read *Monster* in three days. Give me another one just like it." I was thrilled by this muttered demand from a 10th-grader generally regarded as a troublemaker with little interest in academics, much less pleasure reading. This young man had challenged me to find a book he would read, claiming, with some pride, that he had never finished one. Thanks to a simple observation made by me, a voracious reader as well as a school librarian, his demand was an example of the major change that was occurring at Danbury High School (DHS).

Located in Danbury, Connecticut (pop. 80,000), about an hour and a quarter north of New York City, DHS has nearly 3,000 students. Due to a growing immigrant population, 35% of DHS students speak one of 40 languages other than English at home. Nearly half of the students work more than 16 hours per week.

At the end of my first year at DHS, in 2001, I learned that only 14% of the 10th-graders had passed all four sections (mathematics, science, reading across the curriculum, and writing across the curriculum) of the Connecticut Academic

Proficiency Test, and only 24% had passed the reading across the curriculum section. Our staff and administration were stunned.

For most of my professional life, 20 years as a teacher and five as a school librarian, I'd heard that teens did not read for pleasure. The common wisdom was that they were too busy with schoolwork, with sports, with making money; but I didn't buy it or the defeatist attitude that lay beneath it. Research shows that, unless our children became pleasure readers, it's unlikely that they will become analytical readers. Reading comprehension is not only the key to doing well on tests, it is vital to success in many careers. As a school librarian, I felt I could take a powerful role in creating readers, and I was determined to try.

During this upheaval, a veteran English teacher with whom I talked about books, admitted that she was concerned about her students' lack of interest in reading and accompanying lack of skill. Why do we connect so well with books? What motivates us to spend so much of our free time reading and talking about literature of all types, and why don't so many of our students? These questions became the focus of my three-year action research project.

Poor literacy is tied directly to a lack of good books, an absence of reading models, and little time devoted to reading. Most of our students did not have access to interesting reading material in their homes and weren't seeing the adults in their lives reading. Why would they value reading?

I would need to help students discover commonly overlooked genres, get books that they cared about into their hands, and encourage reluctant readers to find the courage to try reading one more time. Each student would have to connect with their perfect book, and I might have only one shot at it.

The official book budget for the library was less than $6,500 per year. While the financial decision-makers claimed they understood that providing interesting books for our students was important, they argued that we couldn't afford it. Curricular books should be the priority, but what is the curriculum? If reading comprehension is the number-one skill needed for success, then pleasure-reading books needed to be part of the curriculum. How could I make that happen?

Getting underway

Finding out what the students wanted to read, acquiring those materials, getting them into the students' hands, and giving them time to read was my vision and drove everything I did. Discovering what they wanted to read was easy. We asked. Once we got suggestions through face-to-face conversations and surveys, acquiring the books was the next hurdle.

DHS is fortunate to have a full-time volunteer who handles many vital functions: running the mentoring program, connecting budding scientists with professionals in the field, and coordinating parent volunteers. She had an office in the library and she heard about our program, "Quick Picks," and offered to help raise funds among her many community contacts to get the project going.

Next my fellow librarians and I shared our ideas with our department chair who helped us lobby the school and district administration using a historical profile of book spending along with a rationale for our request for more money. Over the next three years, we were able to combine funding from foundations, local business grants, donations, and end-of-year district monies to total approximately $150,000. Most of that money was spent on books, including multiple copies of books that would appeal to teenagers for pleasure reading.

I attended department meetings, gave a presentation at a faculty meeting, and

delivered dozens of booktalks. Then I presented the research findings and booktalk ideas at English and reading
department meetings. I had asked my book-loving English teacher to support these presentations with advice that
would give teachers the confidence to try sustained silent
reading (SSR) in class. Some teachers asked nuts-and-
bolts questions that she was able to address. I concentrated
on those who seemed willing, and invited the disinterested
to talk privately with me later. Some teachers allocated 15
minutes a day to SSR, while those who were part of four-curricula teams gave
15 minutes once or twice a week; in effect, that meant that their students would
read daily.

Although I suggested that teachers give no formal assessment of silent reading,
as that is what the research supports, each professional had the leeway to modify
their SSR as long as the students were given time to read. Some had the students
discuss their books, write exit slips, or write brief personal responses. Some required
formal book reports, but most just let their students read. Many teachers modeled
SSR by reading their own literature, a practice recommended in the research. We
knew we were on the right track when our circulation figures rose by 400% during
that first year, but we needed to build momentum.

Going schoolwide

During the second year, another English colleague decided to work with me on
an action research question. We knew more students were reading, but what about
their skills? We spent hours designing methods of obtaining statistics about our
students' reading improvement. Eventually we brought the discussion to our assistant superintendent for curriculum. After listening to our research design, he
helped us refocus on what was important: You don't need to focus on statistics;
you have 30 years of statistics to back your methods. Just find the most reluctant
readers, talk with them, find out what they dislike about reading, and design a
program that will reach them.

We began informally interviewing many students and instituted an open-door
policy for suggestions. We prominently displayed new arrivals with shiny covers.
Local book retailers became familiar with our rush orders, because we promptly
bought nearly every suggested book. We would buy books on our way home, hand
them to students, uncataloged, the day after they requested them. Library heresy;
but we learned that putting the students' enthusiasm and interests first created a
synergy between the library staff and students, many of whom had been leery of
the library.

We bought multiple copies of popular books, including 35 copies of *Monster*,
and replaced at least 20 copies of Tupac Shakur's poetry and lyrics, *The Rose That
Grew from Concrete*, because so many students "lost" their copy. It was a joyous time.

Excitement grew. Teachers reported that whole classes of French, science, and
math students were pulling out books near the end of class to read a few more
paragraphs. Students were reading and talking about books as they walked between
classes. Teens would bring back a book, check it in, then hand it to their friend
who was waiting for it. Girls and guys filled out reserve slips to be next in line for
popular books. One teacher who taught British literature to seniors told his students
to read anything from the *USA Today* best-sellers list every month, British or not.
We realized we needed more books and more funding.

6

Branching out

A social studies teacher who believes passionately in the importance of teaching literacy began to bring her classes to the library for booktalks. She believed if she gave her students time each day for the improvement of reading comprehension skills, using materials they enjoyed, ultimately the students could translate those skills into content-area reading. We discussed how we could incorporate reading strategies into high school classrooms without infringing upon content. She found work done by reading researchers Ann L. Brown and Annemarie Sullivan Palincsar that helped her choose classroom strategies that could be used by content-area teachers.

Then everything changed. We found ourselves in the position of being the most visible stakeholders in a school that had no principal. We were afraid we would lose momentum if we waited until after a new administrator was appointed to implement these ideas. So, we began to attend every meeting that related to our upcoming New England accreditation and No Child Left Behind (NCLB) initiative.

Because NCLB requires district and school improvement plans, we suggested that literacy become the centerpiece of our new plan. We were pleasantly surprised that some department administrators were concerned about literacy, including those teaching mathematics, emerging English learners, science, and even others that we had assumed would not have a strong interest. In response, our leadership team and department administrators decided that every teacher would be asked to include literacy as one of their yearly professional goals. Not all staff members were excited about this new requirement, but it gave our plan credibility and administrative support. Within a few months, a schoolwide reading-strategies goal was in place; all teachers would be trained in reading-comprehension strategies, and their yearly professional goal would include a literacy component.

Positive stories began to drown out the naysayers, and many creative ideas emerged. An art teacher volunteered her Photoshop students to make celebrity READ posters with reading students as the role models. Every age, gender, ethnicity, and ability level was represented. Students were reading in the hallways, bumping into each other as they talked about books. Reading was cool.

A group of students approached us about starting an anime and manga book club, which we agreed to sponsor. Over the year we ordered approximately 400 manga titles and tried to keep up with the plethora of series. Students held weekly meetings after school, showed anime movies, and discussed manga books. The youngster who organized the group grew from being a flighty goofball into a responsible leader. This specialized population became among our most loyal supporters.

To offer assistance to faculty, meetings were held after school where teachers brainstormed and experimented with a variety of classroom strategies. Sometimes they reported that the strategies worked well and produced exciting results. Sometimes they went back to the drawing board. The success stories continued to spread.

The new principal was not scheduled to begin until the first day of the fall semester. Over the summer, assisted by other volunteers and funding from the central district office who had heard the buzz and seen our statistics, we invited author Rosemary Taylor to do a workshop for our school community, as well as all of our school and central office administrators, on leading a school to develop literacy strategies targeted at adolescents. It felt as if we had reached a turning point.

At our first in-service day in the fall, our new principal gave unequivocal support to this literacy work, even posing for one of our READ posters. Because every workshop session was about literacy, all teachers and administrators were armed with strategies and ideas for advancing literacy. It was evident that they felt confident about writing professional literacy goals.

Effect on the library

Our library roles evolved and specialized as our literacy program grew. I became "the book lady." Another librarian specialized in creative, collaborative units with teachers of nearly every department. A third supported and extended students' interests and abilities in technology. Our support staff cheerfully faced new procedures, such as reserved book deliveries to classrooms and enormous numbers of overdue notices. Some students really didn't want to part with their books.

We moved hot titles into the library vestibule for added visibility. A graphic artist at DEMCO created a special Quick Picks label in our school's colors so that students could easily identify the books. Library events snowballed, including poetry slams in collaboration with classroom teachers. Our local newspaper published articles, pictures, and interviews about the initiative, while our school paper created a monthly literacy page and reprinted the reading role-model posters. At that time, the library website included pictures of literacy activities and links to web sources for teen readers.

Oh, yes, about those tests: Those CAPT scores improved. A 9th-grade team used the Stanford Diagnostic Reading Test to pre- and post-test their 80 students. The results: 14 students no longer scored significantly below grade level, 37 improved two grade levels, and 17 improved by three or more grade levels. That was in eight months. In one English class, 50% of those who had identified themselves as reluctant readers at the beginning of the school year reported feeling less reluctant by the end of the year.

The local newspaper ran an article about the rise in teen readership at the Danbury Public Library over the last three years. Although the DHS initiative was not mentioned, we knew we could take credit for part of the increase. We had worked closely with the public library during the project, and one of the public librarians came monthly to sign students up for public library cards. While she often told students about the free videos and CDs available, obviously students found the books, too.

I still live in the Danbury area. Almost daily I run into former students around town. "Yo, miss" and "the book lady" are words from the past. Now they say, "Hi, Mrs. Roberts. I miss you, and I need a book suggestion." One night my husband Ken and I were approached in a superstore by a young man I remembered. Jeff pumped my husband's hand and said, "This woman made me a college student." Ken smiled; I cried; Jeff beamed. What else is there to say?

SOURCE: Adapted from Julia Roberts, "Building a Community of High School Readers," *Knowledge Quest* 35 (September/October 2006): 24–29. Used with permission.

Reaching reluctant readers with nonfiction

by Jamie Watson and Jennifer Stencel

During our years, we've shared books with hundreds of teens, most of whom would describe themselves as not liking to read. Time and again, it is the nonfiction books that teens select first, it is nonfiction that gets passed around and returned much worse for the wear, and it is nonfiction that engages a group enough to talk about issues inside the book.

Most of our teens simply choose not to read, and look at us certain that we could not possibly have anything that interests them. Many of these teens are not committed library users; they are simply in the library because they have nowhere else to go, or they are using the computer, or they have to read for an assignment. Our challenge to find the "right book for the right teen at the right time," and again, nonfiction fills the bill.

Reluctant teen readers think reading = school = assigned fiction. They don't consider nonfiction about rappers, or cars, or their zodiac sign. To the reluctant reader, these interest areas are likely to be their true escape.

Nonfiction also comes in easily digestible pieces, has plenty of pictures and demarcated sections or chapters that make it easy to browse rather than read from cover to cover. The subjects are obvious as well: a sports biography or a drawing book.

The biggest drawback to nonfiction is that it tends to be ephemeral. Pro wrestling titles, which were all the rage five years ago, have waned considerably in popularity. Popular singers come and go as well. Consequently nonfiction has to be strenuously weeded. Titles featuring 'N Sync and Lil' Bow Wow (when he was still Lil') served their purpose admirably, but they can quickly date your entire collection. If you're on a limited budget but want to incorporate some nonfiction, magazines are a great way to acknowledge popular interests with more variety at a lower cost.

Editors' note: An extensive annotated bibliography accompanies the complete article.—*B. W.*

SOURCE: Adapted from Jamie Watson and Jennifer Stencel, "Reaching Reluctant Readers with Nonfiction," *Young Adult Library Services* 4 (Fall 2005): 8–11.

ADVOCACY
CHAPTER SEVEN

Call to action for
library media specialists

by Janice Gilmore-See

School libraries have an image problem with adults. Few adults remember their school library at all, much less how it contributed to their academic success.

Because these adults, who are also decision-makers, often do not know and appreciate the value of the school library, they may see it as an unsupportable luxury. School librarians must focus on the many ways the library is an integral part of the school system and make sure school administrators, parents, and community members know what is going on and how these services directly help students.

Schools that face restructuring may react to low reading scores by cutting the library budget to pay for reading intervention programs. These schools generally serve low-income areas with high-needs students who have little or no access to reading materials at home. Reducing access to the school library only exacerbates the problem. These students often miss out on their favorite subjects—physical education, art, and music—in order to receive double doses of reading instruction, making them less interested in reading.

Dr. Stephen Krashen points out in a July 9, 2008, *USA Today* opinion piece:

> 99% of the U.S. adult population can read and write at a basic level. There is no crisis in basic literacy. The issue is how to achieve higher levels, the ability to read and write complex texts. The only way this happens is by extensive reading. Studies show that if children have access to a plentiful supply of interesting and comprehensible books, nearly all read. The greater the exposure to books, the more they read and the better they read and write. The real problem is that children of poverty have little access to books or high-quality libraries, preventing them from attaining high levels of literacy.

As school librarians, we need to carry Krashen's message to the general public.

One effective way to advocate for school libraries is through the services school librarians can offer students. Librarians become effective library advocates when they:

- create programs and services that attract students;
- loosen policies—lose a few books, gain a few readers;
- recruit and empower advocates;
- update the image of the school library;
- show stakeholders what is happening inside the library.

125

Another effective way is to join local, state, and national library associations and their legislative committees. Calls for action urge school librarians to contact their elected representatives about specific pending legislation. On "legislative days," school and public librarians visit legislators, briefing them about issues affecting libraries.

Another kind of advocacy is subtle and done within any school librarian's sphere of influence. It involves spreading the news of what is happening in the school library.

Some administrators visit and support the library, but many are unaware of what happens there. School librarians often work in isolation. Administrators don't know everything school librarians are doing and don't realize how important the school library is for students. Working inside the school library is only part of the job; school librarians must leave the school library to promote programs and communicate with stakeholders.

School librarians can start by finding out the reputation of the library. They must listen to what parents, teachers, students, and administrators are saying to understand the attitudes and behaviors that follow. If a school board member says, "Libraries are an anachronism, kids can find everything on Google," school librarians need to highlight library features and the technologies that go beyond Google. The library is a place that embraces all students from the high achievers to the students who don't quite fit. The school librarian provides nonjudgmental help and programs to keep students learning every day.

The librarian's attitude lets students know that problems have solutions, that information can be found, and that having accurate information is important. The techniques students learn in the school library will serve them well in life and finding accurate information is a life skill that will help them make better decisions in the future. School librarians help students grow through guided research experiences; they learn from mistakes, try again, and learn to recheck the facts.

What happens when school libraries are targeted as the next cut to balance a budget? The first reaction of school librarians is to attend the school board meeting and proclaim how important they are, timidly stepping to the podium for the brief three minutes they are allowed to try to list the important functions of the library media center (often in terms laypeople don't understand). School librarians need constituents: voters, school administrators, parents, and teachers, to become advocates for the library. When constituents speak up, decision-makers take notice.

School librarians must find thoughtful and creative ways to communicate about the learning that happens in the school library. When possible, students can be given a showcase for their learning and projects so decision-makers can gain an appreciation of the library's contribution to education.

School libraries are not what they were 20 or even 10 years ago. The library may be the only interactive system available to students from home day and night. Students, teachers, and parents use the website to extend the learning day and year. They can access subscription databases and electronic resources from home. They can get online reference assistance 24/7. School librarians should not allow old stereotypes to define what it is now. They can inspire decision-makers. They can recruit and empower others to carry the message forward. They can change the image.

SOURCE: Adapted from Janice Gilmore-See, "Call to Action for Library Media Specialists," *School Library Media Activities Monthly* 25 (January 2009): 51–53. Used with permission.

School library advocacy from an unexpected source

by Carol Heinsdorf

The Association of Philadelphia School Librarians has been actively engaged in school library advocacy since August 2006. The intent has been to inform and educate policy- and decision-makers to the benefits of school library services related to increasing students' academic achievement and literacy. Beginning locally with school district administrators, APSL has steadily enlarged its circle of contacts to include local politicians, news media, the teachers' union, a university, and the Pennsylvania Department of Education.

Recognizing a clear link between high illiteracy rates and high rates of incarceration, we proposed a brief study to the Bureau of Library Development, Office of Commonwealth Libraries. The project and questions were approved by the Department of Corrections, and State Correctional Institution (SCI) librarians who collected the responses.

Respondents are 12 men and six women, ages 22 to 65. Four of the women are mothers with from one to six children apiece. Nine are fathers with from one to 10 children each. One female and one male respondent are grandparents.

The questions asked were:

- In your opinion, what benefits does a school library provide for children?
- Would you like your child to have a terrific school librarian and wonderful school library? Why?

The questions do incline the respondents to answer favorably for making school libraries available to students. Also, SCI librarians would engage inmates known to them in responses to the questions, implying a working relationship with library patron inmates. The thoughtfulness of respondents' answers, however, belies simplistic agreement with the basic assumption.

The benefits of a school library were described from the practical to the sublime. School libraries provide for students "a plethora of reading material, information, and ideas; a place of solace to sit and gather their thoughts; a place to broaden their horizons as well as a place for enjoyment and camaraderie." They provide "research, entertainment, inspiration, imagination . . . and when you start reading, a whole new world to explore." The school library as a place to satisfy curiosity and broaden a child's mind was frequently mentioned. "In their early learning stage, the library provides answers to their many questions." It "provides students with a broader viewpoint and allows children to better understand . . . the ever-changing world they grow up in . . . and learn about life." "It is a fun and relaxing way for children to broaden their horizons, stay out of trouble [this is a mother of six speaking], increase their language skills."

Academic support for the students was a frequent answer. "Books and libraries are where children begin to develop and enrich knowledge." "Information is knowledge. Knowledge on any subject will assist children to obtain better grades." "It provides the opportunity for a child to read, study or research at their own pace." "It gives them the initiative to learn to read better." "It opens the door to discovery and teaches how to research/find answers as well as teaches what question to ask next." "If a child doesn't own a computer he/she can do their research in a library

7

where there's help in need for search of knowledge." "It gives children a quiet place to study, do homework, locate books for book reports or term papers, but most importantly it should help encourage children to learn to read . . . and maybe even more importantly, to enjoy reading."

Librarians were understood to play an important role in helping students in a school library. "When I was a child, when I wanted to learn something, I couldn't learn from my teacher, I taught myself by reading books. When I was a stranger to a library, one librarian guided me to all the rules and regulations of using a library properly. They made me comfortable." "Getting the most out of the materials and resources a library has to offer requires a good librarian to facilitate the operation." Librarians were described as "good people with positive attitudes and behaviors . . . who teach and lead by example." "The librarian will be able to teach my child how to use the library, and all it's resources." "Having a good librarian to guide and direct you in obtaining the required information is a great asset." "A good librarian opens the world to a child." "I want the best for my children."

A thread throughout most of the respondents' answers was the social and family interaction around books and reading. In two different families, grandparents had held on to the books read to their children and then gave the books to the grown children to read once again to their children. Nighttime fears were quelled by parental reading at bedtime; determination to succeed was encouraged across generations through the plot of a picture book passed down, and books were remembered because a parent read them to a kindergartener.

Respondents remembered libraries mostly in public schools, but also in one Catholic and one private school, and a public library. In studying these responses, the greatest impression I take away is the memories generated by significant family members reading to their young children. Now elementary school libraries, with students as "captive patrons," are closing, or certified librarians are replaced with noncertified personnel because school libraries are no longer valued. Consider how many young borrowers lose access to a wealth of books that could be shared with family members at home. Tired working parents do not make the trip to the public library, and in rural areas it is possible that there is no conveniently accessible public library. Where is the level playing field in literacy for these young children?

To finish, one respondent stated that "a good librarian can help shape the mind of a child." Another declared, "The cornerstone of our civilization is books. To hold a book in your hand is a wonderful thing. Failing to recognize this is a great error."

SOURCE: Adapted from Carol Heinsdorf, "School Library Advocacy from an Unexpected Source," *Learning and Media* 35 (Spring 2007): 6–7. Used with permission.

Legislator in the Library Day

by *Christie Kaaland*

Today's school librarians are taking the lead with legislative advocacy for education. In an email interview, school librarian Deb Logan stated that Ohio's school library advocates, working closely with legislators over the past nine years, succeeded in getting language placed in the 2009 House Bill 1 that included funding for the "licensed librarian and media specialist." In 2008–2009, members of the Pennsylvania Library Association worked with Rep. Keith R. McCall (D-Carbon County), Speaker of the Pennsylvania House in 2009–2010, to insert language in the Accountability Block Grant program that allows special funding above the basic education subsidy allocated to each school district to be spent on school library resources (Deb Kachel, email interview with author, November 19, 2009).

Advocacy in Washington State

Advocates for school library programs in the state of Washington made historic legislative inroads in 2009 with the passage of Substitute House Bill 2261. Arguably, the most important factor in Washington's legislative advocacy has been librarians' vigilant participation. During the 2008 and 2009 legislative sessions and, more importantly, during education subcommittee task force meetings leading to that bill, Washington school librarians attended each and every meeting and session. Because of this, many legislators came to recognize that school librarians in Washington truly care about educational policy. They care enough to be involved.

Washington Gov. Christine Gregoire signs Substitute House Bill 2261 into law, May 2009

Both the priority placement of school librarians within the body of the final bill and the language used reflect the high level of involvement that school librarians had in the evolution of this legislation. It is important to note that this priority placement is second only to school administrators; 12 other staff positions follow.

Washington school librarians quickly discovered, however, that it was not enough just to pass a law. Advocacy activity for passing this bill was only the first step; the next step involved the rollout for funding priorities and implementation of this bill, which had an eight-year calendar. Thus, involvement had to be constant and ongoing. Such activism, continuing at its previous and current rate, could help guarantee the future of the profession in Washington.

Legislator in the Library Day

One of the successful legislative advocacy strategies applied in Washington, designed around a similar Pennsylvania model, has been the Legislator in the Library Day. The event involves inviting a local senator or representative to spend a day or part of the day visiting the school library. Washington's school librarians wanted to remain in high profile and Legislator in the Library Day seemed the perfect vehicle for such exposure. It was strategically imperative to select schools whose libraries modeled strong 21st-century programs, because many legislators were still working from an old-fashioned librarian frame of reference.

School librarians who hosted legislators during the fall of 2008 were surprised to discover how nonthreatening and receptive their legislators were, particularly those serving on education committees. Building on the success from the 2008 Legislator in the Library Day, advocacy chairs were able to present the event to select school librarians for this second year in a less intimidating and more celebratory fashion. The state was divided into four regions and school librarians in legislative districts around the state whose libraries modeled strong 21st-century programs were contacted. An email invitation was crafted and sent out to key individuals from the Washington Library Media Association's Advocacy Committee detailing how the visits would transpire, the roles each would assume (advocacy chair and school librarian), and what to expect during the visit.

The effects of these visits have yet to be fully realized. While members of

7

WLMA's Advocacy Committee are still determining what works best, to date these visits have accomplished many of the following goals:

- increased political contact with legislators;
- increased visibility—an issue that often arises with libraries in general;
- improved legislator understanding of services and resources provided by today's school libraries;
- reminded legislators how rapidly school communities change, the importance technology plays in students' educational experiences, and the changing role the library program plays in those experiences;
- opened a dialogue around today's changing information and communication skills (cybersafety, authentication of internet resources);
- showed how the library is the perfect environment for providing equitable access to technology and other resources for all students.

Overall, the most important outcomes for the school librarian hosting Legislator in the Library Day is that it demonstrates that important model of leadership and increased exposure to the school library of the 21st century. Strategies for determining where to focus these visits include the following:

- legislative districts in which a legislator has indicated support for school libraries and an understanding of the role of 21st-century school libraries in education;
- specific schools with high-needs students and/or high level of poverty in which students do not have equitable access to information and resources outside of school;
- legislative districts involving members of educational subcommittees;
- exemplary school librarians who have developed strong library programs.

Carrying the message forward

Obviously, all of these benefits do not occur with every visit, and the process for re-educating educational leaders about what the 21st-century school library can offer is an ongoing task. But, the potential for bringing many members of the political and school community together in a library setting is limitless, not simply for the preservation of school libraries but, more importantly, for moving the profession forward in the 21st century and providing equitable access for all library services to students, WLMA advocates hope other states will build on these strategies for implementation and will carry out this model across the United States.

Legislator in the Library Day

The day was a winning advocacy model for all educational stakeholders:

Children in the schools are able to meet and talk to one of their local legislators, probably for the first time.

Legislators find that this visit is potentially transformative. As legislators meet and engage in dialogue with students in the library, they are able to hear firsthand what today's libraries provide. Principals are able to reinforce with legislators the notion of 21st-century information skills. Additionally, legislators love the positive publicity; visits provide excellent photo ops taken within their legislative districts: meeting, greeting, and reading with children (libraries provide delightful and strategic background images), looking over children's shoulders as they engage in research and use new technologies in the library, and meeting teachers and parents.

Administrators love meeting political leaders under optimal, positive conditions. Principals look good to their administrators; library administrators are seen as political advocates. All this action is taking place in the library, modeling the library as the academic heart of the school.

School board members might also be invited.

School librarians are seen as political activists, concerned educators, and educational leaders, all within the framework of exposing those visitors to a 21st-century school library environment. Here's how to do it:

Samantha shows Pennsylvania Rep. Dick Stevenson how to use ebooks at the Grove City Senior High School Library on April 8, 2011. Photo: Pennsylvania School Library Association.

- Agree to host your legislator for an hour or two in your library.
- Do what you always do: outstanding work with students and teachers. Make sure you have students in the library the entire time and class(es) scheduled on the day of the visit to truly show the legislator what you do, and more importantly, what is possible when school libraries are staffed with qualified, quality professionals.
- You will coordinate with your principal and district office so they know when the visit will be happening and make sure all district policies are followed (e.g., photo release).
- You will invite your principal and parents (if you have any idea of their political affiliation, it would be wise to have parents from the legislator's political party) to come during the visit and talk to the legislator about the impact the school library makes on them.
- Have coffee and treats on hand to host the legislator.
- And at the end, bask in the glory of the experience.

SOURCE: Adapted from Christie Kaaland, "Legislator in the Library Day: A Model for Legislative Advocacy," *School Library Monthly* 26, no. 7 (March 2010): 44–46. Used with permission.

Educating school administrators
by Deborah Levitov

Administrators are identified as key players in the success of school library programs and in the success of school librarians. Yet research has shown that administrators continue to have little understanding of what the school library program is, can be, or should be in the school setting, nor are administrators familiar with the roles a school librarian can play in the school academic program. The school librarian is often the only one who keeps the school administrator informed about the library, the role of the librarian, standards for learning and programs, and the place for the library program in the academic plan.

Upon entry into the position of school administrator, these educators often bring only their personal experience about libraries or brief coverage in administrative coursework (for example, copyright or budgeting) that touches on school libraries, entering their administrative professional careers viewing the school librarian in more traditional library roles. Most are unaware of the standards developed for school libraries, research available about school libraries, resources available to manage and guide them, or the roles outlined for school librarians.

On-the-job training

A traditional solution for informing administrators about school library programs is through one-on-one contact with school librarians. In this scenario, school librarians raise the awareness of the administrator through their actions on behalf of the school library program and through interactions with the administrator. This is a phenomenon corroborated in an interview conducted by school librarian Carl Harvey in which the principal establishes how he came to learn about school libraries and the value of the program through the work of Harvey. This on-the-job training has served as a solution to informing principals and advocating for library programs. Research by Linda B. Alexander and James O. Carey in 2003 supports the important role of the school librarian in educating the school administrator: "The building level professional is the only one with the opportunity for day-to-day influence on the perceptions of the principal."

It is essential for school librarians to realize that they must serve as a central source for educating school administrators about school library programs on a daily basis. Timothy Snyder, a school principal, reiterates the power of the school librarian in *Getting Lead-Bottomed Administrators Excited about School Library Media Centers* (Libraries Unlimited, 2000), stating, "The survival of school libraries depends on the commitment of its stakeholders, and the extent of that commitment rests with its professionals: They hold the key to their destiny; they have the power to shape decisions. They can—and must—sell their programs to critical decision-makers."

Meaningful communication

School librarians must find ways to communicate with administrators about library programs in a way that benefits the administrators' work and resonates with their needs (speaks their language, links to their agenda, reflects their priorities). The American Association of School Librarians' *Standards for the 21st-Century Learner* serves as a perfect example of language alignment. By using the language found in the Partnership for 21st Century Skills (P21) initiative, AASL has done a brilliant job of making the connection through the AASL standards document to common language used in the educational setting through P21.

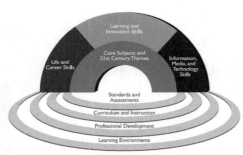

A framework for 21st-century learning, developed by the Partnership for 21st-Century Skills

In a comparison of P21 and the AASL standards, Gail Formanack emphasizes, "The new standards reflect many of the Partnership for the 21st Century Skills of critical thinking and problem-solving, creativity and innovation, and communication and collaboration." She goes on to state, "Substantive discussion about the language in both of these documents is needed to change the culture of library media centers." School librarians need to study, understand, and make use of the language of these documents to make connections to the priorities of school administrators, thus helping them understand how the library program links directly to academic goals for students. Similar links should be made related to other curriculum initiatives as they arise. This is a key component for meaningful communication about school libraries when talking with administrators.

Show, not tell

School principal Steven M. Baule suggests the school librarian should "show (not tell) administrators how the school library program can help them." According to Baule, the goals of the school library program should be linked to the school-improvement plan and requests from the school librarian should be framed in this context. He also emphasizes that the school librarian should not focus on standards you will meet but what students will be able to do that they could not do previously.

Baule states that school librarians should be in regular communication with their administrator, should have a presence on school committees, and should serve the entire school community. As a result, "the school library media program will gain stature through your strategic involvement in all aspects of the school." This type of personal, one-on-one communication and advocacy helps inform administrators about school libraries and helps to raise their awareness.

A worthy and necessary goal

According to Alexander and Carey's 2003 Kentucky survey, fewer than 10% of the principals responding had taken a college course that included content related to school librarians and principal collaboration. Yet principals who had participated in such course work "rated the library media center significantly higher than the principals who had not taken a course." This indicates those who have more background knowledge about school libraries have a more favorable view of programs.

Finding ways to educate administrators about school libraries is, therefore, a worthy goal. Also, since the most reliable methods of educating administrators is through day-to-day interaction with the school librarian, it is essential for school librarians to take a leadership role toward building understanding, garnering support, and building advocacy.

Character traits for the school librarian

In a literature review by Donna Shannon, research shows that "school library media specialists' confidence, initiative, communication skills, and leadership qualities were important factors for those who were active players in the total school curriculum and instructional program." Shannon's review of literature regarding interpersonal and communication skills of the school librarian shows that:

> overwhelming evidence of the importance for school librarians to possess effective communication and interpersonal skills. These competencies appear basic to all aspects of the work of school librarians and are judged essential by school administrators, teachers, and school librarians themselves.

Principals who participated in a study related to the online course "School Library Advocacy for Administrators," offered by Mansfield University of Pennsylvania, described important qualities needed by school librarians with words like "personality, communicator, energizer, cheerleader, voice, leader, or advocate." The role of the school librarian described by these administrators indicated that "personality counts, leadership is key, advocacy is essential, and communication is imperative."

7

In summary

The school librarian remains the main resource for informing school administrators about school library programs and the role of the school librarian in education. Thus the school librarian should not underestimate the importance of communicating with and educating school administrators on an ongoing basis. AASL's *Standards for the 21st-Century Learner* and its *Empowering Learners: Guidelines for School Library Media Programs* give every school librarian reason to make a plan for bringing school administrators up-to-date on these new standards. This can serve as the beginning or continuation of a communication habit that will build better understanding and knowledge of school libraries and the role of school librarians.

SOURCE: Adapted from Deborah Levitov, "Educating School Administrators," *School Library Monthly* 26 (February 2010): 45–47. Used with permission.

Putting students first

by Debra Kay Logan

When we talk about advocating for school libraries, what do we truly mean? Are school libraries an end or a means? Should schools have school libraries just to have a library? Should schools have school librarians simply to have a school librarian?

Before answering these questions, put aside what you know about school libraries and how they support the educational goals of a school. Instead, think about these questions from administrative and budgetary viewpoints. School libraries are traditionally seen as rooms with resources, with school librarians viewed as keepers of materials. Under this pretense, it's no wonder that libraries and librarians are sometimes thought of as expendable.

If the mission of schools is to prepare students to live, work, and learn in the 21st century, many school administrators must be wondering how the school library fits in. Compounding this dilemma is the approach that school librarians have been taking to advocacy: Merely stating that we need school libraries and librarians sounds self-serving and does nothing to align our work with educational goals. When we advocate for school libraries and librarians, we know the many ways our services, programs, and professionalism serve students, teachers, and schools. However, most of our listeners have tuned out.

One definition of advocacy is, "Informed stakeholders standing up for a cause, program, or idea." Under this definition, it is easy to see why decision-makers view school librarians who stand up for their libraries as whiners rather than advocates. That doesn't mean we should stop our efforts to build support. However, it is crucial that we change the nature of our messages while building stakeholder support for school library programs.

To become effective advocates, our profession must shift the focus of our messages from speaking out about school libraries to promoting and supporting student learning and achievement. Student success is the business of schools. Student learning is at the core of meaningful advocacy messages. To be effective school library advocates, we must advocate for students.

Building true advocacy

Since our advocacy mission and messages must be about serving students and must convey that school libraries are essential to meeting student needs, just who is going to come out and say we need strong school libraries and librarians? We need to have stakeholders advocate for them, and it is our job to build this stakeholder support.

Who are these stakeholders? Out best advocates are the members of our learning communities. When students, parents, teachers, and administrators know and experience the benefits of a strong school library program, they can be our most effective advocates. Stop and think about that. Which is more powerful: a librarian who says that libraries and librarians are necessary, or a group of community members fighting for school libraries and access to professional staffing?

How do we foster increased advocacy among our stakeholders? Answering that question necessitates the expansion of our definition of advocacy. But we must also note that good advocacy building is ubiquitous. Building advocacy should be embedded in the school librarians' daily practice.

Motivate stakeholders to advocate

Let's start with what we already know. Wrapping school library advocacy efforts around students and learning is a natural connection. School librarians and libraries are both essential and effective means to helping schools meet their educational missions for students. Study after study shows that school libraries are the means to achieving educational goals common to good schools.

Just flipping through Scholastic's report on school libraries (*School Libraries Work!*) provides an overview of the educational benefits of school libraries and professional media specialists. Projects like the Partnership for 21st Century Skills identify what students need to know to be successful in life and work.

We know that school librarians are teachers who are uniquely qualified to deliver this critical content and help prepare students. To ensure that our students have access to the essential information and skills provided by school librarians, they need access to school libraries. Students without access to professionally staffed school libraries are being left behind. Yet what seems more difficult for our community of librarian-teachers to grasp is how to teach our stakeholders. Clearly, our traditional library message is no longer working. When research evidence is presented in isolation, listeners inevitably question the validity of research. Instead of simply sharing research studies, school librarians need to "mash up" research findings with what we know about our specific programs.

7

Mashing the data

To start, we need to clearly and consistently articulate and highlight the research showing the connections between strong school library programs and student learning and success. This forms a firm foundation for stakeholder advocacy.

Document the connection between research in the library and reading and writing standards as an integral part of weekly lesson plans. Make the library's connection to reading and writing standards part of curriculum maps.

When crafting an advocacy message, focus on specific and essential student needs and how school libraries and librarians are the primary providers of those skills and resources within a school. Share evidence that ties research findings with what is happening in your school. Connect research findings to what your school library provides that can't be found anywhere else in the school. Show that the library's unique services are important to students. Give that information a face with anecdotes from or about actual students.

What do students know and what are they able to do because of your library and instruction? Clearly demonstrate that school libraries and media specialists play vital roles in preparing students for success. True advocacy messages from school librarians are student-centered.

While the goal of evidence-based practice is to improve practice and inform decision-making, the gathering and use of qualitative and quantitative evidence collected for this purpose can be a powerful and multifaceted resource for building advocacy. Asking students to write about what they have learned and how they will use that learning provides qualitative evidence directly from the students. End each lesson with these questions and then share this information with teachers, administrators, and other stakeholders.

Ultimately, students are the library's most persuasive advocates. Their quotes, especially when paired with examples of student work, provide concrete evidence of student learning and of the library's alignment with and support for learning-community goals. Teachers and administrators will realize that their students need the services of the library because the library and librarian make a difference in student learning.

One of the most powerful advocacy benefits from evidence-based practice is indirect and hidden. When students are asked about what they learn and how they are going to use it after instruction, metacognition about learning takes place; Students reflect on learning and its importance. They begin to identify and realize tire value of the library and can become direct and active library advocates.

It's all about the students

All along we have known that school libraries play a critical and unique part in helping schools achieve their goals for students. However, our messages have sounded like school libraries and librarians are ends, not means. It's time to adjust

these messages and become advocates for students and student learning. This means we also need to build support and foster school library advocacy among our stakeholders. We need to help the educational community see that school libraries and librarians are critical in making that happen.

We can no longer rely on the kinds of evidence we have traditionally shared with stakeholders. We need to focus on gathering, using, and sharing data and other evidence that directly shows our contribution to learning. This is essential as we continuously work to build the support of our learning communities.

School libraries and librarians are a powerful means to help prepare students to live, work, and learn in the 21st century. Our students need us to advocate for them to have access to the learning made possible through school libraries and professional librarians. Our message is about what research and our evidence shows about what contributes to student success. Our message is about students and what they need and must have. We are student advocates.

SOURCE: Debra Kay Logan, "Putting Students First," *American Libraries* 39 (January/February 2008): 56–59. Used with permission.

The School Library Link

by Michelle McGarry

As a stay-at-home mom for 10 years who didn't want to go back to work in the frenzy of magazine publishing, I decided to go back to school to become a school librarian. Running a school library seemed like an enjoyable and worthwhile profession, even if I really didn't know much about school library programs and didn't think my potentially fun job in the library would turn into a cause.

A learning curve. During my first year of library studies I discovered how much school library programs contribute to student achievement. The evidence is overwhelming, from the landmark Colorado studies done by Keith Curry Lance to every other study done in other states in this country. All of these studies speak to the invaluable contributions of school library programs, and yet school library programs are among the first to get cut. School librarian positions are the first to be downsized, and lawmakers seem unmotivated to write school library programs into the laws as "essential education." Why is it that no one seems to care about school library programs? Why is no one listening?

It occurred to me that school libraries are a hard sell because they're not flashy— only an extra program and an easy cut to a budget. Why? Because despite advocacy efforts with lawmakers, regular people don't really know how school libraries fit into the school system. As a parent who genuinely wants to support my kids' education in any way I can, even I did not know what my kids were missing. I know now, and my kids are being deprived. With only two certified school librarians in my town, one for the middle school and one for the high school, each elementary school is staffed only by a part-time paraprofessional. Not many parents seem to think there is anything wrong with only paraprofessionals in the elementary libraries. What school library programs do for kids wasn't reaching one important group—parents. If a school administrator announced, "We're going to eliminate all the reading specialists in town and replace them with parent volunteers," parents would come screaming. Say the same thing about school librarians and maybe there would be some disgruntled rumblings, but that's all. It is evident that the image of school librarians needs to be changed with parents.

A grassroots approach. Advocacy was a topic of discussion in every class I took. The idea for a monthly school library newsletter for parents came to me when I was brainstorming what I could do in my own school library once I graduated and got a job. Every school library should have a communication program set up to make contact with parents. What about a newsletter? My classmates looked at me with mixed expressions, "That sounds like a lot of work." I realized that a lot of school librarians may not like to write. So, what if I created a newsletter not only for my school library, but for all school librarians to send home to parents?

The School Library Link is born. I decided to create *The School Library Link* (*TSLL*), a free newsletter, to help school librarians promote their school library programs for parents. *TSLL* is a turn-key promotional tool that school librarians can use to educate parents about the benefits of school library programs. Even though this newsletter is designed for parents, teachers can certainly use it, too. Available for download in PDF (Adobe Acrobat) format, *TSLL* is meant as a quick read for parents to learn about how the school library provides the "link" to a plethora of invaluable learning skills that include reading development, multiple literacies, inquiry, and curriculum learning.

The newsletter is geared for elementary and middle school libraries. By the time students reach high school, not many are bringing flyers home. The aim is

7

also to indoctrinate parents early. Let them know about school libraries when their children are young.

Making the message accessible. In order to get the message out to parents, school librarians have to dole it out in segments. Parents can't be bombarded with all the information at once. It has to be offered gradually, consistently, pleasantly. The message should be offered in short bits that parents will actually have time to read. The newsletter takes a lesson from Advocacy 101 and focuses on benefits to students and parents, rather than features of the school library program. Benefits are the real "money-makers." Benefits are the outcomes of school library programs and how they positively affect students and student achievement. Instead of writing about how many computers, write about some specific lessons students may learn using computers: internet safety or citing sources online. *TSLL* is about the benefits of school library programs because this is the piece parents are missing. Parents see the books; they see the computers. They just don't know what school librarians teach their kids using those tools.

First, to get parents to read the newsletter, I made it simple. *TSLL* contains three headlines maximum and maybe two sidebars. Second, each issue has a theme,

something central to school librarianship that parents need to know and that they are interested in. (Often what is identified as important for parents to know and what parents are actually interested in are two different things.) Each issue has a theme that begins with the phrase, "The School Library Link to . . ." such as "Reading Readiness," "Online Technologies," "Curriculum Learning," and more. Third, every article aims to include two or three practical tips that parents can use right away. A tip might suggest two or three search engines they could use to help their children find kid-friendly websites or the names of three publishers that publish children's nonfiction books that stimulate visual learning. These are two tips that were included in the debut issue of *TSLL*, September 2009, "The School Library Link to Information Literacy."

Address what is important to parents. Parents will respond to information about school libraries if it speaks to their needs and their concerns. Parents already know how influential technology is to their children and are concerned about this; they just don't know that school librarians help teach kids about information and technology.

Parents typically don't know a whole lot about collaboration either. Parents don't know the academic achievement that follows successful collaboration; but they are interested in boosting their children's academics. They just need to be told about librarians who teach students how to use databases to do research, find appropriate websites, and cite their sources.

Creating advocates. The goal is to start communicating with parents on a regular basis. Let them get to know school librarians. Let the importance of school libraries seep into their consciousness. Let them discuss with one another what's going on after they glance at each month's issue. Give parents specific, practical tips to help them help their children learn. After all, that's what school librarians are here to do. Slowly but surely, month by month, perhaps someday there will be scores of parents across the country who will be advocating for us.

SOURCE: Adapted from Michelle McGarry, "The School Library Is the Link to Connecting with Parents," *School Library Monthly* 26, no. 3 (November 2009): 45–47. Used with permission.

UNDERSERVED
CHAPTER EIGHT

Access for students with disabilities
by Helen R. Adams

At one time, few school library professionals considered how to accommodate students with disabilities in their library media centers. This situation changed, however, when Congress passed the following three major laws that impact how students with disabilities are educated:

1. **The Rehabilitation Act of 1973.** This act and its reauthorizations prohibit discrimination against individuals, including K–12 students, on the basis of a disability in programs receiving federal financial assistance. School districts must implement procedures to ensure that students with disabilities have access to the full range of programs, activities, and services, and Section 504 calls for schools to develop specific plans to meet the needs of individual students.

2. **The Individuals with Disabilities Education Act (IDEA).** IDEA requires "public schools to make available to all eligible children with disabilities a free appropriate public education in the least restrictive environment appropriate for their individual needs." Students with disabilities must be considered for assistive-technology use if it is needed to meet the requirement for free and appropriate public education.

3. **The Americans with Disabilities Act of 1990 (ADA).** Under Title II of the ADA, public schools must provide those with a disability an equal opportunity to all programs, services, and activities, and follow specific architectural standards in new construction or renovation of older buildings. However, public schools are not required to make accommodations or modifications that would result in undue "financial and administrative burdens."

Because of this federal legislation, students meeting the various definitions of "disabled" are educated with their peers instead of being isolated, and they have the right to be active users of the school library.

State laws also address the accessibility of instructional resources for those with disabilities. For example, in 2000 Kentucky passed the Accessible Information Technology (AIT) Act, requiring public schools to provide students with disabilities access to information technology "that is equivalent to the access provided individuals who are not disabled." Because state legislation varies, school library professionals should check with local special education staff and/or district legal counsel to determine which laws apply to their respective library media programs.

School library professionals have an ethical responsibility to provide access to the facilities, resources, and services in the library media program for students with physical, cognitive, and learning disabilities, as well as chronic illnesses and disorders. The Code of Ethics of the American Library Association states in Article I: "We provide the highest level of service to all library users through appropriate and usefully organized resources; equitable service policies; equitable access; and accurate, unbiased, and courteous responses to all requests." Every student, regardless of whether he or she has a disability, has a First Amendment right to receive information in the library media center, and it is the responsibility of the school library professional to protect that right. Access to the library media program and its resources and services is an integral part of the intellectual freedom of students with disabilities.

School library professionals provide access to the library for students with disabilities by:

- meeting the requirements of federal and state laws relating to students with disabilities;
- eliminating physical barriers that prevent student users from entering the library and/or obtaining resources and services (such as heavy entrance doors, insufficient width between shelving units, shelving that is too high, furniture set too closely together for free movement across the facility);
- creating a welcoming atmosphere for all students;
- being knowledgeable about positive learning strategies and the needs of individual students;
- selecting resources in various formats that fit students' intellectual and physical abilities;
- building a collection that includes resources that reflect accurate information about persons with disabilities;
- ensuring that students with disabilities can locate, retrieve, and use the selected resources successfully (clear signage, adequate lighting);
- procuring assistive technologies that allow those with special needs to work as independently as personally possible (magnification devices, text-to-voice software);
- providing differentiated instruction in library media and technology skills to ensure students with disabilities are successful lifelong information seekers;
- collaborating with special education staff; and
- advocating for the budget, staff, and services to meet the needs of students with disabilities using the library media center.

SOURCE: Adapted from Helen R. Adams, "Access for Students with Disabilities," *School Library Media Activities Monthly* 25, no. 10 (June 2009): 54. Used with permission.

Accommodating learning differences
by Sandy Guild

Greg sits at the table with a lost look on his face. He is confronted with finding information on Pallas Athena and her relationship to public life in Athens. He is responsible to the other students in his group, who are working on other aspects of public life in ancient Athens, to come up with his contribution. It is clear that he doesn't know where to begin, despite an opening review on how to approach a reference set: Try the index first.

Knowing the issues outlined in his Individualized Education Program (IEP), the librarian offers him the option of using an ebook version of a reference source.

By using that format, all Greg has to do is use the search option to find the relevant material, bypassing the need to come up with the particular keyword that was indexed. Nor does he have to navigate an index page's alphabetic organization, complete with subheadings. The librarian subsequently guides Greg to a source rich in illustration from among those held by the library. On the page on Pallas Athena is a photograph of a Greek statue of Athena which brings some of her attributes to life. Greg comes to understand her as the source of order in the city as he thinks about the warrior's spear in her one hand, the symbol of a conforming civic duty for Athenian men, and the distaff in her other hand, the corresponding domestic symbol for Athenian women.

The need to make libraries and their materials accessible to those with learning differences is, at its most basic, merely the elaboration of a core responsibility of librarians to make a wide variety of ideas and current information available to all within the defined community, whether that community is a city or a school. Greg's librarian, by being aware of Greg's challenges, was able to provide avenues to information using modalities that allowed him to concentrate on understanding the material, rather than using all his mental resources just to access it. As the battle rages over whether mainstreaming or inclusion is the way to go for providing services to the student with learning differences, it is nevertheless clear that, except for the most challenged students, typical school libraries are being expected more and more frequently to accommodate students with learning differences.

Learning differences: The basics

Under the Individuals with Disabilities Education Act (IDEA), a learning disability is defined as a "disorder in one or more of the basic psychological processes involved in understanding or in using spoken or written language, which may manifest itself in an imperfect ability to listen think, speak, read, write, spell or to do mathematical calculations." Learning differences (LD) may result in difficul-

---

IDEA: Individuals with Disabilities Education Act

In 2005–2006, 6.7 million students (14% of the U.S. public school population) qualified for special education services under IDEA; this figure includes students with physical, mental, and emotional disabilities, as well as those with learning disabilities. Six percent of that same population qualified under the definition for specific learning disabilities, the largest disabled group within that 14%.

That number does not include those served in private schools or those without formal identification. With the reauthorization of IDEA in 2004 and the publication of the final implementing regulations in August 2006, the requirements for compliance with IDEA have become more stringent. The 2004 modifications to IDEA align educational achievement with the provisions of No Child Left Behind, placing a new emphasis on measured progress toward meeting defined academic achievement standards. The incidence of students receiving services under IDEA and its predecessor has grown over the last decade, with the largest increase among students who spend the least time out of the regular classroom in specialized instruction. Under the 2004 reauthorization of IDEA, no longer must the discrepancy between intellectual ability and performance persevere in order to qualify for services, thereby contributing to the growing number of students served. These are the students who are finding their way into the school library.

8

ties with memory or organization, or in a lack of focus. A student with a learning difference may read at a level significantly below the norm for his age, be unable to respond to oral directions, or exhibit difficulties in written expression.

Despite this diminished skill level, however, a learning difference does not alter the underlying intelligence of the student. A consistent qualifying measure for the diagnosis of any of these learning differences is a significant gap between the individual's intelligence (as measured by an intelligence test) and his performance. Thus a student who reads significantly below the norm for his age but at the norm for his intelligence does not meet the criteria for a learning difference.

Learning differences make unavailable one or more of the tools used to acquire, process, synthesize, or use information. Successful accommodation strategies create alternate paths to appropriately complex information and its use. By providing accommodations, we are able to help students bridge the gap in the learning cycle created by the learning differences. There is, however, an important difference between accommodations provided to support academic goals and modifications to curriculum content. Accommodations do not simplify the material to be learned, but only the effort required to learn it. In contrast, modifications lower the academic standards associated with the curriculum in response to learning differences.

This dumbing down of curriculum leads to a loss of self-esteem for the student for whom allowances have been made. What is worse, though, is that it consigns students with LD to a diminished potential. The librarian has a core responsibility to prevent this from happening.

By providing ready access to appropriate materials and assistance with supportive technology, the librarian makes accommodation a simpler task for both student and teacher; and with fewer mental resources employed in overcoming processing, memory, or organizational limitations, the students with LD can apply their mental resources to performing the higher-order functions of critical thinking and meaning construction that represent real learning. But the school library's central role in student learning must be supported by adequate resources, appropriate staffing, and administrative engagement to ensure the full academic success of students with learning differences.

Kate Fitzgerald, librarian at Westmark School in Encino, California, provides a vivid example of the difference that a school library can make in the life of a student. Westmark School is a college preparatory school that provides a multisensory approach to learning for students with learning differences. Jared, a 6th-grade student, entered Westmark with a 2nd-grade reading level and low decoding skills. He also came with a bright, inquisitive mind. The challenge was to find the mix of accessible skill level and complexity of content that would provide success while engaging his intellect. Kate proposed he try a children's adaptation of *The Adventures of Tom Sawyer*. The story captured him and he became a reader. He went on to read through every adapted classic he could get, despite the struggles that this entailed. His reading skills continued to lag well behind his academic abilities, and he eventually turned to audiobooks to provide the content he needed. His early eagerness to become literate, born of engagement with the right material, was a mainstay  of his life at Westmark. He is now using audiobooks almost exclusively and doing well in college, free to explore a broadened definition of literacy anchored in the' application of critical-thinking skills to content.

Numerous studies have attested to the importance of good school libraries for student success. School libraries serving an LD population can help ensure that these students join their classmates in their success. Among the important components of an effective program are student supports, including, but not limited to, adaptive technologies; current, diverse, and informative materials in multiple media; and quality services in an accessible environment.

Often, simple adjustments in the normal environment of the library can make significant improvement in student accessibility. For example, the addition of color coding to signage provides an extra cue to aid in location of resources. Thoughtful space planning that allows for quiet seclusion while studying may involve the addition of study carrels with side aprons to help block visual distractions. Numerous and conveniently located electrical outlets minimize the effects of battery power loss for a student body heavily dependent on laptop support.

With the quantum leap in bandwidth, processor speed, and memory capacity, audio and video files are now a convenient addition to the range of media available to teaching and learning in the LD community. Easily integrated into lesson plans, accessibility of audio and video media also makes them a natural resource for student study and exploration. By making the school library a central repository for digital media access and technical support, we make a significant contribution to the learning opportunities for students with learning differences, especially those for whom text presents a problem. In addition, by making visual and audio media a part of the general collection of the library, rather than segregating them as a separate resource for students with special needs, these digital resources are normalized. Similarly, large-print books, extremely useful in working with some types of visual-tracking difficulties, need to be integrated into the overall schema of organization within the print collection as just another vehicle for accessing stories or information.

The issue of normalization cannot be overestimated. Recently I talked with Dave Brubaker, librarian at Delaware Valley Friends School, an independent, college-preparatory middle and high school for students with learning differences in Paoli, Pennsylvania. After some years working with this student population, he continues

Students at Delaware Valley Friends School, Paoli, Pennsylvania

to be surprised by the self-inflicted stigma that surrounds student use of adaptive technology or learning aids in his school. It is not unusual for a student to eschew the use of a visual dictionary because he thinks it will be perceived as childish by others. In a community built upon positive approaches to learning differences and access to learning, students may nevertheless avoid using accommodations or assistive technology; students feel the use of these aids may brand them. The typical adolescent preoccupations with conformity to peer norms of behavior only exacerbate the problem.

Dave also related that the use of adaptive technology can be seen by the student as unnecessarily complicated, despite the positive outcome. Often, this is the result of insufficient experience with the software. By building time into the curriculum to explore the usefulness of learning aids and to develop technical proficiencies, as well as by guiding students as they plan for the additional time necessary to make best use of these accommodations, their use becomes a standard expectation for

8

the community as a whole. Finally, though, it is the successful learning experience designed by a knowledgeable, sensitive, and enthusiastic librarian or teacher, enabled by appropriate accommodations, that will overcome student resistance.

Librarians, whether they serve a primarily LD-challenged population or one into which LD-challenged individuals have been mainstreamed, need to regularly review both their resources and their services for friendliness to students with learning differences.

The first step in this process is to have access to the IEPs (or other learning profiles) of the school's LD students on a timely basis; accommodations are identified and implemented based on the recommendations of the IEP. The second step is to be included in the planning team that creates the framework of support and accommodations for each student. It is here that normalization may often be successfully addressed. Finally, the librarian must enlist the administration's active support. Through adequate funding, necessary staffing and planning time, and diverse materials and technologies the library is able to support the defined learning needs of the student population. This happens only when administrators understand the central role that the library plays in supporting student success.

The reference interview

When LD-identified students come to the library, the librarian should be familiar with their learning profiles. The profile will guide not only the choice of materials and the use of adaptive technology; the profile will also guide the reference interview, instruction, and assistance. Students with difficulties in verbal communication, for example, may be more comfortable using a simple graphic organizer, such as a concept web, to help articulate their questions. Students with attention difficulties may need to be taken to a quiet corner away from distractions to conduct a successful reference interview. A student with task-sequencing difficulties may be precise and articulate in his question, but need structured guidance in planning the steps of his search. A student who has difficulties with spatial orientation may need to be taken to the shelf for a book, rather than being directed to its location. In each case, we need to provide the kind of support that will allow the student to most fully formulate and fill information needs. Above all, we must be willing to experiment with support options to determine the optimal combination for student success.

Concept web diagram

An important facet of working with students with learning differences is modeling metacognitive processes. Teaching students to be metacognitive helps them take responsibility for their success. The librarian may suggest, for example, that one of the criteria for choosing a source might be whether using a resource in that format has proven successful for the student in the past.

Or the librarian may remind the student to make use of concept webbing to help move beyond a pile of note cards toward identifying what material the student still needs and must seek. Reminding the student of accommodations that work successfully for him or her not only helps integrate them into the workflow, it also helps to identify them as part of the normal set of tools that are available in the library. Thanks to the 1996 Roads to Learning: The Public Libraries' Learning Disabilities Initiative under the leadership of Audrey Gorman, that student may find at least some accommodation tools available at the public library as well.

When planning a lesson on library use or research methods, it is best to engage as many modalities as possible in the learning process. In general, instruction should be overtly organized, unambiguous, available to multiple learning pathways, and "short and sweet." Thus, a lesson in finding and analyzing primary sources for research might begin with a video of John F. Kennedy's "Ask not" speech, reinforced by a hands-on group activity in categorizing a number of printed sources as either primary or secondary. Building the lesson on the knowledge of student learning differences within the class, the librarian can provide an optimal learning opportunity for a range of students. A student with reading difficulties, for example, may become so occupied with the task of deriving meaning from printed introductory sources that there is no focus left to respond to the substance of the lesson. By providing the introduction as a video clip, the student may come to a richer understanding of the definition of a primary source, the essential question of the lesson, than he would get by being confined to text sources only. The subsequent reinforcing activity also allows students to immediately engage in application of the lesson while also providing a rich learning environment for auditory learners in the group.

Only when students understand what a primary source is does the librarian introduce the search process for primary sources. By breaking down a process into steps and providing instruction on a "just in time" basis, the librarian frees students with organizational challenges to attend to the requirements of each stage without becoming lost in the task as a whole. Again, individual learning differences should guide instruction. Students with audio-processing deficits may find verbal instructions challenging. By supplementing verbal instructions with a printed pathfinder or a video screen capture of a catalog search, the librarian provides alternate access to the necessary information for the student with audio processing deficits. And with each response to student needs in the design of the lesson, the added pathways enrich the learning experience for all the students participating.

Conclusion

By integration of the accommodations, materials, technologies, and teaching practices necessary for successful learning by students with LDs, the library can become not only a central support for LD-challenged individuals, but also a rich and exciting learning environment for all.

SOURCE: Adapted from Sandy Guild, "LD Accommodations in the School Library: Not Just for the Specialized School Anymore," *Knowledge Quest* 37 (September/October 2008): 24–29. Used with permission.

A parent's view
by Paula Holmes

As a librarian and an advocate for children with learning differences, preparing a presentation for librarians gave me an opportunity to review the journey I began eight years ago. I am the parent of two children who are part of an underserved population. When I look at my children, I don't see their disabilities; instead I see two growing boys with gifts and talents. It is only when we are in situations where people see their disabilities first or don't understand their learning differences that I become a parent of the 20%.

I felt all alone when my kindergartner was diagnosed with myriad learning dif-

ferences, motor delays, and behavioral issues. I found myself in a room with the school officials, who sat on one side of an extremely long table while I sat all alone on the other side.

I can only speak for myself, but the moment when I found out all the things my child couldn't do was overwhelming. I forgot all the wonderful things my child could do. When you confide to friends and family whose children are part of the 80%, they often don't know how to react or they feel uncomfortable. As a parent, sharing was not always rewarding.

I'm lucky to have a background in library science. I researched every term and buzzword the school district used in my first of many Individualized Education Plan meetings. The library is a place to which many parents and caregivers of children with disabilities turn. Libraries are trusted to know reliable sources on the internet, community resources, and the latest published research. Any librarian who has not already done so should consider creating a pathfinder for parents that provides reliable information on disability issues. Making partnerships with parents will, in turn, create advocates for your library.

As deep a love as I have for libraries, I have often felt let down by the library when it comes to my children and my friends' children. At first, my children's disabilities are invisible. To serve them best, allow flexibility and adaptability. Most importantly, as my children adroitly pointed out to me, summer reading prizes shouldn't make you feel bad. For example, a struggling reader does not need to be reminded of his struggles by receiving a prize appropriate for a much younger child. Assistive technology levels the playing field for many kids with disabilities. Consider alternatives to print material. Don't underestimate a child with disabilities. Many of our favorite authors and illustrators are in the same category.

When librarians interact with a child who has a disability, they are modeling behavior for every patron in the library as well as building trust with that child and his family. Librarians represent the view that that child will have of libraries for the rest of his life.

In building trust with a child, librarians help the child become an advocate for himself. They reassure the parents that they are not alone in this journey. My suggestion to all librarians? If you open the door, we will come in. Knowing that a situation is welcoming and safe is a gift. I have found that my journey is one shared by many, and that in sharing my experience, I learn of others with a story. Librarians must continue to partner with patrons so they know the library door is open for them. Improving the view from any side of the desk can be extremely satisfying.

SOURCE: Adapted from Paula Holmes, "A Parent's View: How Libraries Can Open the Door to the 20 Percent," *Children and Libraries* 5, no. 3 (Winter 2007): 24. Used with permission.

The Response to Intervention model
by Deb Hoover

It isn't thrilling to learn you will be spending an hour and a half every day (plus planning and prep time) teaching the enrichment portion of the Response to Intervention (RtI). Create the best enrichment experiences possible with the time and resources available, hoping positive student scores will have something to do with the enrichment the library provides. As more and more librarians find themselves in similar situations, this is my paying it forward with thanks for all those times I borrowed another librarian's work or idea for my students.

For those not familiar with RtI: It is an outgrowth of No Child Left Behind (NCLB) to provide support to identified and unidentified students and provide interventions before they fall behind by working on identified skills, usually identified through a battery of assessments. Students not in need of intervention are provided with enrichment. I began by announcing that I would require collaboration in order to run three grade levels through the library in 90 minutes and be ready to teach the rest of the day. I would not be teaching to the test, but providing students with experiences to deepen background knowledge; require critical thinking skills; broaden technology, math, reading, and writing skills; and be tied to what they were doing in class.

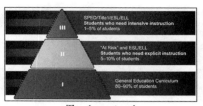

The three-tiered Response to Intervention model

Consulting with the building's literacy coach, the grade level and special education teachers, and especially with the art teacher, who was also providing intervention programming, we started by using the teacher manuals for reading, social studies, and science. We looked for topics that were mentioned or skimmed over but lent themselves to constructivist projects and the essential elements overlay for each topic to embed everything. We created binders of the additional projects or lessons from those manuals and then pieced together our own ideas, often tying several lessons together. We chose projects that were linked by a common theme and covered the theme with specialized projects. We employed group work cooperative learning strategies as students researched, created, and presented their projects. We had to work around schedule glitches and student comings and goings. We often had teachers report that students regularly brought up and shared ideas or information in their classrooms learned through one of these projects.

Education nowadays is all about assessment, and even though we saw the end results of the projects, I wasn't sure if it all added up to anything. With the Pennsylvania System of School Assessment scores as my proof, I spent the summer going through my RtI binders with all my notes, ideas, ramblings, lesson plans, handouts, and text/electronic sources to add a little spit and polish for the next year.

SOURCE: Adapted from Deb Hoover, "Librarian's Role in the 'Response to Intervention Model,'" *Learning and Media* 38, no. 3 (Summer 2010): 15. Used with permission.

8

Advocating for intellectual freedom

by Helen R. Adams

Intellectual freedom is "the right of every individual to both seek and receive information from all points of view without restriction." Unlike school librarians, it is rare for principals and teachers to learn about intellectual freedom in their education classes. Nor is it likely that they are taught about First Amendment court decisions that affirm minors' rights to receive ideas and information in school librar-ies. Therefore, if minors' intellectual freedom is to be protected, school librarians must take responsibility for educating administrators and teachers. The concept of intellectual freedom can be advocated by school librarians to other educators as providing access to a wide range of resources. Use of stories will also make intel-lectual freedom principles more concrete to colleagues.

Prior to beginning an advocacy campaign, the school librarian should first check the status of intellectual freedom in schools locally, statewide, and nationally. The following strategies for promoting intellectual freedom for students are recom-mended by the American Library Association:

- Seek up-to-date information on censorship, privacy, and other intellectual freedom issues in library professional literature and other media sources and through attendance at conferences and workshops.
- Subscribe to intellectual freedom-related discussion lists such as IFACTION (ala.org/offices/intellectual-freedom-email-lists).
- Become familiar with pro–First Amendment organizations and their ad-vocacy efforts (ala.org/advocacy/banned/aboutbannedbooks/firstamend-mentadvocates).

Next, the school librarian can develop an advocacy plan to promote intellectual freedom concepts. The American Association of School Librarians (AASL) has defined advocacy as the "ongoing process of building partnerships so that others will act for and with you, turning passive support into educated action for the library media program." Although one resolute person can achieve a great deal, having administrators and teachers as allies can change a school's climate.

As educational leaders, principals exert a great deal of influence; therefore, winning their support for students' intellectual freedom is critical. To help admin-istrators understand the importance of protecting students' information needs, library media specialists can:

- Assist administrators in making the connection between intellectual freedom and "growing" future citizens. To ensure that today's students are educated for citizenship in a global society, students must be able to use resources on

a wide range of subjects in print and electronic formats.

- Meet with the principal to review the materials selection policy, how materials are selected, and district reconsideration procedures, clarifying any steps that are unclear.
- Initiate a discussion when issues such as the confidentiality of students' library records arise.

Teachers also need to be educated about intellectual freedom. They may not have a clear understanding of the difference between the broad administrative control public school principals and boards of education have on the removal of curricular materials required in courses, and the narrow control administrators and boards have when it comes to removing library resources intended for free inquiry by students. To nurture teachers' development as supporters of students' rights, the library professional, using these strategies, can:

- Meet with new teaching staff to explain library policies related to materials selection, reconsideration, privacy of library records, interlibrary loan, and internet use.
- Plan and work collaboratively with teachers and students on learning experiences incorporating First Amendment speech rights.
- Integrate a different facet of intellectual freedom into each staff development program.
- Select professional materials related to censorship and make them available to staff.

By reaching out to principals and teachers, the school librarian has the potential to create allies who will support minors' access to information when a challenge occurs. The advocacy process is not quick, and it requires more than celebrating Banned Books Week each September. The school librarian must model the principles of intellectual freedom in year-round, day-to-day actions. However, when advocacy is successful, it can change students' lives and impact their effectiveness as citizens.

SOURCE: Adapted from Helen R. Adams, "Advocating for Intellectual Freedom with Principals and Teachers," *School Library Media Activities Monthly* 25, no. 6 (February 2009): 54. Used with permission.

The challenge of challenges
by Gail Dickinson

One of my favorite quotes from John Dewey (right) is: "What the best and wisest parent wants for his own child; that should the community want for all of its children. Any other ideal for our schools is narrow and unlovely; acted upon, it destroys our democracy" (1905). I use that quote when talking about library media center budgeting at the school board. They have the responsibility to act as the best and wisest parents.

When talking about intellectual freedom, that quote loses

some of its altruistic flavor. The "best and wisest" parents now want all copies of Harry Potter removed, or they see any mention of homosexuality as promoting an immoral lifestyle. They earnestly want for every child in the school exactly what they want for their own children. Others, however, see their actions as narrow and unloving, and even as destroying democracy, exactly the opposite of Dewey's intent.

When a challenge gets difficult, it's hard to believe that people challenge instructional materials because they care, to remember that educators want the general public, legislators, taxpayers, and parents to care about education. The challenger may think: As a parent, maybe I can take this one book out of my child's hand, and maybe even take a stand for all of the children in the school.

School librarians and administrators continually strive to understand the concern of the challenger. Tempers flare, and regardless of the responsible efforts to manage the choices made for well-selected collections, headlines trumpet accusations that claim smut has been deliberately placed in the hands of children.

School librarians are the information-resource experts in the school. They are the only ones trained to use the selection principles and criteria. Each school librarian's role in the challenged materials process is to act as informed counsel for the district in the matter of selection, to gather data about the resource, and most importantly, to defend the use of established policy and procedures.

How it got there in the first place

In general, school librarians don't do a very good job of explaining the profession to others. Therefore, one of the most important areas of the job, the selection of materials, is often misunderstood. This lack of shared knowledge about selection comes back to haunt school librarians when there are challenges to instructional materials.

Parents, fellow teachers, and maybe even administrators need to be informed that school board policies govern the selection of instructional materials, and that responsibility to purchase these materials is delegated through the superintendent to the teaching faculty. In the case of library materials, the person responsible is the school librarian. The selection policy, however, applies to all instructional materials in the school whether they are part of the library collection or housed as instructional materials in classrooms. The selection policy applies to materials in all formats and covers materials used in instruction whether purchased through taxpayer funds or through gifts to the school.

School librarians are the only ones trained in selection processes. Selection principles are the reason that school librarians are involved in challenges to instructional materials, whether the challenge is in the classroom or the school library. Librarians are the information-resource experts in the school. They know the interests and information needs of their community within and outside the school. They select materials by reading reviews from authoritative sources and by seeking suggestions from teachers and students.

This means that when a resource is challenged, the librarian's role will be to guide the application of the selection principles to the resource in question. Statements of fact are always preferable to opinion so statements from published reviews are helpful.

9

In choosing materials, the word "appropriate" always causes some concern. When discussing challenged resources, all parties involved should make sure that they know specifically what the issues are. The following definitions of "appropriate" may help:

- **Reading level.** Is the resource appropriate as defined by reading level?
- **Interest level.** Is the resource appropriate as defined by interest level?
- **Intellectual level.** Is the resource appropriate as defined by intellectual level?
- **Emotional level.** Is the resource appropriate as defined by emotional level or maturity of the students? This particular definition of appropriateness will be the one that causes the most discussion. For some students, the material is emotionally appropriate, and for others it may be emotionally inappropriate. Some students may not be ready to read stories or facts that directly contest what their parents or church members believe.

Regardless of the answer to each of the above, they can be used to push the discussion of appropriateness from vagueness into proscribed categories so that each person around the table understands what specific points are under discussion.

Librarians select materials for the school community. It would be nice if the collection were as appropriate for each person in the school community as it is for the average student, but money, time, energy, and lack of available resources precludes any hope of doing this. The selection process should value each child and each parent equally. The goal is to stretch the collection to meet the needs and interest of each child. It's not easy, and it's no wonder that at times parents or other citizens are concerned over materials that do not match the needs and interests of their children.

SOURCE: Adapted from Gail Dickinson, "The Challenges of Challenges: Understanding and Being Prepared, Part I," *School Library Media Activities Monthly* 23, no. 5 (January 2007): 26–28. Used with permission.

Cyberbullying from playground to computer

by Tara Anderson and Brian Sturm

While bullying may affect anyone in any situation, childhood and school are the prevailing age and context for bullying, as children interact with peers and struggle to assert their identity and understand appropriate social behavior. Schoolyard bullying has received considerable attention in psychological journals and child behavior manuals. Society is moving away from the attitude that bullying is just a part of growing up, to understanding the deep, emotional damage it can cause. The recent rash of violence in schools has highlighted just how angry and helpless children can feel. Many schools have begun awareness programs promoting anti-violence and an end to bullying.

The definition of bullying is slowly expanding. Nonphysical aggression has been highlighted in the world of female bullying: rumors, social exclusion, and other forms of quiet aggression to attack other girls. This falls beneath the typical teachers' and parents' radar, and can continue for years without intervention. This quiet, psychological aggression has migrated to the digital world to become "cyberbullying," as bullies take advantage of the anonymity and accessibility of digital technology to harass their victims.

According to a 2004 definition by Canadian educator Bill Belsey:

> Cyberbullying involves the use of information and communication technologies such as email, cell phone, and pager text messages, instant messaging, defamatory personal websites, and defamatory online personal polling websites, to support deliberate, repeated, and hostile behaviour by an individual or group that is intended to harm others.

Cyberbullying is emerging as children become more adept at using computers and cell phones for communication and socialization. Bullies can harass victims about their appearance, sexual promiscuity, poverty, grades, diseases, or disabilities. Glee Palmer Davis, executive director of the Washington chapter of the National Association of Social Workers, said that bullying can also be based on "others' perceptions of a student's value based on gender, race/ethnicity, color, religion, ancestry, sexual orientation or ability level (mental/physical/sensory)."

Several types of cyberbullying, depending on the available technology, allow children to have private conversations with friends, or "buddies," in real time. These combine the instant communication style of the chat room with the personal style of email, creating an arena where youth can establish social networks, providing fertile ground for the bully to send mean or obscene messages to others. Children may be bullied by a friend on their buddy list or by peers with anonymous screen names. Added features, such as buddy profiles, allow buddies to insert derogatory or slanderous remarks about peers for anyone to read, and buddies can also create false personal profiles of their targets that insult or ridicule them. Children can also block other children from a buddy list, creating an effect in which children engage in a hurtful manipulation of peer relationships.

Bullying can also occur through text messaging. Cell phones provide an extremely mobile method for bullying other children. All the bully needs is the target's phone number, and a message or threat can be sent anywhere, anytime. Email bullying works in a similar fashion, and while the originating account can be traced, it is often impossible to prove who actually wrote the message. Phones and email can be used transmit unflattering photos. Digital technology facilitates capturing unprotected moments that can be used as weapons in the wrong hands.

A bully can very easily create a free website or message board devoted to the ridicule of another child, creating the feeling of group bullying, where multiple students post hateful thoughts on a message board. Lists can be posted of reasons the victim is inferior to others with pictures—often digitally altered—that support the prejudice often sent anonymously with a message that convinces readers to visit the site.

Photo: SafetyWeb.com, CC BY 3.0

A bully can use a blog to write derogatory thoughts about a victim (a "bash-board"). If the victim has a blog, a bully could, as an anonymous guest, post mean comments about the victim's personal thoughts.

Older children are the largest group using computers and experiencing cyberbullying. Younger kids may not be able to use communication services without their parents' help, but young adults are often left alone at the computer. Privacy, a huge concern for teens, means parents try to respect their privacy. Young adults with a strong desire for social acceptance shift their dependence from family to peers and may be unable to resist responding to mean messages. They may look at a bully-

9

ing website link they've received. As teens increasingly rely on computers and cell phones for their social networking, they become more susceptible to cyberbullying.

Cyberbullying can happen to anyone. Both the bully and the victim can be very quiet and subtle about the abuse. Most adults in the children's lives may not know that anything untoward is happening. It is a myth that victims of bullying are weak or wimpy; in fact, "people who are targeted by bullies are sensitive, respectful, honest, creative, have high emotional intelligence, a strong sense of fair play, and high integrity with a low propensity to violence" (www.bullyonline.org/schoolbully/myths.htm). These qualities are exactly what makes it easy for a bully to hurt a target.

Bullies may have low self-esteem and act aggressively to overcompensate for their weaknesses, but often bullies are the socially dominant children who ensure their power by degrading others. They have bullied before and have gotten away with it, so they continue to do it. This is especially true where anonymity allows the bully protection from being caught.

Cyberbullying may be worse than face-to-face bullying. The psychological damage caused through online and mobile-phone bullying among girls suggests that such aggression is just as damaging as physical aggression. Victims may experience stress, tension, low self-esteem, and depression. Cyberbullying and bullying can also have extreme repercussions such as suicide and physical violence.

Cyberbullying reaches victims in their own homes. While children can temporarily get rid of cyberbullies by changing screen names, going offline, or turning off the computer, it is unreasonable to ask victims never to use a computer again.

Teens especially may feel alienated from their peers if they must refrain from online communication due to a fear of bullying. Cyberbullying is much harder to escape or avoid than face-to-face bullying.

The anonymity of cyberbullying is also damaging because victims don't know if the bully is a best friend or a complete stranger, or if there is more than one bully involved; they are left confused and distrustful of everyone, even the innocent. The faceless threat is often more frightening than the identified one.

Photo: SafetyWeb.com, CC BY 3.0

Victims often avoid telling adults about the abuse because they fear that nothing can be done to help. Schools have often been helpless with cyberbullying. They cannot take action on something that is occurring outside of school hours or off school property. Parents and school officials are often ineffective against cyberbullying, since children know more about new technologies than many adults.

What can be done?

One easy answer is to tell victims just to ignore it. Turning off the computer or phone deprives victims of their digital social network. Teens should continue to use the technologies but should not respond to the bully's advances, and they should take the time to document all communication made by the bully. Documentation can be used later when discussing the bullying with school officials or with the local police if the situation gets out of hand. If a cyberbully commits a serious offense, parents can try reporting the abuse to their Internet Service Provider (ISP). The ISP can take action against the bully if the actions are malicious and in violation of their privacy or internet use policies.

Before taking the situation to authorities, adults, parents, and children can block users or email addresses attached to hurtful messages (AOL Instant Messenger even offers the ability to block messages from users not on the child's personal buddy list). Children can change their screen names or email addresses, controlling who receives their new contact information. Parents can also contact the phone company to block certain numbers or turn off text messaging services.

S T O P
cyberbullying

As awareness of cyberbullying and its effects on children grows, more information is becoming available on the topic. Educating teens helps victims realize that the aggression is not their fault. Cyberbullying can be minimized if they learn how to recognize the attacks, how to deal with them, and how to stop the bully from contacting them in the future. As parents and teachers learn about the dangers of cyberbullying, they can reduce future problems by monitoring children's online behavior, helping them set up their online accounts, asking them about their online friends, and watching for sudden changes in their children's attitudes toward the internet. Bullies need to be held accountable for their behavior whenever possible, and victims need to have the support of caring adults. Schools may need to extend their disciplinary purview beyond school walls to match the information services they provide, although this is currently a legal nightmare. Finally, ISPs need to continue to improve their methods of handling misuse of their services.

If parents, caregivers, and technology experts work together, they can help children cope with this potentially devastating form of abuse. We must also try to protect our children's privacy, their freedom of expression, and their right to access these new communication and information technologies. It is difficult, but as information professionals who work with children, it is our responsibility to accept this challenge, and to mentor children in socially beneficial ways.

SOURCE: Adapted from Tara Anderson and Brian Sturm, "Cyberbullying: From Playground to Computer," *Young Adult Library Services* 5, no. 2 (Winter 2007): 24–27. Used with permission.

What to do about cyberbullying
by Kathy Fredrick

From Arkansas to Iowa and from Nebraska to Washington, state legislatures are enacting bills that extend anti-harassment measures to the electronic world, both in school and out of school. The tragic deaths of teens that are linked to extended cyberbullying by classmates and adults make shocking headlines. Other teens and preteens who have been bullied online suffer anxiety and depression. Stories of the victims of cyberbullying have left deep impressions on all educators. What can be done about it?

A definition

A basic definition of "cyberbullying" is provided by Nancy Willard, director of the Center for Safe and Responsible Internet Use, who defined cyberbullying as using the internet or other mobile devices to send or post harmful or cruel text or images to bully others (csriu.org). This type of bullying takes a number of different forms, and appears to be particularly compelling because of its relative anonymity. The

9

advent of social networking has highlighted cyberbullying. Email, instant messaging, chat rooms, and web pages are all venues for cyberbullying.

What do victims experience?

1. repetitive messages that are angry or vulgar or intimidating;
2. messages with cruel, false, and harmful statements about them are sent to other people with the intent to embarrass or discredit them with classmates and friends; and
3. a bully who masquerades as another person.

Unlike the face-to-face bullying, cyberbullying continues 24/7, tormenting the victim without an opportunity for intervention.

Even though legislatures are enacting measures against cyberbullying, schools can, at the district level, develop an Acceptable Use Policy. Make sure there is a statement requiring students not to post information about other students, particularly not information that is incorrect or harmful. This goes hand-in-hand against posting personal information that identifies location, contact information, or other items that would make it easy to find a student. This will also come in handy for other Web 2.0 technologies being used such as blogs, podcasts, and other social networking tools. Some districts are also rewriting student codes of conduct to reflect Web 2.0 technologies and their interactive nature.

To judge how prevalent this problem is for students, school librarians could survey students and parents about the issue. Before doing the survey, gauge awareness of this issue among colleagues and with administrators to determine the best approach. Based on what is learned from this evaluation, staff development may be in order. Online safety sites like i-SAFE, Media Awareness Network, and McGruff have materials that will help in this process.

The role of the school librarian

After researching the topic, school librarians can be advocates in fighting cyberbullying. They can work with teachers to instruct students about cyberbullying and how to combat it. Since students are reluctant to tell when they are bullied online, it is important to let them know there are ways to combat the problem. Working with students is a natural extension of instruction related to web evaluation and using online resources. Students can develop strategies to share with other students, produce anti-cyberbullying materials, and talk with others about how to combat cyberbullying. As policies are in place, school librarians can go over them with students regularly.

Information can also be shared with parents through the school library website and at parent meetings. The same materials and video clips that work with students will also work with parents. The parents' first reaction may be to say they won't let their kids online. As an alternative, the school librarian can talk with them about extending rules for online use to include ways to guard against cyberbullying, keeping information private, knowing how to block access and change passwords, and knowing when to tell an adult what's going on.

The role models provided for children should not include a roadmap for cyberbullying. They need to be given the resources they need to make good choices online and to have the resilience to respond to those who would tear them down.

SOURCE: Adapted from Kathy Fredrick, "Mean Girls (and Boys): Cyberbullying and What Can Be Done about It," *School Library Media Activities Monthly* 25 (April 2009): 44–45. Used with permission.

What is the "first-sale" doctrine?

by Rebecca P. Butler

Social responsibility recognizes the importance of information and the teaching of ethical behavior to a democratic society. Copyright issues for clients of school librarians—students, teachers, administrators, parents, and community members—require teaching ethical behavior.

For your high school algebra teacher, one of the least favorite parts of the job is creating test questions. Test questions should not come from the textbook, but should be new questions that cover the same material as that of the textbook. However, teachers are often tired of writing up new questions for every chapter. Then comes a great discovery: An algebra book in a college bookstore covers much of the same information. As the teacher reads through this new book it appears that test questions could be taken from this new book. They would work well with the students, and questions would not need to be reinvented. Because you, the school librarian, just conducted a copyright in-service, your teacher asks if this is feasible.

Your questions for the teacher: Do you have permission from the copyright owner to borrow these questions? Does the use of the questions you plan to copy fit under the fair-use guidelines? Have you purchased a license to use the college algebra book in this manner? Is the college algebra book in the public domain? When the teacher says the answer to all of these questions is "no," you respond:

> The way to legally use the book—*for one student only*—is to tear the college algebra book apart, cut the needed questions out of the pages, and paste them into a test. If you need the same questions for the whole class, then you would have to purchase the same number of the college algebra books as there were students in the class, and do the same thing as you did for the first student.

This will sound crazy to the teacher, but you are talking about the "first-sale doctrine." This doctrine, "rooted in contract law ... basically states that the owner of a particular copy of a work has the right to dispose of that copy as she or he sees fit." (See Rebecca P. Butler, *Copyright for Teachers and Librarians*, Neal-Schuman, 2004.) This means that if teachers purchase a copy of the college algebra text, they can do whatever they want to do with that copy: sell it, give it away, put it in a library, even cut it up and tear it apart. However, if teachers do not have the proper permission or license, the use is not covered by exemptions of the copyright law (such as fair use), or if the textbook is not in the public domain, the teacher cannot *copy* the questions out of this book to use.

SOURCE: Adapted from Rebecca P. Butler, "What Is the 'First Sale' Doctrine?" *Knowledge Quest* 34, no. 4 (March/April 2006): 32. Used with permission.

9

APPENDIX

Periodical publishers

This list includes information about the publishers who so generously allowed us to use articles that would help readers better understand how school libraries function, their management, and their role in the education of students. We thank them for sharing their authors and the contents of their publications with us. In some cases, the editor is able to provide permission. In others one must go to the parent company. For that reason we have included the name of the publisher and the name of the editor of the periodical, although in many cases, editors of periodicals change frequently.

American Libraries
American Library Association
50 E. Huron Street
Chicago, IL 60611
Telephone: (800) 545-2433, ext. 5105
Fax: (312) 440-0901
Email: americanlibraries@ala.org
americanlibrariesmagazine.org
Editor: Laurie D. Borman

CSLA Journal
California School Library Association
6444 E. Spring Street, #237
Long Beach, CA 90815-1553
Telephone: (888) 655-8480
Email: info@csla.net
www.csla.net/index.php/publications/journals
Editor: Jeanne Nelson

Children and Libraries
Association for Library Service to Children, a division of the
    American Library Association
50 E. Huron Street
Chicago, IL 606011
Telephone: (800) 545-2433, ext. 2163
Fax: (312) 280-5271
Email: alsc@ala.org
ala.org/alsc/compubs/childrenlib
Editor: Sharon Korbeck Verbeten

Knowledge Quest
American Association of School Librarians, a division of the
American Library Association
50 E. Huron Street
Chicago, IL 0i6011
Telephone: (800) 545-2433, ext. 1396
Email: aasl@ala.org
ala.org/aasl/knowledgequest
Editor: Markisan Naso

Learning and Media
Pennsylvania School Librarians Association
Email: nflncf@ptd.net
pslawiki.wikispaces.com/learningandmedia
Editor: Michael Nailor

Library Media Connection
P.O. Box 292114
Kettering, OH 45429-0114
Telephone: (800) 607-4410
Fax: (937) 890-0221
Email: lmc@librarymediaconnection.com
www.librarymediaconnection.com
Editorial Director: Gail K. Dickinson

School Library Journal
A division of Media Source, Inc.
160 Varick Street, 11th Floor
New York, NY 10013
Telephone: (646) 380-0700
Fax: (646) 380-0756
Email: slj@mediasourceinc.com
www.slj.com
Editor-in-Chief: Rebecca Miller

School Library Monthly
3520 South 35th St.
Lincoln, NE 68506
Telephone: (805) 880-6812
Email: dlevitov@abc-clio.com
www.schoollibrarymonthly.com
Managing Editor: Deborah Levitov

Teacher Librarian: The Journal for School Library Professionals
16211 Oxford Court
Bowie, MD 20715
Telephone: (301) 805-2191
Email: dloertscher@teacherlibrarian.com
www.teacherlibrarian.com
Editors: David V. Loertscher and Elizabeth "Betty" Marcoux

Young Adult Library Services

 Young Adult Library Services Association, a division of the
  American Library Association
 50 E. Huron Street
 Chicago, IL 0i6011
 Telephone: (800) 545-2433, ext. 2128
 Fax: (312) 280-5276
 Email: yalsa@ala.org
 www.yalsa.ala.org/yals/
 Guest Editor: Linda W. Braun

Index

You may also be interested in

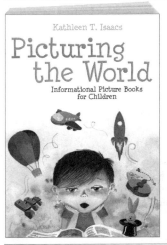

PICTURING THE WORLD
Informational Picture Books for Children
KATHLEEN T. ISAACS

Enrich your library collection with outstanding informational books that children really want to read. This annotated resource by veteran children's book reviewer Isaacs surveys the best nonfiction/ informational titles for ages 3 through 10, helping librarians make informed collection development and purchasing decisions.

ISBN: 978-0-8389-1126-6
216 pp / 6" × 9"

GRAPHIC NOVELS IN YOUR SCHOOL LIBRARY
JESSE KARP,
ILLUSTRATED BY RUSH KRESS
ISBN: 978-0-8389-1089-4

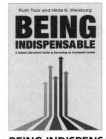

BEING INDISPENSABLE: A SCHOOL LIBRARIAN'S GUIDE TO BECOMING AN INVALUABLE LEADER
RUTH TOOR AND
HILDA K. WEISBURG
ISBN: 978-0-8389-1065-8

LIBRARY SERVICES FOR CHILDREN AND YOUNG PEOPLE: CHALLENGES AND OPPORTUNITIES IN THE DIGITAL AGE
EDITED BY CAROLYNN RANKIN
AND AVRIL BROCK
ISBN: 978-1-8560-4712-8

EMBEDDED LIBRARIANSHIP: TOOLS AND PRACTICES
BUFFY J. HAMILTON
ISBN: 978-0-8389-5857-5

TWENTY-FIRST-CENTURY KIDS, TWENTY-FIRST-CENTURY LIBRARIANS
VIRGINIA A. WALTER
ISBN: 978-0-8389-1007-8

BOOKS IN MOTION
JULIE DIETZEL-GLAIR
ISBN: 978-1-5557-0810-8
